JUSTICE FOR ALL
AND HOW TO ACHIEVE IT

Citizens, lawyers and the law in the age of human rights

JUSTICE FOR ALL
AND HOW TO ACHIEVE IT

Citizens, lawyers and the law in the age of human rights

Geoffrey Nice

SCALA

First published in 2017 by
Scala Arts & Heritage Publishers Ltd
10 Lion Yard
Tremadoc Road
London SW4 7NQ, UK
www.scalapublishers.com

ISBN 978-1-78551-123-3

Designed by Park Studio
Printed and bound in Turkey

10 9 8 7 6 5 4 3 2 1

Cover: Two children walking beside the West Bank Separation Barrier, Abu Dis, Israel, 2004. (© Alessandra Sanguinetti / Magnum Photos.)

To

Amelia, Mahalah, Nena, Philippa and Taffa

Who, perhaps unknowingly, shared values with one another and with me, and provided support and inspiration throughout

Contents

Illustrations

Between pages 108 & 109

Between pages 188 & 189

Abbreviations

AU	African Union
CFREU	Charter of Fundamental Rights of the European Union
CPS	Crown Prosecution Service
DB	Serbian State Security (Državna bezbednost)
DRC	Democratic Republic of Congo
ECHR	European Convention on Human Rights, drafted by the Council of Europe and entered into force in 1953
ECtHR	European Court of Human Rights, established by the Council of Europe in 1959 to ensure member states of the Council observe the terms of the Convention
ECJ	European Court of Justice
EEC	European Economic Community
EU	European Union
FGM	Free Gaza Movement
FRY	Federal Republic of Yugoslavia
HRA	Human Rights Act (of the UK Parliament, 1998)
ICC	International Criminal Court
ICCPR	International Covenant on Civil and Political Rights
ICJ	International Court of Justice
ICRC	International Committee of the Red Cross
ICTR	International Criminal Tribunal for Rwanda

ICTY	International Criminal Tribunal for the former Yugoslavia
IDF	Israel Defense Forces
IED	Improvised explosive device
IHH	Humanitarian Relief Foundation (Turkish NGO)
JNA	Yugoslav People's Army (in Serbo-Croat: Jugoslovenska narodna armija)
JSO	Special Operations Unit (of Serbia – Jedinica za specijalne operacije); also known as Red Berets
KLA	Kosovo Liberation Army
MoD	Ministry of Defence (UK)
MUP	Ministry of Internal Affairs (of Serbia – Ministarstvo Unutrašnjih Poslova)
NGO	Non-governmental organisation
NIOD	Netherlands War Documentation Centre (Nederlands Instituut voor Oorlogsdocumentatie)
OPCW	Organisation for the Prohibition of Chemical Weapons
OTP	Office of the Prosecutor (of the ICTY)
PA	Palestinian Authority
RPA	Rwanda Patriotic Army
SCSL	Special Court for Sierra Leone
SDC	Supreme Defence Council (of Federal Yugoslavia)

SFRY	Socialist Federal Republic of Yugoslavia
SPS	Socialist Party of Serbia
UN	United Nations
UNESCO	United Nations Economic, Social and Cultural Organization
UNHRC	United Nations Human Rights Council
UNRWA	United Nations Relief and Works Agency for Palestine Refugees in the Near East
VJ	Yugoslavia Armed Forces (in Serbo-Croat: Vojska Jugoslavije)
VRS	Bosnian Serb Army (in Serbo-Croat: Vojska Republika Srpska)

International Protocols

Extracts of what the world – and later Europe – could agree when World War II was a vivid memory and something to be avoided at all costs. It is by no means clear whether these or similar international instruments – in force though they are – could be agreed to now; and many in the UK wish to withdraw from the European Convention.

UNITED NATIONS CONVENTION ON THE PREVENTION AND PUNISHMENT OF THE CRIME OF GENOCIDE (1948)

Adopted by the United Nations General Assembly on 9 December 1948.

Article II

In the present Convention, genocide means any of the following acts committed with intent to destroy, in whole or in part, a national, ethnical, racial or religious group, as such:

(a) Killing members of the group;
(b) Causing serious bodily or mental harm to members of the group;
(c) Deliberately inflicting on the group conditions of life calculated to bring about its physical destruction in whole or in part;
(d) Imposing measures intended to prevent births within the group;
(e) Forcibly transferring children of the group to another group.

UNIVERSAL DECLARATION OF HUMAN RIGHTS (1948)

Adopted by the United Nations General Assembly on 10 December 1948.

Article 1: All human beings are born free and equal in dignity and rights. They are endowed with reason and conscience and should act towards one another in a spirit of brotherhood.
Article 3: Everyone has the right to life, liberty and security of person.
Article 4: No one shall be held in slavery or servitude; slavery and the slave trade shall be prohibited in all their forms.
Article 5: No one shall be subjected to torture or to cruel, inhuman or degrading treatment or punishment.
Article 7: All are equal before the law and are entitled without any discrimination to equal protection of the law.
Article 13.1: Everyone has the right to freedom of movement and residence within the borders of each state.
Article 19: Everyone has the right to freedom of opinion and expression.

EUROPEAN CONVENTION ON HUMAN RIGHTS (1950)

Not universal; ratified and entered into force on 3 September 1953.

Article 1: Obligation to respect human rights
Article 2: Right to life
Article 3: Prohibition of torture
Article 4: Prohibition of slavery and forced labour
Article 5: Right to liberty and security
Article 6: Right to a fair trial
Article 7: No punishment without law
Article 8: Right to respect for private and family life
Article 9: Freedom of thought, conscience and religion
Article 10: Freedom of expression
Article 11: Freedom of assembly and association
Article 12: Right to marry
Article 13: Right to an effective remedy
Article 14: Protection from discrimination

STATUTE OF THE INTERNATIONAL CRIMINAL COURT (2002)

Not universal; entered into force on 1 July 2002.

Article 5: Crimes within the jurisdiction of the Court

(a) The crime of genocide;
(b) Crimes against humanity;
(c) War crimes;
(d) The crime of aggression [*not yet in force*].

Article 7: Crimes against humanity

1. For the purpose of this Statute, 'crime against humanity' means any of the following acts when committed as part of a widespread or systematic attack directed against any civilian population, with knowledge of the attack:

(a) Murder;
(b) Extermination;
(c) Enslavement;
(d) Deportation or forcible transfer of population;
(e) Imprisonment or other severe deprivation of physical liberty in violation of fundamental rules of international law;

(f) Torture;
(g) Rape, sexual slavery, enforced prostitution, forced pregnancy, enforced sterilization, or any other form of sexual violence of comparable gravity;
(h) Persecution against any identifiable group or collectivity on political, racial, national, ethnic, cultural, religious, gender, or other grounds that are universally recognized as impermissible under international law, in connection with any act referred to in this paragraph or any crime within the jurisdiction of the Court;
(i) Enforced disappearance of persons;
(j) The crime of apartheid;
(k) Other inhumane acts of a similar character intentionally causing great suffering, or serious injury to body or to mental or physical health.

Article 8: War crimes
1. The Court shall have jurisdiction in respect of war crimes in particular when committed as part of a plan or policy or as part of a large-scale commission of such crimes.

2. For the purpose of this Statute, 'war crimes' means:
(a) Grave breaches of the Geneva Conventions of 12 August 1949, namely, any of the following acts against persons or property protected under the provisions of the relevant Geneva Convention:
(i) Wilful killing;
(ii) Torture or inhuman treatment, including biological experiments;
(iii) Wilfully causing great suffering, or serious injury to body or health;
(iv) Extensive destruction and appropriation of property, not justified by military necessity and carried out unlawfully and wantonly;
(v) Compelling a prisoner of war or other protected person to serve in the forces of a hostile Power;
(vi) Wilfully depriving a prisoner of war or other protected person of the rights of fair and regular trial;
(vii) Unlawful deportation or transfer or unlawful confinement;
(viii) Taking of hostages.

Article 8 (2): War crimes (cont.)

(b) Other serious violations of the laws and customs applicable in international armed conflict, within the established framework of international law, namely, any of the following acts:

(i) Intentionally directing attacks against the civilian population as such or against individual civilians not taking direct part in hostilities;

(viii) The transfer, directly or indirectly, by the Occupying Power of parts of its own civilian population into the territory it occupies, or the deportation or transfer of all or parts of the population of the occupied territory within or outside this territory.

(c) In the case of an armed conflict not of an international character, serious violations of Article 3 common to the four Geneva Conventions of 12 August 1949, namely, any of the following acts committed against persons taking no active part in the hostilities, including members of armed forces who have laid down their arms and those placed *hors de combat* by sickness, wounds, detention or any other cause:

(i) Violence to life and person, in particular murder of all kinds, mutilation, cruel treatment and torture;

(ii) Committing outrages upon personal dignity, in particular humiliating and degrading treatment;

(iii) Taking of hostages;

(iv) The passing of sentences and the carrying out of executions without previous judgement pronounced by a regularly constituted court, affording all judicial guarantees which are generally recognized as indispensable.

(d) Paragraph 2 (c) applies to armed conflicts not of an international character and thus does not apply to situations of internal disturbances and tensions, such as riots, isolated and sporadic acts of violence or other acts of a similar nature.

(e) Other serious violations of the laws and customs applicable in armed conflicts not of an international character, within the established framework of international law, namely, any of the following acts:

(i) Intentionally directing attacks against the civilian population as such or against individual civilians not taking direct part in hostilities;

(ii) Intentionally directing attacks against buildings, material, medical units and transport, and personnel using the distinctive emblems of the Geneva Conventions in conformity with international law;

(iii) Intentionally directing attacks against personnel, installations, material, units or vehicles involved in a humanitarian assistance or peacekeeping mission in accordance with the Charter of the United Nations, as long as they are entitled to the protection given to civilians or civilian objects under the international law of armed conflict;

(iv) Intentionally directing attacks against buildings dedicated to religion, education, art, science or charitable purposes, historic monuments, hospitals and places where the sick and wounded are collected, provided they are not military objectives;

(v) Pillaging a town or place, even when taken by assault;

(vi) Committing rape, sexual slavery, enforced prostitution, forced pregnancy, enforced sterilization, and any other form of sexual violence also constituting a serious violation of Article 3 common to the four Geneva Conventions;

(vii) Conscripting or enlisting children under the age of fifteen years into armed forces or groups or using them to participate actively in hostilities;

(viii) Ordering the displacement of the civilian population for reasons related to the conflict, unless the security of the civilians involved or imperative military reasons so demand;

(x) Declaring that no quarter will be given.

(f) Paragraph 2 (e) applies to armed conflicts not of an international character and thus does not apply to situations of internal disturbances and tensions, such as riots, isolated and sporadic acts of violence or other acts of a similar nature. It applies to armed conflicts that take place in the territory of a State when there is protracted armed conflict between governmental authorities and organized armed groups or between such groups.

JUSTICE FOR ALL
AND HOW TO ACHIEVE IT

Citizens, lawyers and the law in the age of human rights

Preface

Laws and legal systems pilot us along the puzzling path from birth to death. Good laws, properly applied, can save us from harm; when not so good they can expose us to risk – or worse.

But the law in all its forms actually does much more.

It may be thought that the citizen who spends an entire life obedient to national laws can die confident of her or his goodness, or at least without any sense of having done wrong. Thus, the 19th-century judge who sentenced Oscar Wilde to imprisonment for homosexual offences will have died a contented death. Likewise, the 20th-century judge and jurymen who between them brought intellectually limited Timothy Evans to conviction and death by hanging for a murder he did not commit. Similarly, the judge who sentenced brilliant mathematician Alan Turing, who had broken the Nazi wartime codes, to submit to medical treatment for homosexuality, or the Home Secretaries who refused to commute death sentences on Ruth Ellis, the last woman in England to be hanged for murder, and 19-year-old Derek Bentley for the 'joint enterprise' shooting of a policeman by his younger fellow burglar. These courts would now be regarded as having done serious wrong; there can be no real excuse for their actions, save through blaming the fact that the laws they followed reflected moral standards that are never universal over time and place. The judges' sense of contentment at the end of lives in which they had damaged or killed fellow citizens – their sense of personal goodness – was allowed only by laws that can now be judged immoral and wrong.

Of course the jurors – and maybe the judge – in the Timothy Evans case could claim dilution of culpability because they followed the law's 'superior orders', and I include *them* as an example to add difficulty to our thinking about the issue I raise. The Home Secretary in the Bentley case, to his great credit, drafted much of the European

Convention on Human Rights; what he failed to do for Bentley shows just how fractured and incomplete can be human goodness. But, despite this, would we not all like the last closing of the eyes to come with at least some comprehensive concept of goodness against which we can calibrate our own?

The world's religions – in conflict, often violent conflict, with each other – offer no such comprehensive concept, and national and international law provide no conclusive and comprehensive code of goodness. Assessment of the individual's worth must, ultimately, lie squarely on her or him.

This became for me – not necessarily for my audiences – a recurring theme as I worked through the 24 Gresham lectures of which 17 form the basis of this book. To give 24 lectures with a legal content but for general audiences over four years was difficult but a great privilege; there were things I knew about and *wanted* to discuss and things I thought I *should learn about* and try to convey. There were also other topics I felt I *had* to talk about given the times in which we live. I was and am truly grateful to Gresham College for having given me the opportunity.

A second theme – this one probably apparent to the audiences as well as to me – was that national and international legal systems are just like the national or international bodies that created them: they will always put their own interests above the interests of the ordinary citizen and the ordinary victim. Victims count for little if state interests, or if the interests or even reputations of legal systems, are at risk. But this theme, for me, is thicker and more profoundly serious than that.

It is just understandable, however appalling, that major powers may well suppress information that could tell more truth of the Srebrenica massacres because that information would reveal more about the major powers' complicity in those crimes. Less understandable, once considered rigorously, is the general hypocrisy of most states that pretend that criminal wickedness is intrinsic to some citizens. Overlooking all evidence of conditioning as a major engine of crime, they then ask for confession from criminal citizens despite states themselves confessing to nothing if they can possibly avoid it.

Who really doubts that if the 2013 London rioters had been switched at birth with the children of the then ruling Gloucestershire elite that the behaviour of both groups of children would have been reversed? But yet, who could fail to understand the desire of the owner of a family-run furniture store in Croydon burnt to the ground for wanting to see the arsonists punished?

Might the question of whether wrongdoers should be punished be more generally subordinated to the underlying question of whether doing wrong is a reflection of the failings of the society in which the offender lives or of intrinsic at-birth personal wickedness? Theoretically yes, but it is almost impossible to make that subordination without exposing the hypocrisies necessary to the efficient functioning of societies, even democratic ones. And so wrongdoers – to include historical sex offenders and others at home just as much as genocidaires abroad – must reach the end of life unable to test the level of their goodness or badness by codes set, or punishments imposed, by societies that pretend to morality; they, like those never caught offending, will remain obliged to calibrate their own conduct. But how?

A third theme, observable to some, was that I, and I assume many of us, remain until the end our parents' children. Valuing and evaluating parents is, I think, a recurring companion to the process of ageing, and for the four years of Gresham lectures I thought of my parents often. They were both remarkably good people, in my view. But my father's determined blue-collar modesty could embarrass me at school – something he clearly recognised by disguising his 'blue collar' job behind some formula about being 'engaged on secret work for Her Majesty's Stationery Office'. His declining a management position when I was a teenager at the local excellent direct grant school – St Dunstan's College, Catford – added to my bowed-head shame in conversations when other boys could brag of their fathers' jobs or of the new family car.

My father justified his refusing promotion to manager, when he did, because he did not want to bring home work worries to the detriment of my elder brother and of me. I suspected that he was actually stubbornly stuck in his background, mildly bitter about those with money and power. But, as the trade union representative of his fellow employees – 'Father of the Chapel', for he worked 'in the print' – he came home regularly enough worried and unhappy about what was happening to them. In particular, I recall his extended anxieties about following a rule (almost a law?) – 'LIFO', last in first out – that meant he *had* to approve his boss Robert Maxwell – the employer who stole his employees' pensions – kicking one of my father's members out of a job.

Was my father's modesty a spur to the worldly ambition I surreptitiously disguised for fear of failure but that otherwise drove me on?

My mother successfully contested the rule against women continuing to work as teachers after marriage when she needed to return to work; but she too declined promotion, to headmistress, in favour of teaching disabled children in London's East End once my brother and I were old enough for her to leave us alone at home and make the long daily journey from Bellingham in South London where we lived.

My parents inspired me quietly all my life.

And yet to acknowledge, as I reached my eighth decade, that I could still be influenced by the approach to life – absolutely admirable – of my parents only adds to the puzzle I *first* identify. How can any of us, guided or not by religion or by our nation's laws, think sufficiently freely to evaluate our own lives and not be trapped by standards set by others? I remain conditioned, happily, by how my parents thought. Can I truly claim more genuine freedom of thought than a citizen of Kim Jong-un's North Korea or a Mormon, or the child of fiercely Zionist parents?

Which brings me to justice. While working at the UN's tribunal for war crimes committed in the former Yugoslavia (ICTY) I often spoke to visiting groups of schoolchildren, university students or other lawyers. To open a discussion, I usually asked why there should be war crimes tribunals. Most groups answered in a similar way and for nearly all groups 'justice' was a first or second reason. But when asked what justice was, every group floundered, as I confess do I. Is it fairness of the law? And if so whose laws, a nation's laws, international law, sharia law, which? Is it fairness of process? Is it fairness of outcome to defendants or to victims or even to a lawyer? I have never found a conclusive resolution. But that may not matter.

Asking what justice is and whether it has been delivered are often at the heart of the lectures from which this book has been drawn. And, as in discussion with visitors to the tribunal, I rarely venture a firm answer.

Was – is – my asking questions but not providing answers a way of avoiding responsibility? I hope not. Justice may be impossible to define but *in*justice is something easily sensed or felt. Non-lawyer citizens own the law – lawyers and judges do not; indeed it is quite often lawyers and judges as well as politicians who will act so as to cause injustice, and the non-lawyer needs to know how limited should be the trust s/he (hereafter 'he' for brevity) reposes in them and to understand how difficult it can be for institutions to deliver justice. Acknowledging how injustice occurs can lead non-lawyer citizens and lawyers to ask what they can do personally, and what institutions *should* do, to achieve justice, however impossible to define. On this very last question, the aspirational principle which I sought to promote in the very last lecture – 'that I may place others' causes before my own' – may be some answer or perhaps little more than a dream. But if we do not sometimes dream we may never change.

Chapter 1

International Criminal Tribunals: Experiments? Works in Progress?

In the last 20 years several international courts have been established to try crimes committed in armed conflicts. Public expectation of what these courts may achieve is high; but are the courts living up to that expectation? Even if not, have they done enough to chart an irreversible path along which international law and courts will advance in the service of communities or countries at war?

Original lecture delivered on 12 September 2012.

War crimes courts and tribunals have changed the way the world citizen can think. Now – never before – he can say of someone seen as responsible for horrors in conflict 'send him [occasionally her] to The Hague'. He probably has in mind one of the courts, of various kinds, that are the modern successors to earlier models that attempted to deal with war by law.

There are three types of modern international criminal courts.

First, there are two tribunals set up by the UN under its Chapter VII peace-keeping powers for particular conflicts: the International Criminal Tribunal for the former Yugoslavia (ICTY), established in 1993 to prosecute persons responsible for serious violations of international humanitarian law committed in the territory of the former Yugoslavia since 1991; and the International Criminal Tribunal for Rwanda (ICTR), established in 1994 to try offenders for genocide and other such violations committed in Rwanda and the territory of neighbouring states, between 1 January and 31 December 1994.

Second, there are other hybrid courts with limited conflict-specific jurisdictions usually set up and operating in the country of the conflict that are run by international and local judges and lawyers working together: these court's deal with conflicts in Cambodia, East Timor, Sierra Leone and Lebanon.

Third, there is the treaty-based International Criminal Court (ICC) set up and maintained as a permanent court not by the UN but by those 124 countries that have now ratified the Rome Statute.

These tribunals and courts resemble ordinary national criminal courts in many ways. As a result the world citizen may assume that they, like national courts, are part of a coherent, judicial crime and punishment system that happens to be international. Nothing could be further from the truth.

Comparison of national and international 'systems' can help our understanding of both. A nation's judicial system is very familiar to its citizens, especially if they have ever been involved in it as victim, defendant, witness, lawyer or judge. Both the law of the system and its procedures will be generally known and, more important, in most countries the citizen can approve, disapprove or seek to change them through his vote or by becoming a legislator. More easily for the citizen – and without his having to take any direct action – in developed and open societies newspapers and other media of communication will be reflecting his and others' views on the legal system of the country every day. Open any newspaper, from a serious broadsheet to a tabloid, and be surprised at how many stories are actually testing and challenging the law and its operation: straight legal reporting reflects the law and legal practice as it is; criticism of existing law and especially of sentencing challenges the law and seeks its change; professional or personal errors by judges or lawyers are always good media 'copy'. In modern academic jargon the citizen 'owns' the law and the legal system by which his day-to-day conduct is regulated.

He has no such proprietary rights over the international law under which he may live or die.

If the often expressed desire by humans to live in peace is genuine – despite all evidence to the contrary – then international law and the procedures by which it is applied could hardly be more important. World War II showed us that we have the potential to destroy ourselves through the atomic bomb. The Holocaust demonstrated how we have the potential to persuade each other and ourselves to do the worst possible, unimaginable things to fellow humans. So perhaps a period of time spent considering international criminal law is justified, and to this end differences between national and international legal systems may be quite informative.

SELECTION OF CONFLICTS FOR INTERVENTION

In a national system any serious crime committed today can and will be investigated and may be prosecuted this year, next decade or even later. The legal system is with the citizen until death – whether to help him if a victim or to turn on him if a villain.

Crimes in armed conflicts are treated very differently. In the list of major conflicts since 1900 it is unsurprising how few conflicts have been subject to any form of investigation.

Highly selective though the process of choosing conflicts for judicial intervention has clearly been, some choices are easy enough to understand. Both world wars could not be missed. Once the political situation permitted, Cambodia might be thought of as an obvious candidate because of the numbers killed. The selection in 1993 of Rwanda and of the former Yugoslavia for war crimes trials may seem similarly obvious now, although these choices are considered by many to have been responses to UN and EU failures to prevent mass killings and have only been possible because neither country had a sufficiently powerful patron to stand in the way of investigation.

Of the African countries with cases running or pending at the ICC, some, in particular the Congo (DRC), Uganda and Kenya, referred *themselves* to ICC investigation. But those 'self-referrals' are, at least in part, said to reflect the desire of the referring governments to have the ICC on their – the governments' – sides in continuing conflicts and to make the governments' enemies international pariahs, fairly or not.

And what about negative selection, or rather non-selection, for judicial intervention? No one, of course, has sought to investigate the mass killings of millions by the Soviet Union under Stalin before and during World War II. No one has sought to inquire judicially into crimes committed in the Korean War or – yet – into the gross violations of human rights by North Korea since.[1] Similarly with Burma. Interestingly, when the Burmese generals showed some signs of movement and Aung San Suu Kyi was allowed a world tour with full publicity, pressure for international judicial review of mass crimes committed in recent history reduced. Respect – or some other form of reasoning – for territorial neighbour China stands in the way of investigation. The victims of some country conflicts are better overlooked. The Russian invasion of Georgia or the wars in Iraq and Afghanistan – all of which could engage ICC jurisdiction – may be seen as conflicts that have escaped selection for various reasons, including the identity of the states involved. The late Robin Cook, when British Foreign Secretary, observed that the ICC was 'not a court set up to bring to book prime ministers of the United Kingdom or presidents of the United States'.

The permanent ICC suffers a further, significant and probably irremediable defect, especially apparent in the selection of conflicts to investigate, that may be seen as distinguishing it as a court from any national court.

While purporting to represent the will of the modern world citizen for some form of world order, the treaty-based permanent court has been ratified by only two-thirds of the approximately 200 countries of the world. The US, Russia and China in particular have not ratified. The court is not good enough for their citizens, it would appear. Yet they are happy to send citizens of other non-ratifying countries like Sudan or Libya to the court for trial through a Security

Council Resolution. Interestingly, four tiers of international justice are created: ratifying countries like the UK; non-ratifying countries which are members of the Security Council 'permanent five' and which will never face the court; non-ratifying members like Sudan or Libya which may face the court; and Israel which, although nominally like Sudan, has a patron on the Security Council.

Discrimination that applies the rule of law selectively, saying 'the law is for you not me', may well be understood and practised in both Russia and China; but for the US or for the rest of the so-called 'West' it must be odd to have anything to do with, or to show any respect for, a legal system that applies to this group of people but not to that group.

And will the US, China and Russia ever sign up? Probably not. Will the court survive without them? For the time being a country may be sufficiently under the influence of one or other of these 'super-powers' to feel obliged to allow its citizens to be tried by a club whose rules are not good enough for three of the 'permanent five' members of the Security Council. But things change and once any country says it will withdraw from such a selective court then the seeds of self-destruction in the court may germinate. How serious could this be?[2]

Selection or non-selection of a conflict for investigation seems often to be a highly political act. Should this worry us? Return to what may be thought of as Lilliput and ask this question: what confidence would you feel if, in the UK, you knew that rioting in London in 2011 would be investigated but rioting in Birmingham the year before (had there been any) would not be investigated; or if crimes in London were, but crimes in Manchester were not ever to be investigated?

SELECTION OF DEFENDANTS

You may say: 'Well, political choice of which conflicts to investigate is inevitable; the world cannot try them all.' True. So consider next the selections actually made of possible defendants once a particular conflict has been selected.

And this time let us start with a form of analogy: what would you say if the riots of Peckham were to be investigated but only where crimes were suspected of having been committed by members of the tribe of Capulets, but never if suspected of having been committed by members of the tribe of Montagues? How confident in your society would that make you feel, especially when the Montagues start marching up and down your street in paramilitary outfits?

During and after World War I there was an appetite to try leaders for war crimes. This is what the Treaty of Versailles had in mind for the Germans:

> **Article 227**
> The Allied and Associated Powers publicly arraign William II of Hohenzollern, formerly German Emperor, for a supreme offence against international morality and the sanctity of treaties.
>
> A special tribunal will be constituted to try the accused … guided by the highest motives of international policy, with a view to vindicating the solemn obligations of international undertakings and the validity of international morality.
>
> **Article 228**
> The German Government recognises the right of the Allied and Associated Powers to bring before military tribunals persons accused of having committed acts in violation of the laws and customs of war. Such persons shall, if found guilty, be sentenced to punishments laid down by law.

Not a word about bad things done by the Allied and Associated Powers.

Kaiser Wilhelm had been granted sanctuary in the Netherlands and Queen Wilhelmina refused to have him extradited. US President Wilson also rejected calls for his extradition, arguing that punishing Wilhelm for waging war would destabilise international order and lose the peace.

Many of the problems that still face international war crimes trials were touched on then: the responsibility for crimes in war of a political leader; the sanctity of sanctuary once granted; the political risks associated with criminal trials that might outweigh the advantages of an amnesty or of a criminal trial. Yet how interesting might have been a trial of the Kaiser, who early in the war in a letter to Austrian Kaiser Franz Joseph wrote the following revealing description of his state of mind:

> My soul is torn, but everything must be put to fire and sword; men, women and children and old men must be slaughtered and not a tree or house be left standing. With these methods of terrorism, which are alone capable of affecting a people as degenerate as the French, the war will be over in two months, whereas if I admit considerations of humanity it will be prolonged for years. In spite of my repugnance I have therefore been obliged to choose the former system.[3]

Mental state of some kind, '*mens rea*' in lawyer's Latin, has to be established for any criminal offence. Had the Kaiser stood by this justification would this articulated mental state have amounted to a defence? If not, how would past judicial condemnation of the Kaiser, had such a defence failed, have looked to President Truman when he authorised the use of atomic bombs on Japan or to Churchill when he approved the Dresden attacks? Each might have foreseen having to rely on the same defence.

Trials of other war criminals were limited. There was no tribunal that explored the conduct of the war generally, and although there were notorious executions by the Allies of their own servicemen for desertion or other wrongs, I have found no record of Allied soldiers being tried for the equivalent of war crimes.

Tribunals established after World War II in Germany and Japan – often enough described as examples of 'victor's justice' – resembled or perhaps mimicked trials in national systems to the extent they could. But reflecting the same intent manifest in World War I they only ever tried one side – the Germans or the Japanese. And they were very different from national trials.

First, they only continued for a time and only ever tried for criminality a selected few of those who might have been involved in crimes.

Second, there is a considerable amount of evidence – nearly all untested by any court – of war crimes committed by all Allied forces: rapes, executions, torture, starvation. There was no tribunal set up to investigate such crimes and, although there were a few courts martial for regular crimes, evidence of possible offences was generally swept under the nearest convenient carpet. For events that could not be covered up and that would cry out today for judicial consideration as possible war crimes – Dresden, Hiroshima – there was no process of judicial assessment of any kind.

Will we or later generations have uncomfortable discoveries of unprosecuted horrors to integrate into our heroic history of 20th-century conflict just as descendants of those who were colonial officials in Kenya may now have to accept that their forebears committed atrocities against the Mau Mau in the interest of the Empire?

In the absence of any post-World War II judicial appraisal of the conduct of the Allied forces, Japanese courts did eventually dare to consider the atomic bombings. In 1963 *Ryuichi Shimoda et al. v The State* found that 'the attacks upon Hiroshima and Nagasaki caused such severe and indiscriminate suffering that they did violate the most basic legal principles governing the conduct of war'.

In 2007 an informal 'International Peoples' Tribunal' delivered its verdict, stating:

> The Tribunal finds that the nature of damage caused by the atomic bombs can be described as indiscriminate extermination of all life forms or inflicting unnecessary pain to the survivors … [The] use of nuclear weapons in Hiroshima and Nagasaki was illegal in the light of the principles and rules of International Humanitarian Law applicable in armed conflicts, since the bombing of both cities made civilians the object of attack, using nuclear weapons that were incapable of distinguishing between civilians and military targets and consequently caused unnecessary suffering to the civilian survivors.[4]

The Allies got away with little formal examination of any criminal responsibility.

INVESTIGATING ALL SIDES, OR AT LEAST TRYING ONE SIDE PROPERLY

Modern international criminal courts do not so easily fall into the trap of prosecuting one side only. Their mandates typically allow for trial of all sides. To some extent that did happen at the ICTY, although not without difficulty as we will see. However, a number of somewhat surprising decisions challenge the notion that these various courts are being punctilious in observance of the rule of law when other interests collide.

Rwanda

In Rwanda attempts to try the victorious Tutsis, then in government, sought by Prosecutor del Ponte were successfully blocked by the government and not pursued by her successor. Tutsis, although victims of genocide, had also been suspected of grave war crimes.[5] Del Ponte told the UN Security Council that the Rwandan government was manufacturing reasons to block cooperation with the court after her announcement that she would investigate the country's present leaders for alleged war crimes.

The government of Rwanda submitted to the UN that 'The Government of Rwanda does not believe that abuses committed by the Rwanda Patriotic Army should be equated to the crimes committed by the perpetrators of genocide … It would appear that the proposed indictments of the RPA are merely intended to appease advocates of a so-called "ethnically balanced justice".'[6] Del Ponte responded to political pressure from the UN and the EU; the government won, and the Tutsis have not been prosecuted. Was this the rule of law in action?

Sierra Leone

The Special Court for Sierra Leone (SCSL) on 7 March 2003 issued an indictment against Charles Taylor, serving President of Liberia. Taylor filed a motion to quash his indictment, arguing that he enjoyed absolute immunity from prosecution as a serving head of state, and that exceptions to diplomatic immunity can only derive from other rules of international law unavailable to the SCSL because it was effectively a national court.

On 11 August 2003 Taylor resigned as president and went into exile in Nigeria pursuant to an arrangement brokered by the African Union (AU), the UN and the US in which Nigeria offered Taylor exile. But pressure to hand Taylor over to the SCSL was then put on Nigeria by the US, the European Parliament, Western non-governmental organisations (NGOs), Nigerian civil society, bar associations and academics.[7]

In order to overcome head-of-state immunity the SCSL Appeals Chamber decided in May 2004 that, though the court was a hybrid court, 'the principle seems now established that the sovereign equality of states does not prevent a head of state from being prosecuted before an international criminal tribunal or court.'[8] So Taylor could be handed over.

The decision has been heavily criticised not least because fundamental interests of states are at stake – and insufficiently addressed – in situations where the Security Council purports to abrogate, through the creation of a tribunal, the immunity of a serving head of state.[9]

Libya

Another example now rich with irony is that of Colonel Gaddafi of Libya. The first Chief Prosecutor of the SCSL, David Crane, wanted to indict Gaddafi for his direct participation in the conflicts in Sierra Leone and Liberia. Gaddafi was alleged to be one of masterminds of the war in Sierra Leone, and a key financier. The US however, was not interested in indicting Gaddafi because at the same time the US was engaging with Gaddafi over the removal of chemical weapons. French Foreign Minister Dominique de Villepin encouraged French business in Libya. British Prime Minister Tony Blair met with Gaddafi in Tripoli and signed an agreement for Shell to have rights to oil exploration on the Libyan coast. The US re-established diplomatic relations with Libya, and Gaddafi was never indicted.[10]

Favoured at one international court acting under political pressure to meet Western interests, was he later 'disfavoured' by another when the ICC indicted him at unprecedented speed as if to assist in recognition of the Transitional Council by which Gaddafi's regime was finally changed?

Cambodia

The Extraordinary Chambers in the Courts of Cambodia was established by the Cambodian government and the UN to try senior figures in the Khmer Rouge. Nominally independent, the court has, at crucial times, been subjected to improper influence by Hun Sen, Cambodia's prime minister. Almost all Cambodian prosecutors and judges are active members of the Cambodian People's Party, Hun Sen's own party. Conflicts over loyalty and independence are commonplace amongst Cambodian legal staff. Five cases were shut down without any examination of the evidence, without suspects being notified that they were under investigation, without witnesses being interviewed or crime sites being examined.[11] Disgracefully, a senior international UN official was instrumental in these decisions.

Hun Sen's motive for shutting down the court on his terms is assumed to be to stop it digging up evidence that could implicate serving members of the ruling elite. The UN and the US State Department have nevertheless defended the decisions of the judges – one of whom resigned specifically over the pressure imposed on him by the Cambodian government.

International co-prosecutor Andrew Cayley made public the glaring deficiencies in the investigation of the dropped cases. He tried to get the judges to investigate properly cases that he determined should be investigated in accordance with the express mandate and jurisdiction of the court. The investigating judges threatened him with contempt on spurious grounds. He was left without support by the international community, the UN in particular. Cayley's experience in being left to sustain as much as possible of the rule of law without the support of the UN or of the countries which participate in the ICC is not unique.

Overall, the selection of those to be prosecuted within any conflict chosen for investigation may well be as political as was the choice for inquiry of the conflict itself.

THE TIMING OF INTERNATIONAL JUDICIAL INTERVENTION

The ICC can investigate all sides of a conflict but faces another difficulty that would never face national courts, which rarely, if ever, get involved in acts that are, or may be, criminal as they are happening. Recent war crime trials – Rwanda, Cambodia, most trials arising from the Yugoslav conflicts – are also after-the-event trials and deal with activities and states of mind of the accused that crystallised before the trial started – hard though they may be to prove.

ICC cases, on the other hand, are often started while conflicts are continuing and this has led to the recurring suggestion that African countries engage the ICC in order to attack their opponents, thereby to make the court itself an instrument of war.

In any democratic country decision-making about international treaties that generate international law can *theoretically* be traced through various government bodies back to the elector citizen. In reality elections are rarely, if ever, fought on the detail of some international treaty. In the result the international law with which we are concerned has developed piecemeal and at a distance from the voting citizen anywhere.

Racing by the instructions for conduct of war to be found in Deuteronomy 20: 10–18, the Lieber Code for the American Civil War, and the Hague Conventions of 1899 and 1907, we may eventually arrive at the drafting of the statute for trials at Nuremberg. This did much to define, and led to further definition of, the modern law, but that was – as Professor William Schabas argues – done in a calculated way.[12]

To understand his argument it is necessary first to remind ourselves that crimes are not in any sense absolute, whatever the informed modern citizen may think about, for example, the crime of genocide. Crimes are selections by category of human behaviour and the same name for a crime is often differently defined in one nation from how it is defined in another. Murder in the UK may be different in definition – and thus in the category of acts identified as murder – from murder in the US. And crimes once defined can easily enough be divided further, as some crimes (although not murder) have been in the UK according to whether they are or are not 'racially aggravated'.

On analysis, genocide is a sub-set of crimes against humanity, as now defined. The phrase 'Crimes against Humanity' had been in use in ordinary language for over 200 years. One attributed early use is to French revolutionary Maximilien Robespierre, who described Louis XVI as a '*criminel envers l'humanité*' ('criminal against humanity'). In 1860 the electoral platform on which Abraham Lincoln stood for president included the following statement: 'We brand the recent re-opening of the African slave trade, under the cover of our national flag, aided by perversions of judicial power, as a crime against humanity.'

The term started its shrinking of meaning to a usable legal term in the 1907 Hague Convention preamble, which codified the customary law of armed conflict based on existing state practices as being derived from those values and principles deemed to constitute the 'laws of humanity', as reflected throughout history in different cultures.

Its first formal appearance was in a declaration concerning the Armenian massacres made by the governments of France, Great Britain and Russia on 24 May 1915 ('In the presence of these new crimes of Turkey against humanity and civilization ...'). Interestingly – and connected to what follows – the US did not join in this denunciation and US Secretary of State Robert Lansing referred to what he called the 'more or less justifiable' right of the Turkish government to deport the Armenians to the extent that they lived within the zone of military operations.

After World War II, the Nuremberg trials included allegations of crimes against humanity. In the London Conference of 1945 that preceded the Nuremberg trials, where the crime was defined, US prosecutor Justice Jackson, echoing World War I Secretary of State Lansing, made it quite clear that it was no part of the US's functions to interfere with the internal affairs of another country, even if they were exterminating their citizens. Jackson explained – candidly – that this reflected how a broader definition of crimes against humanity that could allow the Allies to try the Nazis for acts *not* linked to war could expose the US to the same pursuit for things it had done in the past. No doubt the UK agreed with the outcome and the reasoning.

But the Nazis *were* to be tried for what they had done not just to the populations of other countries but also to their own people in the course of the war. Thus, although it was possible to draft an offence as a 'crime against humanity' that covered what the Nazis did to the Jews in the war, such crimes were only to be justiciable by the tribunal if they involved:

> murder, extermination, enslavement, deportation, and other inhumane acts committed against any civilian population, before or during the war; or persecutions on political, racial or religious grounds *in execution of or in connection with any crime within the jurisdiction of the Tribunal*, whether or not in violation of the domestic law of the country where perpetrated.[13]

The Tribunal's judgment in 1946 followed the Statute[14] and Raphael Lemkin, the man who had coined the word 'genocide' in

1943 and brought it into some general usage by the time of the Nuremberg trials, was driven to go to New York, explains Schabas, to ensure that, in future, peacetime acts such as those committed by the Nazis against the Jews could be covered. This would require genocide to become a specific, identifiable crime.

But for this course of events, then, the activities of the Nazis – as of the Turks in Armenia, the Hutus in Rwanda, the Khmer Rouge in Cambodia, the Serbs in Bosnia – would not have been found by any retroactive opinion or court verdict to have been 'genocide' but rather to have been terrible acts that might qualify in ordinary parlance as genocide but in law as a category of crimes against humanity.

The Genocide Convention was passed in 1948 and has now been ratified by some 142 states. The definition of genocide – significantly different from Raphael Lemkin's first definition in 1943 – has been followed closely or precisely in various national and international statutes since that time, including in our own UK law that outlaws the crime.

Curiously, it may seem, many of those closely involved with international courts do not see the power to charge genocide as a crime always to be a good thing. I recall a colleague at the ICTY writing a book on genocide when we both worked there titled 'Crime of Crimes'. And that, in a way, is where the potential for difficulty lies. People – victims as much as some lawyers – live in an age of superlatives and celebrity. Victims may want to have their suffering described as the worst of all possible; lawyers may want to be seen working on a case that is the worst of all possible. Celebrities may want to stick their names to eye-catching words when they support victims of a particular conflict. And, of course, once any trial has attempted to deal with a genocide allegation – as with the allegations made about Srebrenica in the ICTY and in the world's senior civil court, the International Court of Justice (ICJ), also in The Hague – it is essential that the correct legal record is left.

A truth – that introduces a puzzle – is that killings in large numbers and terrible circumstances can be as bad whether characterised as crimes against humanity, war crimes or genocide. The only distinguishing feature of genocide is the intention that has to be established, namely the intent *to destroy, in whole or in part, a national, ethnical, racial or religious group, as such* – an intention that might seem less sane than the state of mind of someone who commits a war crime by killing all prisoners in his control, as Henry V did at Agincourt, for the more practical reason of not allowing them to rise again as combatants. Which motivating force is the more criminal?

CONDUCT OF TRIALS

Staffing

These tribunals are either run by large organisations like the UN, or the participating countries of the ICC or by one-off combinations of local and national lawyers. It is hardly surprising if these last arrangements generate cross-cultural difficulties. As for the UN and the ICC, people are sometimes surprised to hear the insider's view that these large organisations are much like other large organisations: they do not contain a staff of highly committed idealists and they frequently 'default' to mediocrity at best. They do not necessarily attract the best of the world's lawyers and the judges they recruit have a varied reputation.

In most of the courts the judges have to be nominated by a nation and elected in New York. Some judges are ex-diplomats or academics with no previous judicial experience, and there are those owed favours by the governments that nominate them. Although the UK judges have generally been very well thought of, it is of note that only in Sir Adrian Fulford at the ICC and Lord Iain Bonomy at the ICTY did the UK nominate candidates of the level of High Court judges because there was limited appetite from the senior or very senior judiciary to take on this work.

Location of hearings

At the ICTY I wondered how different it might have been for the judges to uproot themselves from the comfortable life in The Hague and fly south. There, in suits not robes, they might have taken evidence day after day in local public halls, perhaps showing willingness to work long hours in circumstances where local residents, who would have experienced the horrors of war, could walk in to see justice being done. It was never going to happen for a thousand practical reasons. And there would have been no judicial appetite for it in any case. Weekend travel to and from the judges' home cities, which many liked to visit regularly, or even simply back to The Hague would have been too difficult; and long days in dusty halls insufficiently agreeable. Such an exercise might, I thought, have given considerable impetus to whatever effect the trials could have on reconciliation, but here I dream.

Legal staff

The lawyers in these courts are in a different position from that of the judges. Their privileges are limited and they have to fit into normal management systems even if, like me, they come from private practice where it is comparatively easy to be independent and respectful of ethical duties owed to a court or to a defendant on trial. Employed lawyers are in a far more difficult position – often thousands of miles from home, with partners and children to support, they may find the exercise of independent judgment in the face of being instructed to do something on the edge of, or beyond, propriety hard to resist.

My own experience at the ICTY was revealing of the politicised nature of such institutions and the pressures brought to bear on individuals within them (see also Appendix 1). Three examples follow.

The very best collection of documents the prosecution obtained was a stenographically recorded series of meetings lasting nine years attended by Slobodan Milošević and the presidents of Montenegro and the rump Federal Republic of Yugoslavia. Serbia made a deal with the prosecutor to have the best – or rather the worst – parts blacked out from public view. Lawyers and judges could see the totality. Citizens could not. Extraordinarily the ICJ trying the case brought by Bosnia against Serbia for breaches of the Genocide Convention worked on the basis of the blacked-out documents and never saw what lay beneath. The deal served Serbia's purposes. There was no conceivable reason that I could see why they should have been blacked out and the deal was made against my written objection.

Within those records there is this passage, finally public although too late to generate much interest now in Bosnia, sadly. In the session of 14 August 1995, the first reference to the fall of Srebrenica and Žepa was made. Milošević referred to his communication with General Ratko Mladić, leader of the Bosnian Serb forces, commonly regarded as responsible for – and at the time of publication on trial for – the Srebrenica genocide, saying:

> Momo remembers well my conversation with Mladić on the occasion of attack on Žepa and Srebrenica. On that occasion I said: 'Ratko, you are now measuring the military price of that success. The military price is six persons killed, 20 wounded, one vehicle destroyed, etc. It is inexpensive. However, the political price could be a million times higher because there might be a concern for the interests of 12 million people!'[15]

There was plenty of intelligence on the Internet and elsewhere to the effect that *intercepts* of these conversations between Milošević and Mladić existed, as was confirmed in the official Netherlands War Documentation Centre (NIOD) report on Srebrenica – that said:

> The existence of these intercepts was confirmed by a Western diplomat. During a meeting at the White House between Gore and Bildt, the Swedish negotiator tried to convince the US vice-president that he should not form an excessively black-and-white image of President Milošević. Gore responded to these statements by reading from US intercepts, which showed that Milošević had consulted with Mladić about the attack on Srebrenica. Gore then reportedly said to Bildt: 'Forget about this. Milošević is absolutely not the friend of the West.'[16]

I sought by every means to get the intercepts and had a target entity waiting to face the court to explain whether, as suspected, it had them to hand over. A different entity entered the office and instructed the prosecutor to withdraw the application. She complied. Whose interests were served? Serbia's? Maybe. The interests of any other entity that would have preferred less to be known about its knowledge of events at the time? More than maybe. I would have had to reveal how the prosecution succumbed to pressure if Milošević had said that the West knew what was about to happen – had he not died.

My final example relates to Ramush Haradinaj, prime minister of the small entity of Kosovo, which was in the process of gaining its independence at the time. The prosecutor was determined to indict Haradinaj, arguably for political reasons, because Serbia was complaining about an insufficient number of Kosovars being pursued. Qualified lawyers refused to indict Haradinaj because there was insufficient evidence. Lawyers in the prosecutor's office who *never* appeared in court to act as advocates were instructed to indict Haradinaj – and did as they were told. He was tried to acquittal and released. He was returned to custody for a partial retrial, arguably in defiance of even the most modern standards of permitted 'double' jeopardy that only allow someone to be prosecuted a second time in extreme circumstances. Between March 2005 and November 2012 he was in custody or on 'provisional release' (bail) before being acquitted a second time and returned to Kosovo. His political career did not flourish, and in early 2016 he was detained in France on an extradition warrant obtained by Serbia. The outcome of this case is awaited. One thing is clear: prosecuting this successful politician was contrary to normal standards and arguably deprived a fledgling state of the leader under whom it might have flourished in what had been a difficult period.

THE FUTURE OF INTERNATIONAL CRIMINAL TRIBUNALS

Are trials of what may be criminal wars, or of criminal actions in otherwise lawful wars, processes the citizen can trust? Are they, in reality, processes whereby selections of conflicts and individuals within conflicts to pursue are political or politicised decisions? Is the law by which those selected for trial will be tried itself politicised in a way that is out of reach of the citizens affected?

Suppose the very worst of interpretations can be put on the developments of the last 20 years; do we face return to a reality explained in Shakespeare's *Henry VI, Part 3* when Northumberland says to York immediately before York is butchered,

> It is war's prize to take all vantages;
> And ten to one is no impeach of valour.

If resolution, including by war crimes trials, of armed conflicts remains subject to influence of the victors, does this give everything to the victors, both as to spoils and as to reputation? I think not and invite consideration of the following as immensely positive outcomes of war crimes tribunals.

First, all trials leave an enormous record of evidence that would never have come to light or never have come to light so soon. And – something for which the adversarial system can be praised – the evidence is usually tested in court by cross-examination on behalf of, or even in person by the accused against whom it is aimed. Future generations who may wish to abuse history for cynical political reasons may be able to complain about verdicts – which will perhaps count for far less than some think when they are rendered – but will have to be able to surmount a wall of more or less unbreakable evidence.

Second, individual nations have been compelled by the existence of the ICC statute to add to their own statute books laws that cover more crimes of war, just as the UK has done with genocide.

Third, states involved in conflict – such as Rwanda, Serbia, Bosnia and Croatia – have found themselves conducting domestic trials for war crimes that are beyond the finite capacity of the international courts to try. This reality on the ground – together with the expectation that it should happen – adds in a practical way to the general raised expectation in the world citizen of 'sending people to The Hague'.

And if you think this may be encouraging it is only, I believe, the start.

African countries are beginning to resist the attempted reach of the ICC. Is this necessarily a bad thing? In 2014 the African Union made first moves – yet to be completed – to establish a criminal component of its African Court of Justice and Human Rights. This may be to keep Africans out of ICC jurisdiction, but note the intended scope of its statute, which would include, unprecedentedly, the crime of unconstitutional change of government and establish mercenarism as a crime along with corruption, money laundering, trafficking in persons, trafficking in drugs, trafficking in hazardous wastes, illicit exploitation of natural resources, and the crime of aggression. Genocide would be extended beyond the ICC law to cover acts of rape that are intended to change the identity of a particular group. The prohibited age for conscription of children into armed forces would be raised to 18.[17]

Regional, locally 'universal' courts – all Africa; all South America; all the Far East – could well be a more realistic way forward than the non-universal ICC that not too subtly attempts to impose Western standards in a political way on countries not strong enough to resist. An African country reluctant to surrender one of its citizens to The Hague for trial may be far less unwilling to have the issue dealt with in Arusha in Tanzania.

And even if this optimism is justified it is by no means all. The work of the courts to date has added to the citizen's understanding of how to react to conflict. Research shows that it is the existence of courts that has made citizens less cowed by grand institutions and governments and more aware of their ability to act and react within political systems, turning to the law when they need it – the 'Mothers of Srebrenica' who have tested the conduct of the ICTY are a prime example.[18] But the context in which all this is happening – the 20 years in which these courts have emerged – is of an age of previously unimaginable advances in computers, the Internet, social networks, Skype – and this may turn out to be significant.

I have never been the victim of conflict violence and thus cannot know how such victims feel about the need for retribution through convictions and sentencing of offenders. And I do not diminish their potential importance. However, it seems clear that after conflicts a principal concern of the affected citizen is to know what happened and to be confident that the best possible narrative of events is left behind. A belief that this can, or should, be done through a form of criminal trial process was held as possible by Hartley Shawcross at Nuremberg but dismissed as outside the law's scope by Hannah Arendt in her seminal book *Eichmann in Jerusalem*. But they never knew the World Wide Web. Neither did Bertrand Russell when he established his peoples' tribunal for Vietnam.

These days for the purposes of leaving a record of events the citizen no longer has to show respect to great institutions if they fail to serve him well. By way of example, an international group of diaspora Iranians created in 2007 a Lord Russell-style tribunal to deal with massacres of Iranians during the 1980s in Iran's prisons (see chapter 7). The two-stage process of that tribunal was intended not just to leave a record but to hold the Iranian regime accountable for its crimes against humanity. Internationally respected figures agreed to serve unpaid as commissioners and judges of the two-part commission and trial process. At modest cost – and with the benefit of Skype – 80 witnesses from around the world were heard in the first week in London in June 2012 and the Commission's report of this evidence together with other critical witnesses was heard in The Hague that October. The decision of the tribunal was delivered in 2013. This condemned the regime and identified individuals against whom evidence existed of the commission of grave crimes.

To go back to where I started, this is a conflict that would never be selected for international attention despite its gravity. The informal tribunal shows that the world citizen can *hope* courts will serve him well but can easily find the means to do the job himself if they don't. Courts – in particular the ICC – should perhaps be seen as part of larger projects and not so much as ends in themselves. This may encourage them to perform with less attention to political interest, to recognise that courts that are genuinely respected are those that simply perform to a high standard without seeking to engage in politics along the way. These courts – ICTY, ICTR, ICC and so on – have stimulated expectations for the future and they can now benefit from the criticisms of them that exposure has created. Whether they come to be seen as experiments or works in progress may matter less than the title of this chapter suggests.

Those who claim that international courts and legal systems will end impunity would do well to remember the following: making a crime of murder or rape did not stop killing or raping. It may have reduced the times these things happened but deterrence – a good ambition – is probably the product of politicians, social scientists, and many other parts of our open societies working hand in hand, sometimes with lawyers, and building on knowledge from wherever generated. These courts have added to knowledge immeasurably and *may*, properly deployed and when functioning at their best, increase the prospects of a reduction of future conflict. For that to happen in the long term, extraordinary universal and 'multi-disciplinary' determination will be required that sets as objectives universal justice *for all victims* together with a reduction of armed conflicts. To be legitimate and acceptable the objectives would have to be for all countries and for any conflicts – regardless of the disinclination of powerful countries or groups of countries to allow their conduct in conflicts to be tested. Until that determination is found – if it ever is – keeping the present courts going despite their shortcomings may be as good a first step as any other.

Chapter 2

The End of Slobodan Milošević

Slobodan Milošević faced three indictments covering the three major conflicts of the 1990s in the western Balkans: Croatia, Bosnia and Kosovo. He was surrendered to The Hague for trial in 2001 by the successor government of Prime Minister Zoran Đinđić, himself assassinated by those loyal to Milošević in 2003.

The trial lasted 467 days; 350 witnesses gave evidence in person; 59 written witness statements were read. The transcript of the trial occupies 49,191 pages and there were approximately 150,000 pages of prosecution paper exhibits and 25,000 pages of defence exhibits. The prosecution served on the defence at least 1,000,000 pages of 'exculpatory material'. Milošević died in his cell shortly before the end of the time allowed for his case, on 11 March 2006.

There were no closing arguments and no judgment.

Original lecture delivered on 2 October 2012.

This is how I might have started a closing argument in the Milošević case:

'Your Honours. In deciding on the guilt of Slobodan Milošević on the specific charges in this indictment may you be assisted by a separate and single question: did a time come when, by any modern standard, this man crossed the line that divides the lawful from the unlawful in circumstances when he knew full well that he had crossed that line?

'An answer to this question is significant because the subjective mental state that has to be proved for any crime is inevitably confirmed, or reinforced, by an accused's private recognition of having crossed the lawful–unlawful divide. More significant may be that politicians pulled into wrongdoing over time – as Milošević *may* have been – can have numberless different states of mind as days pass: today a real intent to make negotiations work; tomorrow an intent to become a statesman; the day after that an intent to kill enemies by fair means or foul. In truth, for such people the forensically precise analysis of a mental state associated with a particular – sometimes single or momentary – action may be hard to prove. But not when he has already crossed over to mental territory he knows to be outside the law and from which he may be unable to return, given loyalty to a driving cause that he may be unable to recant.

'Milošević trained as a lawyer and became a banker. The prosecution found nothing criminal or violent in his past. By the end of the 1980s he was a man who had tasted power and found the taste to his liking, but who faced difficult problems for which he fashioned responses that were, or became, criminal.

'Were Milošević simply a deranged monster, then it would be easy to regard his trial as irrelevant to the world of rational democratic politicians we like to think we inhabit. However, it is sometimes those very politicians for whom the tragic history unleashed by this man's deeds may be a lesson; as it must for him be both a lesson and the route to sanction of this court.'

SOME OBSERVATIONS

First, I offer a few general points about this and other similar trials. Evidence in such cases cannot be frozen or sealed before the case starts. Investigations will continue; the topic is too important to stop investigating, and more evidence will always be available, some of it freed by the very process of a public trial: people produce documents they might not otherwise have produced but for seeing the trial, and some witnesses find courage to give evidence once they see the trial progressing.

Milošević represented himself and took swiftly to cross-examination, a feature of the adversarial system of trial that was adopted arbitrarily, or by cultural imperialism, for these trials and that is outside the experience of most continental European and Balkan countries that have inquisitorial systems. He was soon able to intimidate witnesses. But he was, I thought, a terrible advocate because he chose the bad points, not the good, and revealed too much of himself by his demeanour in court, something that could have been obscured by a smooth lawyer. Such a lawyer could have painted him in a very different light: it would have been a very good case to defend.

Eyewitnesses or victims of the terrible things done in conflicts are unlikely to be other than honest. Cross-examining them is unlikely to serve the cross-examiner well. Milošević unwisely cross-examined every witness. This stretched further a trial timetable already extended by his recurring ill health. In this 'extra time' thus made available the prosecution was able to find and present much more, and much better, evidence than it could have done had Milošević been represented by a smooth lawyer who, on the first day of the trial, could have told the court that all the evidence of crimes could simply be read into the court record without troubling the victims and that he, the lawyer, would look forward to dealing with the evidence connecting those crimes to Milošević. The prosecution would have been very embarrassed by such an approach.

After Milošević's death the judges, I understand, destroyed any notes they might have made. No judgment will be forthcoming from them on a man who, under the principle of the burden of proof, died free of the stain of any conviction. However, at the end of the prosecution case, arguments were advanced about the sufficiency of evidence for some counts. The court reviewed the prosecution's case as presented and gave a judgment about which counts were sufficiently well evidenced to require Milošević to put a defence if he chose. That judgment, readily available on the ICTY website, is a valuable document of judicial analysis on some of the evidence presented by the prosecution.[1]

THE BALKAN CONFLICTS OF THE 1990s

Yugoslavia, the country of the South Slavs created after World War I, existed in two slightly different forms until World War II when, in 1941, it disintegrated, with an enlarged Croatia becoming a Nazi puppet state, Serbia falling under direct Nazi rule and Serbian Četniks and Yugoslav Partisans dividing ideological loyalties. Immediately after the war Marshal Tito forged the People's – later Socialist – Federal Republic of Yugoslavia (SFRY), and kept it together until his death in 1980. When dismantling of the Soviet communist bloc proper loomed, national interests surfaced in the former Yugoslavia and disintegration of that state into individual republics became a reality.

There were at least two serious underlying problems. First, Tito needed to deny Serbia perpetual hegemony over the other much smaller republics. This had been achieved by Kosovo and Vojvodina, two provinces of Serbia, being granted autonomy equivalent to that of full republics. Nationalist Serbs never accepted this reduction in the effective size of Serbia.

Second, many Serbs lived in Croatia and Bosnia; separation or secession of these republics from Serbia or from the rest of the former Yugoslavia would leave Serbs living under Croat, or other, control. The war in Croatia and the following war in Bosnia were largely about carving out autonomous Serbian areas in those republics that could then be connected together by Serb-controlled 'corridors', eventually to be joined with Serbia to form a Serbian state in which 'all Serbs could live'. Serbia was never itself at war in these conflicts but rendered support to Serbs in both the other republics. At material times for these two conflicts Milošević was president only of Serbia.

There is a concept of 'Greater Serbia' that permeates different aspects of the trial just as of Balkan history itself. According to the classic Serb version, the Serb defeat by the Ottomans in 1389 on Kosovo's Field of the Blackbirds reflected Tsar Lazar's conscious preference for a 'heavenly' rather than the 'earthly' empire he was told would come with victory. His choice made the Serbs by extension into a 'heavenly' people chosen by God who wished to reclaim their lost lands as 'Greater Serbia'.[2]

After the Dayton Accords halted the conflicts in Croatia and Bosnia, problems in Kosovo continued. Should Kosovo remain in or separate from Serbia? This led to the third conflict. As Kosovo was still part of Serbia itself and Milošević was head of that state his criminality was thought, by some, easier to prove than for the earlier conflicts. The Kosovo conflict ended with NATO bombing Serbia into a defeat that led later to Milošević's surrender to The Hague by a successor government for trials for war crimes.

The different conflicts – although very clearly of the same general theme – tended to be supported by different categories of evidence. I will deal with different types of evidence for each of the three conflicts.

THE CROATIAN WAR

The 110-paragraph indictment charged Milošević with 32 counts for offences alleged between August 1991 and July 1992, on the grounds that he had worked with other Serbian and Serb-Croatian politicians, police and military to exterminate, imprison, torture, destroy homes and property of, deport and forcibly transfer non-Serbs. It alleged specific attacks including on Vukovar and Dubrovnik – all crimes said to be committed through the agency of others. Casualty estimates included some 16,000 Croat soldiers and civilians killed or missing and 4,000 Serbs killed (mainly paramilitary troops).

This part of the case was well evidenced by senior figures from Serbia and Croatia. The overall case was that Serbs in Croatia – in various locations but starting at Knin in 1990 – wanted to create Serb enclaves that could detach from Croatia and join Serbia.

The 'Log Revolution'

Things took off under a man called Milan Babić in Knin with a 'Log Revolution' when Serbs blocked vital transport routes by felled tree branches. Milošević advised Babić on this, and it could be said to be his first truly criminal act by the incitement of unlawful behaviour in another republic. But it was hardly the stuff to excite emotion or justify the billion dollars and more the Yugoslav tribunal has cost or the millions the Milošević case itself cost.

High-level witnesses called by the prosecution included Borisav Jović, President of the Socialist Party of Serbia (SPS) before the conflict and a colleague of Milošević. We needed him to confirm that Milošević held absolute authority with the people and within the SPS. No single important decision in Serbia was taken without his consent and he wanted to know everything. In June 1990 the accused told Jović that the secession of Croatia was to be carried out so that various regions of Croatia would remain with Serbia – this evidence from Jović was the prosecution's overall case in a sentence.

President Stipe Mesić of Croatia (as he was when a witness) spoke of the 'Log Revolution' around Knin that blocked vital Croatian transport routes and of how the Yugoslav People's Army (JNA) lent its support to the rebels by preventing the Croatian police forces from getting rid of the logs. In the summer and autumn of 1991, Mesić said, paramilitary groups were gathering, arming and obtaining logistical support from Serbia. They arrived bearing arms, and Serbia did nothing to stop those who were on their way to Croatia to kill people and to destroy Croatian towns. Paramilitary groups, he explained, operated under the command of the JNA.

Milošević met Mesić many times, very often explaining that, were Yugoslavia to collapse, he could not leave more than two and a half million Serbs outside Serbia. Slovenia and part only of Croatia could secede from Yugoslavia, but Milošević would insist on the parts of Croatia inhabited by Serbs remaining in Yugoslavia.

Vukovar

The JNA Guards Division attacked and destroyed much of Vukovar as part of a regionally widespread campaign, apparently aimed at creating some form of a 'Greater Serbia'. These units were all under the command, ultimately, of Milošević. Those who carried out liquidations in Vukovar were given decorations by Serbia and promoted.

Before the war, Vukovar had a mixed population of approximately 45,000 people. During the JNA attack, 22,360 people were expelled. Vukovar was completely surrounded for three months by tanks; planes flew almost daily over the hospital, which was not a military target in any way, attacking it and other surrounding buildings. From 25 August until 20 November 1991, 2,250 wounded persons were admitted to the hospital. It was undefended. Dr Vesna Bosanac, Director of the Vukovar General Hospital, alerted the international community to the shelling. On 4 October 1991, two bombs hit the hospital. Cluster bombs and gases were used. JNA planes on several occasions dropped phosphorus bombs causing fires. In the space of two days 174 wounded persons were transported from the hospital under compulsion; 260 people were ultimately unaccounted for.

Some 200 people left the hospital and were killed at Ovčara and buried in a mass grave, the largest single massacre in Europe since World War II and until Srebrenica.

Dubrovnik

Dubrovnik was under siege from all sides by Serbs in October 1991. It was attacked not least to satisfy part of Serbia's desire to have access to the sea. The town was never taken.

General Nojko Marinović took over the defence of Dubrovnik, arriving there on 20 September 1991. He testified he had a mere 670 soldiers under his command. On 1 October 1991, the JNA launched a massive attack against the wider Dubrovnik municipality from both Herzegovina and Montenegro. The total strength of the JNA forces engaged in Dubrovnik was 5,000–7,000 men. The combined units involved had at least 36 howitzers, 60 heavy mortars, 240 bazookas, 60 anti-aircraft guns, and 44 tanks. They had total air superiority and deployed three missile boats and two patrol boats, along with surface-to-surface missiles with an 80-km range.

The only heavy weapons that were used inside the city of Dubrovnik (not in the Old Town) were two truck-mounted 20-mm anti-aircraft cannons. No weapons were placed in the proximity of the Old Town or the hospital. All military activity there was forbidden and the Old Town walls were marked with UNESCO flags and the hospital with a large red cross. As it was a UNESCO-protected site much of the civilian population had taken shelter there. The three worst attacks on the Old Town occurred on 23–24 October, 8–13 November and 6 December 1991. On all three occasions, nothing had occurred on the Croatian side which justified targeting of the Old Town.

The JNA military campaign failed because the JNA was not expecting any resistance, and when they started experiencing casualties their troops quickly lost their motivation. An international outcry resulted from their launch of unprovoked attacks against a UNESCO-protected city of no military significance. As the most intense shelling of the Old Town occurred within a wider JNA battle it would not be without the prior knowledge, planning, participation and supervision of the chain of command all the way to the top of the JNA.

Pero Poljanić, Mayor of Dubrovnik, spoke of the shelling that began on 1 October 1991. The shelling lasted until 31 December 1991 with the worst bombardment occurring on 6 December. In total, some 1,056 shells fell on the city. Specific buildings were not targeted; the entire city was the target. Petar Kriste, a Croatian government minister, explained that Dubrovnik was attacked in order to annex it to Greater Serbia. If Serbia had taken Dubrovnik and other Croatian territory to the north – and then some or all of Bosnia – Serbs could have lived in one state right up to the Karlobag–Karlovac–Virovitica line, favoured as a border by Serb extremists, a result that would have left Croatia as a small butterfly-shaped state about the size of Slovenia.

Hrvoje Šarinić, Chef de Cabinet of President Tuđman of Croatia, met Milošević many times, including at an infamous meeting on 26 March 1991, with Tuđman at Karađorđevo facility, where Tuđman confronted Milošević with his support of the 'Log Revolution' and the 'Greater Serbia' concept. To which Milošević said, 'Surely we can find the common language to solve those problems,' and it became clear to the witness from what was said by both Tuđman and Milošević afterwards that this statement was about dividing up Bosnia.

On 15 April 1991, the second meeting of this series with Milošević took place, this time at Tikveš. Tuđman told the witness that his objective was to get Milošević to influence Serbs in Croatia to come to their senses, to withdraw, 'so we could again establish our sovereignty in the entire Croatian territory, and then we can talk about Bosnia'. They probably reached an agreement, the witness thought, but it was never fulfilled, and that is why the war occurred.

After this second meeting in Tikveš, Tuđman showed the witness a paper that he received from Milošević, which spoke about the great danger posed by expansion by Muslims in Bosnia–Herzegovina. Roughly, it said that the Muslims were a major evil and that Serbs and Croats should be careful of the so-called green transversal, *zelena transverzala*, going from Turkey through Bulgaria, Western Macedonia, Kosovo and Sandzak.

Šarinić had a further meeting with Milošević in Belgrade on 20 September 1995, after the fall of Srebrenica. They spoke about the organisation of the Bosnian state. Milošević said:

> We, Hrvoje, are going to solve our problem and without the international community. We are each going to annex our part of Bosnia–Herzegovina. The United

> States are cradling this bastard but they don't understand a thing. We are going to put forward the formula, and the symmetry of two entities, and you should support us in that. We must not allow a unitary Bosnia–Herzegovina.

After the Croatia and Bosnia wars ended with the Dayton Accords, the two met on 10 March 1998 and discussed Kosovo. Šarinić asked him: 'How far are you prepared to go?' Milošević replied: 'All the way to wide-ranging self-rule, but any autonomy is out of the question.' Šarinić said: 'But this is less than the Albanians had in the 1974 constitution.' Milošević replied: 'Probably so, but that's history, and that was a big mistake which we have corrected, and we are never going to repeat it, regardless of how high the price might be.'

Witness C48, a true at-risk 'insider', worked as a waiter and in other capacities at the Royal Casino in the Hotel Pudnik in Novi Sad where he was trusted to be present at meetings of high-level SPS officials. In the first weeks of March 1993, the accused himself attended a meeting at the casino, where Milošević asked Jovica Stanišić, a Serbian intelligence officer, about the situation in eastern Slavonia and Baranja. Stanišić replied that everything was going according to the plan, that the terrain had been cleansed of Croats, and that the situation on the ground was stable. Milošević then said: 'Very well. So we have completed the main part of the job. Carry on like that but in a subtle way.' Milošević thus expressed his approval of the successful campaign of ethnic cleansing.

C36, another insider with good access to the leadership, was an excellent witness, but so detailed was his evidence that journalists in the region rapidly guessed it was Milan Babić himself – the leader of the Serbs in that part of Croatia who had been working to cut their area off from Croatia and join up with Serbia. He had to abandon his pseudonym and anonymity. Babić testified about the extent to which Milošević controlled the army, and that the parallel structures of military formations in Croatia all answered to Milošević.[3]

These witnesses proved the case, it may be thought, and no arguments about the sufficiency of evidence in the Croatian part of the proceedings were raised by the court's amici curiae at the end of the prosecution case.

The Kula Camp video

The best piece of evidence in the entire case was probably the Kula Camp video. This video showed an event initially misunderstood until the tribunal's top researcher, Nevenka Tromp, realised what had been missed by others in the office. The video, made in 1997, had Milošević making an error. Although he was never known to be with his troops on front lines or to visit those affected by the wars or even to don a military uniform, he did for some reason feel obliged to attend in 1997 the annual ceremony of a brigade called the Red Berets. This unit – a paramilitary group funded by Serbia and properly known as the JSO – had operated extensively in criminal activities in other republics.

At the ceremony the group's notorious and famously unphotographed leader welcomed Milošević and in a speech explained how the unit was formed in May 1991 – only part-way through the Croatian conflict. He went on with other senior Serb officials to explain, by reference to maps and place names, the various battles in which the unit had fought in both Croatia and Bosnia. There was no need to discriminate between the two because, as the prosecution argued, the plan in both republics was the same – to ethnically cleanse areas the Serbs wanted to carve out and join up with Serbia. Jovica Stanisić, who controlled the Serbian State Security – Državna bezbednost, or DB – said the following to the accused: 'Mr President, everything we have done so far we did with your knowledge and with your consent.' At the same ceremony, the accused said to a member of the Red Berets, Radojica Bozović, that he 'read the reports' from Bozović.

The content of the video was quite explicit and absolutely clear. Milošević establishing a paramilitary-style group to fight on the territories of others was an unlawful act – it was, we would have argued, that irrevocable criminal step that Milošević knew full well took him across the line. There was no other evidence showing other than by inference that he established this particular group, infamous as it was to become, but this piece of evidence was, as he was aware, conclusive – it denied him the chance to plead a non-criminal state of mind for other events. This was the dictator as criminal – and he knew it.

BOSNIA

An indictment of 79 paragraphs charged Milošević together with other Serbs and Bosnian Serbs with genocide, complicity in genocide, persecution, extermination, murder, wilful killing, unlawful confinement, deportation and other inhumane acts, wanton destruction and plunder, in 29 charges, for the period between March 1992 and December 1995. Of course, all acts were committed through the agency of others.

Between 90,000 and 104,000 people were estimated as killed, 8,000 of them in the Srebrenica massacre of July 1995.

As with Croatia, witnesses included senior government, military and police officials, all of whom were able to speak of Milošević's power and of the crimes committed. But there was no Babić to speak directly of Milošević's instruction to commit crimes.

Documentary evidence was prominent for this indictment. Two crucial documents were created in the territory of the Bosnian Serbs. First, a document came into existence at the end of 1990 setting up Variant A and Variant B of what was to happen in municipalities according to whether Serbs were or were not in a majority. There may have been little difference between the two, but taking control of a town where Serbs were not in a majority was bound to lead to violence and ethnic cleansing.

Second, on 12 May 1992, at a session of the Bosnian Serb Assembly, Radovan Karadžić announced the six 'strategic objectives' of the Serbian people in Bosnia–Herzegovina, reflecting policies the conception, consideration and implementation of which were common to the Bosnian Serbs and the Serb leadership:

1. Establish state borders separating the Serbian people from the other two ethnic communities;
2. Set up a corridor between Semberija and Krajina;
3. Establish a corridor in the Drina river valley to eliminate the Drina as a border separating Serbian states;
4. Establish a border on the Una and Nerteva rivers;
5. Divide the city of Sarajevo into Serbian and Muslim parts and establish effective state authorities in both parts;
6. Ensure access to the sea for Republika Srpska.[4]

Objectives 1 and 5 show how committed both Serb leaderships had to be to ethnic cleansing; objective 6 reflects in part what had already happened in Dubrovnik even if the objective could not be pursued.

Intercepts

Intercepts made by the Bosnia–Herzegovina official state security unit from May 1991 to February 1992 of conversations between Milošević, Karadžić and others[5] showed common planning and that Karadžić did nothing without Milošević's consent. The plan to keep all Serbs in one state was an evolutionary process that would require ethnic separation in Bosnia and for Serb territories to be conquered by force.

Milošević never publicly used the words 'all Serbs in a single state' to describe the Serb state's plans for the post-Yugoslav era, words widely associated with the ideology of a 'Greater Serbia'. However, Milošević sometimes used different wording to express the same, or a similar, concept. In one of his conversations with Karadžić he said: 'The Serbs will not be divided into several states. That should be the premise of your thinking.'[6] On another occasion, Milošević lost his temper, shouting: 'Please let's move. We don't give in to anybody any more. And if they want to fight, we'll fight ... And they should go to hell, whoever wants to fight us, we'll fight and we're stronger.'[7]

The records of the Supreme Defence Council (SDC)[8] – a council of which Milošević was clearly in charge – provided important information. There were nine years of meetings, roughly every month, with audio recording and stenographers' transcripts available. They revealed:

- How Serbia supported the Serbs in Croatia and Bosnia effectively in secret;
- That Milošević and his colleagues were aware of the functioning of paramilitary groups, and of the need to deny knowledge of them;
- That there was a very clear plan to take territory from the other republics and to join it to Serbia proper;
- That Milošević, unlike his Bosnian Serb colleagues, recognised that taking half of Bosnia was as

> much as could reasonably be achieved – not for him the full Greater Serbia plan.

As with all investigations of crime the careful observer or lawyer checks for what is missing. For the period in 1995 when Srebrenica fell and 8,000 men and boys were massacred, an event that could not possibly have been unknown to the people sitting round the table, *no* reference was seemingly ever made to it by the SDC. None. Further, the records produced can be seen – on careful analysis – not to be remotely complete. Nevertheless, they are of great value. Milošević went from these meetings to be an international negotiator, never once condemning Mladić privately or in public. What does that tell us?

Within these fascinating if incomplete records the following may give a flavour. At the meeting on 25 August 1995 General Mladić arrived late and was greeted respectfully. No remarks were made about the crimes in Srebrenica and other nearby towns, but at his belated arrival they were all effectively sworn to secrecy. In the discussion that followed there was no criticism expressed about what Mladić's troops might have done. On the contrary, Milošević congratulated the generals who had done their work with honour. Milošević described Goražde as a trap for the Serbs, implying that they shouldn't take it but that it could be exchanged for other territories. (Goražde, Srebrenica and Žepa were the three UN-protected 'safe areas' the Serbs might take to create a contiguous Serb region in Eastern Bosnia.) He also expressed the view that the enclaves would not need to be exchanged as they would blend into the Serbian surroundings without a fight, continuing: 'If the Muslims refuse the peace solution they will be told that they are to be left alone with the sword of Damocles hanging over them in the form of General Mladić.'[9]

An expert witness

We also called another important witness: Dr Ton Zwaan, Professor at the Centre for Holocaust and Genocide Studies at the University of Amsterdam. He spoke not a word about Yugoslavia, at least not during my questioning of him. Instead he spoke about other conflicts and other massacres. He testified about the importance of ideology and use of propaganda in setting the context for genocide. As stated in the judgment at the end of the prosecution's case:

> Ideology plays a major role in processes leading to the commission of genocide, involving various types of radical nationalism, which dehumanise the targeted group, also using collective historical memory (where applicable) in an attempt to create a 'them' and 'us' culture. These nationalist ideologies are later used to legitimise, rationalise, and justify the genocidal process. Although individual motives for participating in the acts may be varied, ideologies give an overall sense of direction to what should be done and impart a sense of purpose and intent to individual perpetrators. Dr Zwaan testified that scholars generally agree that genocide is a crime of state, i.e., the overall perception, attitude, behaviour, and decision of the central political leadership are decisive factors in the emergence of genocidal crimes. According to Dr Zwaan, genocidal crimes never develop from the 'bottom up'; they are 'top down' affairs. Such crimes occur with the 'knowledge, approval, and involvement of the state authorities'.[10]

The evidence was immensely powerful; people came up to me afterwards and said it was the best evidence in the case *because* it did not mention Yugoslavia. You could 'read across' to the facts of Yugoslavia, and infer that of course there was leadership, control and direction for these terrible things that were happening, and that these actions could be characterised as genocide.

Demography and maps

Demographic research displayed in maps became a remarkable tool for forensic deduction. Use of census and voter material allowed preparation of maps showing composition by ethnicity of relevant parts of Bosnia and of how that composition changed in line with the Serbs' plan, and in particular how the sites selected for charges in the indictment changed most dramatically. This all suggested effective and purposeful ethnic cleansing.

KOSOVO

Here Milošević faced an indictment of five counts, charging murder, crimes against humanity, violations of customs of war and persecution, between January and June 1999. There were probably between 8,000 and 12,000 deaths.

The conflicts had started in Kosovo in the 1980s when the Kosovo Serbs sought a champion to represent their alleged suffering at the hands of the Kosovo Albanians, some of whom wanted independence from Serbia. Milošević was the Serbs' second choice, in a way, after his best friend, mentor, *kum* or 'best man' and political senior – Ivan Stambolić – let them down. As his first and greatest political coup in Serbia Milošević was then able to annul the autonomy of Kosovo. With this to his credit he became the leader of all Serbs in the Croatian and Bosnian conflicts, even if technically only leader of Serbia.

After the Dayton agreement – that extraordinarily allowed the Bosnian Serbs to profit from genocide – he could have become an international statesman. He might never have been unearthed for what he had actually done and never tried in court. But the Serbs remained demanding and the Kosovo Albanians suffered a crack-down. Without this crack-down Milošević's victory in the annulment of autonomy might have become a focus of potential conflict; his supporters would not tolerate that.

There was an immense amount of evidence in the case about Kosovo, including from victims, experts of various kinds, and international figures. It revealed killings and ethnic cleansing on an extraordinary scale. Milošević could raise no defence except to blame the Kosovo Liberation Army (KLA), saying they forced their own people out and killed them.

A great deal of eyewitness evidence showed the attack on the Kosovo Albanians to be a reality. Lord Paddy Ashdown was an interesting and extremely valuable witness. He had visited neighbouring Albania in the conflict and had clandestinely observed Kosovo from a mountainous part of the Albania–Kosovo border – hardly to be expected by the Serbs. He explained:

> There were some houses below us, which I would estimate at about two kilometres range, perhaps slightly less, that were being individually targeted by a tank ... there were collections of armoured personnel

> carriers and tanks gathered, waiting to conduct further attacks ... two tanks going away from me, towards Djakovica ... were systematically, and in turn, firing at one house in the village after another, from the roadside ... it was perfectly possible to hear small-arms fire as well as tank fire ... although I cannot, of course, say to the court that there was no return fire from any of these houses, I can say that I never heard or observed any return fire from these houses.

Milošević went to great efforts to prove that Lord Ashdown could not see from Albania what he saw. A large amount of time and money was involved in proving or disproving this. In reality he protested too much – the evidence was impossible to deal with and something that revealed criminal conduct when Milošević thought his troops were unobserved.

During another visit to Kosovo in September 1998, Ashdown saw evidence of organised mass destruction of Albanian villages and heard of killings of civilians. He also saw the site of what he believed to be a KLA execution of Serbs.

Jacky Rowland, a BBC journalist, went to Dubrava prison on 21 and 24 May 1999. Dubrava prison was huge and it had housed a large number of senior KLA prisoners – political prisoners as they may have been. On the first visit she saw a pile of bodies; on the second the bodies had been moved. She gave evidence of the uniforms of the soldiers supervising her second visit.

Later in the case we came to learn that this was a crime where we just might have been able to trace direct responsibility to Milošević. I am often asked if we should have tried Milošević for everything or found a single crime and dealt with him for that, rather as Saddam Hussein was dealt with for a single crime. The difficulty with most of the crimes against Milošević was that the whole picture had to be revealed to prove his responsibility; we could never be certain that we could establish his guilt of any single crime in isolation. In fact, even if we had been alert to material about Dubrava and had been able to prove it as Milošević's direct responsibility I doubt if our decision to charge all crimes we reasonably could for the three wars would have been different.

Nevertheless, and to explain what we should have considered, journalists were first allowed into Dubrava to see bodies of those allegedly killed by NATO bombing – although the visiting journalists saw no wounds consistent with that kind of killing. After the first journalists' visit the regular prison guards had been stood down. Another unit arrived – the JSO or Red Berets unit that had fought for Milošević in Croatia and Serbia and that was the subject of the Kula Camp video – and a massacre of the prisoners followed. These bodies were buried. On the second journalists' visit it was clear that these JSO soldiers wore different uniforms from those seen by Rowland on her first visit. Paperwork in our possession showed that the prison authorities, who were replaced between journalists' visits in order that the JSO could get on with the killings, had queried what happened with Belgrade. The paper trail reached an assistant minister. We got no further. But no assistant minister would have authority – nor even a minister – to authorise use of the JSO in such an event. This line of reasoning, if investigated by us in time, could have 'nailed' Milošević for a very grave crime.

In April 1999 a refrigerator with dead bodies in it was found in the Danube in Serbia. Suppressed at the time, the information eventually led to an investigation that showed the bodies had come from Kosovo and were bound for reburial on a site near a military installation in Serbia. Why?

General Obrad Stevanović kept a diary of his meetings. One page was ultimately revealing. It showed a meeting in the President's office with the following sequence of notes:

> 'President'
> 'No corpse – No crime'
> 'Back-breaking work on … On that issue.'
> 'They will use evidence on crimes to justify aggression.'
> 'Clearing up.'
> 'Simultaneous clearing up of territories.'
> 'When the mission arrives …'
> 'Clearing up the terrain the most important.'[11]

Stevanović attempted to put an interpretation on the contents different from the obvious one that the bodies had to be moved to put the incoming international observers and peacekeepers off the scent. He did concede that the 'president' referred to was the accused.

CLOSING ARGUMENT

How might this enormous case, with its many themes and strands of evidence, have been concluded by the prosecution? There were in reality always two questions: What part did forces under Milošević's control or supported by him play in the atrocities committed? What was his state of mind at the time? A detailed analysis would have dealt with the first question. As to the second I might have argued on these lines to the judges:

'It is well to consider how clever this man was. From an educated background, of which he could be proud, he showed cleverness in court regularly and you sometimes thanked him for it: he could read the instantaneous English-language transcript of evidence while listening to the one or two languages of the questioning without interpretation and correct the transcript for us – but only when the correction was in his favour. He never corrected errors against himself. That, in a minor way, shows the man, the man in the respectable business suit, never in casual clothes, never in military uniform. The man who, when young, had the looks and skills of a businessman, banker or a mid-level party or government official but who, offered power by the Kosovo Albanians, turned those boons to his perceived advantage and became leader of all the Serbs. A man without clear political philosophy apart from maintaining his own power, dependent though that made him on achieving Serb objectives that could only be satisfied by extreme violence and mass atrocities.

'That same cleverness has to be in mind when the court contemplates his years in office receiving accurate information from Yugoslav/Serb embassies of what was reported as happening, including detailed reports of human rights abuses from NGOs. He received international figures of stature – often one-to-one – and heard their accounts of what was being done.

'A clever politician receiving such information these days is bound to be clever enough to know of the cause and effect mechanism that operates in a violent world: politician says and does this; citizens he leads or speaks for will do that – and the 'that' may very well be extremely criminal. Milošević cannot properly suggest that what Dr Zwaan told us about the aetiology of mass violence is a mystery. It isn't. It is commonplace and all modern politicians, if they are to do their job, have to know what their actions may bring.

'Avoid front lines as he might; fail to meet the Serbs kicked out of Croatia when Croatia won back its territory as he might – he knew what he had done and was continuing to do.

'His avowed intent may have been to keep Serbs in one state, not in itself a criminal act – but from the start of the offences alleged in the Croatia indictment, and without doubt from the day he established the Red Berets paramilitary unit to commit crimes on his and Serbia's behalf, to the last Kosovo Albanian killed or forced from home, he knew what he was doing and that it was wrong. Did he start a bad man or was he coarsened and corrupted by the temptations and difficulties he faced? After the conflicts were over, when his one-time best friend, *kum*, political mentor and promoter Ivan Stambolić decided to stand against him politically, Milošević had him shot dead in cold blood by members of the same JSO / Red Berets and laid to rest in a shallow grave – as a Belgrade court found.[12] The common criminal acting through others was the same man who had – acting through others – knowingly committed seven years of crimes in war. There is only so much that the white shirt and tie of respectability can hide; not enough, the prosecution would argue, to shield him from the judgment of this court.'

Chapter 3

Legal Process as a Tool to Rewrite History

The war crimes trials at the ICTY produced a huge record of trial evidence. ICTY trials had several objectives, including bringing retribution and achieving deterrence, but they never sought to write history; every trial record produces at least two competing narratives, a prosecution narrative and a defence narrative or narratives, none of which may be accurate. Yet outside the courtroom, the trial record will be used – or abused – for shaping the collective memory of the peoples and nations involved and for providing an overall account of the wars themselves.

Original lecture delivered on 13 February 2013.

The law has become something of a religion to which international bodies representing the citizen turn in need, treating lawyers and judges as priests and oracles able to provide not just arguments and judgments but truth. Hannah Arendt, discussing the role of the law, said: 'Even the noblest of ulterior purposes, the making of a record of the Hitler regime which would withstand the test of history … the supposed higher aims of the Nuremberg trials, can only detract from the law's main business: to weigh the charges brought against the accused, to render judgement, and to mete out due punishment.'[1]

Even assuming her narrow view of the function of the law is right, it is not that easy, even with the best will in the world, to confine its output or effect in the way she might have preferred. It is all too tempting for the citizen casually to allow law's wider potential to do things beyond its proper scope. In this chapter I consider the potential of the trial process, and of trials in war crimes courts, to go further than just to deal with individual criminal responsibility for actions in conflicts and to write or rewrite history for parties to the conflict.

It may be helpful to compare aspects of what is new and untested – as the war crimes trials of the last 20 years are – with aspects of what is familiar, tried and well tested – the domestic national criminal trial. Such trials are immensely significant to the individual, who is found guilty or not guilty, who is punished or not punished.

Some trials may also be of a higher significance in that they reveal something about the societies and nations in which they take place: the Dreyfus Affair and the trials that were part of it revealed much about French society, corruption within the army and anti-Semitism. It became part of French history but essentially remains the case of a single man.

Similarly with the trials of Oscar Wilde, revealing though they are of those times, they are not substantially usable as the instruments of misdescription of history – only of revelation. The *Oz* obscenity trial in 1971 showed a great deal about then current standards of morality and of the seeming corruption of the legal process, given the conduct of the judges. It did not, however, rewrite or even write history. This is the same with the trials of IRA offenders that showed up some corruption in police forces and the need to change legal procedures.

Exceptionally a trial can, in itself, change the history of a society. The trial of Penn and Mead in 1670 established a jury's right to acquit a defendant in the teeth of direction and intimidation by the judge; that right, once established, became part of our history and of our continuing and existing legal system.

International and war crimes trials are, it seems to me, very different in potential effect and can readily have a real effect on history. To explore such a proposition, where might we start?

PRECURSORS OF MODERN WAR CRIMES TRIALS?

James Gow proposes that the trial of William Wallace is arguably the first example of an international war crimes trial.[2] Edward I's victory over his Scottish opponent in 1305 had Wallace taken to Westminster Hall. Notwithstanding the rights to proper trial enshrined 90 years earlier in Magna Carta, Wallace – with nothing more than the indictment read to him – was condemned to the most savage of deaths, imposed immediately. Although this was the very century in which the profession of barristers developed, Wallace was without representation and not allowed to speak. Why bother with a trial at all? The court of noblemen acting under the king's direction no doubt reflected the sovereign's understanding that a statement of Wallace's crimes in a form of trial, reinforced by an unspeakably barbaric death, would confirm the accuracy of the victor's view of the history and better guarantee the future peace.

The trial of Peter von Hagenbach, a royal official in Alsace, in 1474 is cited as one source for the legitimacy of modern international humanitarian law and can also be viewed as the first international war crimes trial. It can even be seen as a trial in which the origins of crimes against humanity may be found and as a first example of a trial where rape was charged as a crime and the defence of superior orders was rejected. There were international judges and Hagenbach was allowed to put his case before his predictable beheading. Some argue that it was in fact a 'show trial' meant to rebuff the territorial ambitions of Hagenbach's master, Charles the Bold, with confessions obtained through torture. Whether it was in any sense a real trial it was the last known such process with international oversight until nation-state supremacy and immunity from outside supervision was subjected to post-World War I scrutiny and, much more significantly, post-World War II Nuremberg and Tokyo trials. Gregory Gordon describes it as a 'historic and conceptual pillar of international criminal law's "pre-history"'.[3]

The trial of King Charles I is an example of the audience being more important for the process than the defendant, the prosecution or the law itself. In the words of Justice Michael Kirby:

> The 'Court' had no legal authority. It was the creature of the power of the army. The King had no advance notice of the charge. No one was appointed to help him with his defence. The court did not even pretend to be impartial ... Eventually the King's refusal to answer was deemed not to be a plea of not guilty (requiring the accuser to prove the charge) but a plea of guilty to treason ... The King never accepted the authority of the court.[4]

Expressed differently:

> The trial and execution were part of the dramaturgy of state, designed to convince its audience that the text of Charles's life must be read as treason, his death as 'exemplary and condign punishment'. By staging the trial as a public display, the regicides strove to justify but also exposed to open challenge the legitimacy of their cause.[5]

The revolutionaries may be seen to have made efforts to give a semblance of justice to the proceedings. The fact that they felt an obligation to conduct a trial at all is noteworthy as a reflection of the power of the trial process on the imagination of the English people, even at that time.

These trials were not legal processes reflecting the rights of accused persons and victims. They were manifestations of the use of power, and not necessarily the abuse of power.[6] In each case, given the possibility of summary execution, a trial process was used for objectives that included, or may have had as the principal component, the writing of a history.

In these cases we see an understanding of the power or use of trials that follow conflict. The Nuremberg trials may demonstrate that same power. There was never a possibility of leaders of the Allies having their actions even *considered* for investigation in the way that perhaps they should have been. Does this fact, this elimination from consideration, make it easier – even today – to think badly of Germans in ways that we do not think of North Europeans generally? Trying the Nazis *and only the Nazis* was a choice that has left records, including photographic images of the trials, of immense, enduring power. Churchill famously favoured summary execution – just as did the citizens of Romania once Ceauşescu was at their mercy. How different would our knowledge and view of World War II be if firing squads had 'tapped out' short summaries of history for the victors?[7]

WRITING HISTORY?

And so to modern war crimes trials. Has the potential to try all sides of conflicts in the modern era of codified rights of accused and of victims changed or limited the way trials may shape history? Is it reasonable to expect modern states to act differently in their approach to trials after conflict?

First, however, we must recall that all judges at all these courts say that they *do not* write history in their judgments. This was noted by the ICTY chamber in the Kupreškić case when the chamber stated that:

> The primary task of this Trial Chamber was not to construct a historical record of modern human horrors in Bosnia–Herzegovina. The principal duty of our Trial Chamber was simply to decide whether the six defendants standing trial were guilty of partaking in this persecutory violence or whether they were instead extraneous to it and hence, not guilty.[8]

Former ICTY judge Patricia Wald made the following observations:

> Initially the Tribunal was urged to make detailed findings about the ... events leading up to the atrocities on trial. This, it was suggested, would provide an antidote to revisionist history ... However, commentators, citizens, and officers of the implicated countries increasingly suggest that the adversarial trial process and the findings of judges may not produce the best approximations of history. Moreover, the 'adjudication' by ICTY of who started, prolonged, or

> ended the war and why in the context of criminal proceedings without the states themselves having input is basically unfair, or at least does not contribute to future reconciliation.[9]

However, this says nothing of the actual power of the trials to write the history, no matter what the judges may say, of states involved in trials; and nothing of the use states may make of trial processes, or trials themselves, to write history as they choose it to be. African cases at the ICC show how the courts can be engaged in a cynical way to become instruments of conflict; that is itself a method of writing one-sided history. If one side of a conflict gets the court to prosecute only the other side, then leaving behind a balanced history of the conflict will always be a much more difficult task.

DOCUMENTATION: DELAYING TACTICS AND DECEIT

Returning to the conflicts in the former Yugoslavia, what may we learn on this issue from the work and judgments of this most successful of the recently formed family of international courts? The statute and the rules of the ICTY oblige states to cooperate in all ways with the tribunal in the surrender of individuals and documents but then go on to provide a regime that allows the greatest possible delay in provision of documents.

How could it ever have been realistic to expect a court system stuck in a remote northern European country, with no police force and limited powers of securing documents from states that had been at war, to rely on the good will of these states to help to prove cases against their own nationals? Especially unrealistic if, as for ICTY cases, delaying tactics allowed postponement of provision of documents for up to five years, during which time other documents could be created and originals destroyed.

The ICTY's rules allowed in principle for every conceivable tactic by Serbia (and no doubt other third-party countries) to avoid handing over what might have been interesting, and the judges did not seem keen to cut the red tape and allow the prosecution to race to the vault.

Many would argue that, from the creation of the ICTY, Serbia knew that it had to take the tribunal seriously, not in order to assist genuinely in the prosecution of serious offenders but in order to do what it could to preserve its, Serbia's, long-term reputation to the extent possible. Serbs had been assessed by almost all independent observers as having committed most crimes, and the most serious ones, in conflicts where some six states and entities were involved. Serbia, however, wanted and wants to create some kind of moral equivalence with those other parties to the conflicts and in this way to rewrite its history and the history of others, in particular the histories of Bosnia and Kosovo.

Serbia proclaimed a policy of cooperation in the extradition of high-level indictees, such as Slobodan Milošević and others who were citizens of Serbia and who were known to be in its power to surrender, but had a different approach to allowing the tribunal to have access to documents from the federal and republican state archives. The prosecution requested many documents on many occasions between 2001 and 2004 and was always met by Serbia using procedure to block production. Belgrade's position on the fate of Kosovo-related documents varied from a denial that the documents existed, to claims that the documents requested were destroyed during the NATO bombing, to statements that the documents could not be located.[10] When documents were eventually provided it was found that they were selected in a way that was not responsive to the request made or were exculpatory for Serbia or for the accused concerned.[11]

When challenged on this the Serbian legal representatives reminded the court that Serbia was following the court's orders, and the court's excessive respect for Serbia allowed them to assert this. When deciding on ordering the production of the documents listed by the prosecution, the trial chamber ruled against production of critical 'war diaries' as 'over broad' although – as later emerged – they were easily identified documents sitting on an archive shelf and of immense potential value to the tribunal's trials.[12]

Serbia sought to present itself as conscientious in its endeavours by creation of the VJ [Army] Commission for Cooperation with the ICTY in 2002. In a written submission to the court of May 2003, the prosecution argued that this commission actively assisted the ICTY indictees in preparing their defence.[13] The prosecution quoted a media report which stated that a 'select team of general officers and ranking officers searched documents in the military archives in search of evidence in favour of persons indicted by the ICTY'.[14] The same report raised the issue of the commission's direct support of Milošević's defence:

> Milošević is posing very precise questions to witnesses which are based on very high-quality information on battlefield events, the engagement of personnel and units and the political background of steps taken by the warring sides … the way his questions are posed indicate access to extensive information which only the Army of Serbia and Montenegro has in a number of military sites.[15]

The commission was abolished in April 2003 by Boris Tadić after he became the Minister of Defence in Serbia. It appeared that in its short-lived existence the commission collected over 10,400 documents of relevance for the wars in Croatia, Bosnia–Herzegovina and Kosovo. At the same time it created new material specifically for use at ICTY trials.[16]

One defence witness, General Božidar Delić, explained how the preparation of his own testimony took place. He received a list of events from the commission and was asked to deal with them in graphic and textual form. In order to do that the VJ Commission provided access to all contemporaneous documents he needed to prepare for his testimony. To demonstrate how well prepared he was, he showed the court the copies of the operational logs and the war diary of his brigade.[17] The prosecution identified them as some of the documents it had sought from Belgrade and Delić was compelled to hand over the war diary despite his protest. Delić initially claimed that the reason why the prosecution did not get any of the contemporaneous VJ documents was because the prosecution had never requested them.[18] Eventually, he was compelled to accept that the prosecution had requested many contemporaneous military documents via official channels including those relating to his unit, protesting that 'they asked for the documents of practically the whole army, referring to the whole army. What they should have done was to ask specifically which document they were interested in: which unit and which specific document.'[19]

Why should the prosecutors at The Hague investigating such grave crimes have been limited to asking only for what they already knew might exist, when their duty was to investigate grave crimes thought, justifiably, to have been committed by bodies that held their own original records of what they had done?

By controlling – manipulating – provision of genuine and newly minted documents to the ICTY the commission *through a court process* was seeking to affect not just criminal trials but the historical record of the conflicts.

Supreme Defence Council records

Supreme Defence Council records were the most important document collection the prosecution came to know of and to receive. The SDC succeeded the Presidency of the Socialist Federal Republic of Yugoslavia (the old Yugoslavia that broke up in the conflicts) as the top defence body of the successor Federal Republic of Yugoslavia (FRY), composed of just Serbia and Montenegro. The SDC consisted of three voting members, Slobodan Milošević, the President of Serbia; Momir Bulatović, the President of Montenegro; and the Federal President. From 1992 to 2006 the SDC was a federal body with the mandate of commander-in-chief of the armed forces of the FRY. Knowing what the SDC did and the decisions it made was essential to understanding the level of engagement of the Serbian armed forces in the wars in Croatia, Bosnia and Kosovo.

SDC stenographic notes were made available but only for inspection by the ICTY's Office of the Prosecutor (OTP) researchers in August 2003. Based on the preliminary assessment of these stenographic notes, the OTP made an official request for all the records. The Serbian authorities handed over some records in December 2003, two months before the end of the prosecution part of the case.[20] As I explained earlier, the SDC records were provided on terms accepted by the chief prosecutor that the most interesting parts of the documents were blacked out from public view even though ICTY judges and lawyers could read the documents themselves in full.

The SDC records provided by Belgrade were not complete. While minutes were provided for all sessions, stenographic notes were not provided for 21 of those sessions. It is significant that most of the 'missing' records were from 1995, the year of the Srebrenica genocide. Further, the Serb authorities claimed that the SDC stopped convening meetings after 24 March 1999, the time of the third Kosovo conflict. No satisfactory explanation has ever been given by the Belgrade authorities as to which political body replaced the SDC in supreme command of the armed forces during the war in Kosovo. From the way the situation was presented by Belgrade in its communications with the OTP, it appeared as if the army had no civilian oversight during the military intervention in Kosovo. This was an improbable tale.

Bosnia – like Serbia – was aware of issues broader than just those of individuals facing personal trials or being witnesses in trials (and Bosnians were pursued as defendants at the tribunal, even if they much more regularly featured as witnesses against Serbs and against some Bosnian Croat defendants). Bosnia brought a civil case in the International Court of Justice in The Hague, a court that usually deals with issues concerning the law of the sea or border disputes but which on this occasion – and over a period of nearly a decade – confronted an allegation by Bosnia that Serbia as a state had committed genocide.[21]

The ICJ, surprisingly, worked on the basis of the blacked-out documents and declined to ask for the full 'un-redacted' version. The court's decision, delivered in 2007, was a profound disappointment to Bosnia. In a tantalising judgment[22] the court went step by step towards, but stopped short of, a finding of genocide by Serbia or of Serbia's complicity in genocide. It made this decision, arguably, because it had been deprived of material that would have filled a gap; some argue that what lay behind the blacked-out parts of the SDC records could have been enough to have brought a different verdict. Of course it is always possible that political influences were at work in the minds of some of the judges at the ICJ, for all international courts have such vulnerability asserted against them. What is certain is that the processes that allowed Serbia to manipulate or control evidence at the ICTY did much to allow this unsatisfactory verdict to emerge.

Theoretically Bosnia could have sought to reopen the case by a process known as 'revision', but the opportunity to do so expired at the end of February 2017. An application for revision was in fact filed at the very last minute but was refused by the court on procedural grounds. In the end the litigation history – and any future litigation narrative – must acknowledge that courts can only act on evidence available at the time of their judgments and that they are largely at the mercy of states when it comes to getting their hands on relevant documents.

A SMEAR CAMPAIGN THAT WILL NOT GO AWAY

Finally, to Kosovo – a case study not just in what can be achieved by a state within an actual trial but what mere exposure to investigation of those in conflicts can bring. Kosovo was the beginning and the end of the Balkan wars of the 1990s. Milošević devoted a great deal of the time allowed him by the court for his defence to deal with Kosovo and needed to make the Kosovo Albanians out to be as bad as could be in his own defence. There was, as explained above, active support for him at government levels in Serbia, as a minimum when it came to cooperation or non-cooperation with the tribunal over production of documents. Did that support go further?

For whatever reason, an allegation was made in 2003 to the tribunal's prosecutor during the Kosovo segment of the Milošević trial that Kosovo Albanian leaders had in the late 1990s been organising the execution of Serb prisoners in Albania to harvest their internal organs for sale on the black market. The allegation, once it surfaced, was as unlikely as the one Churchill advanced in World War II about Russians eating their babies – until the Russians became our allies and he had to correct the propaganda. It is exactly the sort of story heard often in war, but it was being made against leading Kosovo Albanians, including their then prime minister Ramush Haradinaj.

Papers have since been leaked in various forms and show obviously genuine ICTY prosecution documents and internal reports of various kinds constituting an investigation into the allegation. On analysis there is nothing in the leaked paperwork that justifies the otherwise unsupported allegations of organ-harvesting and, as a result, the investigation came to nothing.

I knew nothing of it at the time, although I was to discover how strong were the forces determined to have Haradinaj tried for war crimes. As already explained, he was eventually tried and acquitted, then retried and exonerated yet again. That is another sorry story. Haradinaj surrendered himself to The Hague immediately he was indicted and, of some significance to what follows, Hashim Thaçi became prime minister.

Once the chief prosecutor – who had been so determined to have Haradinaj charged – left office she published a book in which this unsubstantiated allegation was raised again – but this time and for no accountable reason against Thaçi, who barely featured in the pages of the original documentation (that had yet to be leaked to the press).

Later still the Council of Europe became involved and launched an investigation that sought to find substance to back the allegations against Thaçi, still the serving prime minister. Some say the Council of Europe is dominated or heavily influenced by Russia and Russia is certainly Serbia's ally.

Through endorsement of its statehood by UN members, Kosovo seeks practical confirmation of the independence it took from Serbia and Serbia would no doubt like to discredit Kosovo's application to become a full UN member and a member of the European family of states.

The allegation in the Council of Europe was made by a former Swiss prosecutor called Dick Marty, who has since been the subject of bruising encounters with EU parliamentarians over the quality of the report he presented and the evidence on which he relied, which was substantially the same evidence that came to nothing in 2003. The first publication of his report to the Council of Europe coincided with the first leaking of the 2003 ICTY documents concerning the allegation. At this first leaking the documents were heavily redacted in black ink, and nothing is as good as a blacked-out document to raise suspicions. It was only later, when the un-blacked-out documents appeared, that they could be seen to contain neither compelling evidence of the alleged crimes, nor any mention of Thaçi. And there was no evidence of substance additional to what was first seen and rejected as inconsequential in 2003.

One would think the full disclosure of these documents would see Thaçi publicly exonerated at least in the court of public opinion in the way his predecessor has now been acquitted in court. Not at all. Further official UN investigations continue, and he remains tethered by a rumour that would have got nowhere at all had it not been raised within the seeming solemnity and seriousness of a tribunal process. To date not one piece of eyewitness testimony or forensic/scientific evidence has been produced to support the organ-harvesting allegation, yet Thaçi finds himself forever tainted by the rumour and unable to prove a negative. The rumour, and the lack of investigation into the origins of the rumour, taint all Kosovars and play into the hands of those who are determined to see their claims for full statehood thwarted.[23]

And who raised the allegation? There is little doubt there: the same body that revives the allegation whenever it needs to in its pursuit of leaving a record of moral equivalence with the David that stood up to its Goliath.

SOME LESSONS

What comes out of all this? Nothing, if it is accepted that victory in conflict allows the victor to take all prizes including the prize of setting the record; nothing, if trials after conflicts are treated as conflicts themselves. Victors or vanquished should be allowed to do all they can according to the rules of the game to create what record they like.

Where, in earlier times, trial processes were used by victorious states to achieve political objectives of pretty straightforward kinds, modern war crimes trials can be used by any party involved in ways that can affect or corrupt the setting of a record of events, the very history of what happened.

If modern trials are driven by objectives of long-term reconciliation not just of victory in conflict, and if trials are being conducted according to concepts of human rights for victims as well as for perpetrators then there are problems revealed here of which we need to be aware.

And what can Bosnia or Kosovo do to redress the imbalance they say harms them and will or may harm their future?

The following conclusions may emerge.

First, those of us reading about these international trials can work on the basis that the lawyers and judges are doing their best with the material available to them, but we would be wise to keep in the backs of our minds that there may have been significant political manipulation of what has been made available as evidence.

Second, those who establish these courts and trials – the UN and the states parties of the ICC – might have as a priority establishing systems that will allow documents to be obtained in hours or days, not in weeks, months and years, and for documents obtained to be made public to the maximum extent possible as early as possible. That may mean that obtaining documents (and witnesses) should be an active responsibility of the political body that establishes the court and that may have the ability to sanction a country for non-compliance.

And finally, countries turning to courts to leave accurate records of conflicts should understand the limitations that court decisions inevitably involve. They should recognise that it is the responsibility of a country that has been in conflict to ensure that an adequate record is left of its own history – whether by truth commissions or modern computer-assisted evidence projects – and the countries concerned must recognise that if they do not take this responsibility, subsequent generations may hold them responsible for whatever may follow from their histories being inaccurately recorded.

Chapter 4

State Involvement in War Crimes and War Crimes Trials

International war crimes courts deal only with the responsibility of individuals for crimes they committed. It is vital not to overlook collective and state criminal responsibility, but state responsibility can only be dealt with formally at a different court, the International Court of Justice. Has this allowed states to escape attention that should have been paid to their responsibility – as states – for conflicts, a responsibility different in kind from the responsibility of their leaders?

Original lecture delivered on 10 April 2013.

Considering the role of states in the aftermath of conflict has led me to a conundrum, crystallised by those who speak of the Iraq invasion only by reference to UK Prime Minister Tony Blair and US President G. W. Bush. There are only ever just these two names, which is puzzling because open government and any form of cabinet rule involves collective responsibility. Of course it is easier to have a single villain to attack, and sometimes with real dictatorships it is appropriate to pursue one leader because he really did exercise solitary control. But – usually – the leader's apparent decisions will have been made by a collective, or endorsed by a collective, or – at a very minimum – will not have been resisted by a collective of other politicians and military leaders. The tension here is between individual politicians and a state or government about who should stand up to be indicted.

It may be pertinent to ask what is more likely to deter wrongful war, or bad conduct in war, in the future: having a single leader in some conflict under examination or prosecution picked out for punishment *after* the event and allowed to assume, by publicity and popular opprobrium, *all* responsibility? Or having the leader's cabinet colleagues understand – *when they make the decision to go to war or to press on with war or not to resist war* – that they may all be pursued for collective responsibility if they make the wrong decision? To ask the question is to provide some, at least, of the answer, even if to answer that all government ministers in such cases should be held to account could freeze or clog much governmental decision-making.

And of course 'state' and 'government' are very different things that should not be equated too readily.

One way and another it is on differences between *individual* criminal responsibility and other responsibility, whether of the state or government, that I will focus.

STATE RESPONSIBILITY AND INDIVIDUAL RESPONSIBILITY

Lawyers have detailed definitions of what a state is and of conceptions of state liability. The earlier concept of the state alone being responsible in international law for the unlawful acts of its citizens, even if unauthorised, has changed over time so that individuals now fall for consideration under international law when crimes may have been committed in armed conflicts. But how wide should the net be cast?

Theoretically it can be claimed of a modern state that, 'Even in a perfect democracy ... it cannot be said that every citizen is the author of every state policy, though every one of them can rightly be called to account.'[1] More practically, with modern mass communication, citizens of a state in armed conflict – *or* citizens of a state oppressing some or all of its own people – are unlikely to be unaware of what their state is doing in the name of some component of the population. They might, as a result, share collectively some of the consequences of the state's failure to live up to its legal and moral responsibility and should 'in any event, be aware that their society's tolerance of, or complicity in, illegal and harmful conduct cannot be expiated by the punishment of a few leaders'.[2]

Or, as Volker Hüls makes clear:

> Any acts of aggression or human rights atrocities on a large scale cannot simply be attributed to individuals, especially when they have been organised and directed through a command structure ... in a post-conflict situation only a state can come up with the amount of financial compensation required to cover the damage to infrastructure and the economy.[3]

Interesting though these concepts are, the ordinary citizen may have a ready understanding of the difference between an individual and a state and maybe between each of these and a government. He will understand that among individuals who commit war crimes, some are truly evil, while in many others the hand of government will have operated invisibly but irresistibly to lead them to do what they did. And he may not be very interested in allowing legal definitions to affect what might seem obvious solutions to present problems.

The germ of an idea

In one century we have moved from a position where judicial trials of war crimes were considered almost inconceivable to a position where they are taken for granted and expected. There is a very limited mechanism for state accountability for some criminal acts but essentially it is only individuals, not states, who may stand accused of crime in war before a criminal court. How did this come about?

We may look back over two unimaginably violent world wars to citizens living at the end of the 19th and start of the 20th centuries with a brutalised eye and assume that they somehow accepted the terrible violence that was to come. Nevertheless, let us go back a hundred years or so to trace steps to where we are.

How were wars conducted? Like many others I have looked at Carl von Clausewitz's *On War*, written in the early 19th century but said to have continuing relevance to the conduct of war. In this work there is no reference that I could find in the index of the edition I consulted to any topic connected to modern concepts of post-conflict judicial accountability.[4] Indeed, the only topic in the index that I could find of conceivable relevance were six 'cold' references to the use of taking prisoners (but not to the way of dealing with them once they were imprisoned); treatment of prisoners was only later to become a starting point in the development of international humanitarian law.

The 19th century saw the development of new ideas on the conduct of war and positive change. The Lieber Code of 1863 regulated the conduct of the Union forces in the American Civil War and, based on that, other countries developed similar codes.

The first Geneva Convention of 1864 dealt with:

- Immunity from capture and destruction of all establishments for the treatment of wounded and sick soldiers;
- Impartial reception and treatment of all combatants;
- The protection of civilians providing aid to the wounded;
- The recognition of the Red Cross symbol as a means of identifying persons and equipment covered by the agreement.

This led to the first unequivocal proposal for the creation of a permanent international court in 1872 by Gustave Moynier of Switzerland[5] who suggested this as a forum to address violations of the 1864 Geneva Convention in the Franco-Prussian War of 1870–71.

The Hague Peace Conferences of 1899 and 1907 imposed obligations on states, while the 1902 Treaty of Vereeniging that concluded the Boer War allowed for proper war crimes trials. In fact, at the beginning of the 20th century there was a considerable peace movement – hard though that may be to believe. Planned, hypothetical interventions of legal processes in war and the conduct of war were seen as possible ways to end war *altogether*; but, if not, then as ways to achieve the more modest aims of deterring some wars and ensuring better conduct in others. That idealistic hope may have disappeared under battlefields of blood, but deterrence was, and remains, a principal objective of all judicial and other interventions in wars.

For a reason to which I will return, it is interesting to become acquainted with what debate there was then for what is fashionable to discuss now. Before, during and immediately after World War I trying and punishing the Kaiser was high on the agenda of British politicians and voters. The Reverend Arnold Page, in a letter to *The Times* published on 16 September 1914, expressed in general terms what many then felt:

> We may be far still from the abolition of war, but we should not be far from the end of atrocities in war if those responsible for them in whatever rank had the risk before their eyes that they might have to suffer just penalties as common felons.[6]

The phrase 'Hang the Kaiser' featured strongly in the rhetoric of Lloyd George's campaign in the British election of 1918.

Even before 1914 Baron d'Estournelles de Constant de Rebecque devoted himself to working for peace and arbitration, and his long-term solution for European problems was a political one – the formation of a European union. With others he lobbied for judicial treatment of international conflicts and was influential in organising the second Hague Conference and establishing the Court of Arbitration. He argued that trials having the appearance of victor's justice should be avoided, and favoured creating a high court to provide impartial judgment of individual crimes contrary to international law, arguing that in this way the example of previous wars might advance the prospects of future peace and justice.[7]

One particularly significant feature of the Hague conferences in which Baron d'Estournelles was influential was the participation of Japan and other extra-European powers in creating a new 'concert of nations' with interests in a new internationalism. This was based on universal participation of states, relying on the principles of equality, disarmament (and pacifism), and the pacific settlement of international disputes through due process of law instead of war. Disarmament and arbitration, something considered at the 1907 Hague Conference, is still reckoned as one workable route to better international security.[8]

Into World War I the debate about war and international affairs, in public and among parliamentarians and governments, had much else to deal with – from the use of submarines sinking merchant and passenger ships including the *Lusitania,* widely identified as a war crime, to the development of the League of Nations with so much hope pinned on it.

In the aftermath of World War I, politics prevailed over international justice, if only by a short head. The US president started to doubt whether the Kaiser really was the originator of the war and the Kaiser's sanctuary in the Netherlands just held. Only six of the twelve men tried in Leipzig for war crimes were convicted. Attempts to try war criminals more generally became an embarrassing failure. The Turks did not have to face international jurists over the massacres in Armenia. The Permanent Court of International Justice created by the League of Nations (and the Permanent Court of Arbitration) had no criminal jurisdiction and expired in the 1930s as rising tension made such a largely optional court redundant.[9]

Throughout there was an acceptance that it was individual criminal responsibility, if at all, that had to be considered. Even to think of states or governments – as opposed to individuals – being held to account would have been more than enough to frighten the political leaderships' horses. The world was, for a time, more concerned with the new world order that the League of Nations would usher in; and then it had to be concerned with Nazi Germany.

So the – arguably odd – idea of individual criminal responsibility for what happens in war had been brought to life by many developments – but though alive was not yet really kicking.

DEVELOPMENTS SINCE WORLD WAR II

After World War II it could be said any principle of state responsibility, even for the wrongful unauthorised acts of officials, yielded to the concept of individual criminal responsibility for grievous atrocities and mass human rights violations. Indeed, this concept was the driving idea behind the Nuremberg and Tokyo trials.[10]

The Charter of Nuremberg Article 6 thus provided a tribunal:

> for the trial and punishment of the major war criminals of the European Axis countries … [to] have the power to try and punish persons who, acting in the interests of the European Axis countries, whether as individuals or as members of organizations, committed any of the following crimes …
>
> (a) Crimes against peace
>
> (b) War crimes
>
> (c) Crimes against humanity
>
> Leaders, organizers, instigators and accomplices participating in the formulation or execution of a common plan or conspiracy to commit any of the foregoing crimes are responsible for all acts performed by any persons in execution of such plan.

In the Tokyo trials the defence challenged the indictment, arguing both that crimes against peace, conspiracy and aggressive war had yet to be established as crimes in international law and that there was no basis in international law for holding individuals responsible for acts of state, as the Tokyo trials proposed to do.[11]

The outcome was imperfect, with plenty of evidence of political influence in who should or who should *not* be tried (including Emperor Hirohito). One highly respected judge who gave one of many dissenting opinions, Justice Röling of the Netherlands, observed, 'I think that not only should there have been neutrals in the court, but there should have been Japanese also … they could have convincingly argued issues of government policy which were unfamiliar to the Allied justices.'[12] This observation, although made in the setting of a trial of *individuals*, may say something about the influential presence of governments and states in all war crimes trials of political or military leaders.

Having a judge of the same country as a party to a case sitting as a member of a multi-judge court is practice at the International Court of Justice (where 15 judges sit) and that deals largely with state *v* state non-criminal issues. It has never been attempted with international criminal courts. Perhaps it should be. A Serbian judge sitting as a fourth or fifth member of a trial court where a Serb was on trial would have provided a fascinating balance from many points of view. If the judge always sided with the defendant he would be disregarded by observers. But if he were to be true to a judicial oath and decided on the evidence, even against his own countrymen and women, how much stronger and impregnable would the judgment of the court be? Is this naive idealism or daring lateral thought? Röling, a much respected judge, would have said the latter.

THE INTERNATIONAL COURT OF JUSTICE

The International Court of Justice was established in June 1945 and its jurisdiction, somewhat broader than that of its predecessors, is to decide, in accordance with international law, disputes of a legal nature that are submitted to it by states. It also gives advisory opinions on legal questions at the request of the United Nations or specialised agencies.

However, alleged *criminality* of states has come before it on only a few occasions, most famously in *Nicaragua v United States*, in which Nicaragua was able to challenge the US for recruiting, training, arming, financing and otherwise encouraging, supporting and directing military and paramilitary actions by the Contras in and against Nicaragua, and for violating various treaties. The allegations went further, asserting coercion and intimidation of the Nicaraguan government, the use of force and the threat of force against Nicaragua, and the killing, wounding and kidnapping of Nicaraguan citizens. The US was said to be under a duty to cease and desist immediately from all use of force (whether direct or indirect, overt or covert) and to have an obligation to pay reparations.

The US challenged the jurisdiction of the court and when it lost that argument declined to involve itself further, save to block in the Security Council what might have followed by way of reparations had the court's decision favourable to Nicaragua been respected.

The ICJ's ruling dealt with the responsibility of the US for violations of international humanitarian law by the Contras, identifying two tests. The first test 'deals with the control a state

[US] exercises over the entire functioning of a group [Contras] … equat[ing] *de facto* controlled groups with state organs'. The second test looked to effective control and 'deals with the state's control over the conduct of a specific operation in the course of which violations have been committed, when the conditions of the first test are not met'. These tests, accepted by all judges of the court, set a very high evidentiary standard for fixing a state with liability for the actions of a paramilitary or similar group operating in another country.[13]

The high threshold was apparent again in the ICJ's 26 February 2007 ruling on the *Application of the Convention on the Prevention and Punishment of the Crime of Genocide* (*Bosnia and Herzegovina v Serbia and Montenegro*), when the court found that Serbia had not committed, conspired to commit, incited the commission of, nor been complicit in genocide but that Serbia had violated the obligation to prevent genocide, contrary to the Convention on the Prevention and Punishment of the Crime of Genocide, in respect of the genocide that occurred in Srebrenica in July 1995.[14]

An academic review of this case suggested that:

> For the first time in legal history, and of the four genocide cases that have come before the ICJ,[15] the Court unequivocally held states can be found responsible for genocide … [But t]he core difficulty remains: 'The [Genocide] Convention definition of genocide requires proof of specific intent. It is hard to conceive of a state with specific intent.' Without evidence proving that a state's leaders possessed the specific intent at the crucial time, it is impossible to prove genocide. This intent requirement is what defeated Bosnia's Article IX claim.[16]

To which comment I respond with a resolute 'Yes' and 'No'. 'Yes' hard, but 'No', certainly not impossible – why else did so many states sign up to the convention in the first place? Further, and more important, the citizens of states, having been provided with the language of genocide and the laws for dealing with criminal genocide, want to see states dealt with for the crime. And it is not for lawyers, judges or academics to be too willingly dismissive of those legitimate expectations.

If, as Bosnian Muslims (Bosniaks) certainly believe, it is important for Bosnia to have recorded for its history that a state – Serbia – committed genocide against Bosnia then there is no court other than the ICJ where that can be properly recorded as a finding of law.

BRINGING THE LEADERSHIP TO ACCOUNT

Before we come to that, there could, of course, be another route to establishing what may *look* like state responsibility – the Nuremberg route. Although you try people only for individual criminal responsibility, by 'bagging' the leadership – as it might be a cabinet or a president and his secretaries of state – you effectively establish government / state responsibility for crimes. At Nuremberg as many as available of the Nazi government leadership were on trial. The non-lawyer citizen might readily equate government criminal responsibility to state responsibility and state responsibility means, in a way, that every citizen is responsible through the state for what may have been done in their name. We may all know that what happened in Germany was caused by events that conspired in a way that could have drawn any or many of us, had *we* been living there, into following the Nazi leadership. Yet, perhaps because of the Nuremberg process, we still treat that particular state and its present citizens, nearly all born after the war, as irremediably marked by the crimes found proved against earlier government leaders.

Might the same process have been used to assist Bosnia in whatever purposes may be served by setting the record straight? Might a trial of the Serbian 'government' have done the trick?

Well, again, yes and no. Individual criminal responsibility courts such as the ICTY and ICTR have regularly enough pursued leaderships just as was done in Nuremberg. Indeed, in Rwanda two cases were known by shorthand as the 'Government 1' and 'Government 2' cases. But two problems arise. First, you may simply not be able to 'bag' enough of the leadership in the way achieved in the dock of Nuremberg to make it look as though the government is on trial. Second, in all cases where as many government members as possible have been tried, it has been on specific evidence attributable to individuals that guilt or innocence has been pronounced. There has not been any example of a government member being convicted on the basis of mere failure to act in circumstances where he might be expected to shoulder collective responsibility. We have not yet reached the stage where a minister sitting at the cabinet table may be held to account for doing nothing when, by being in a position to act by virtue of the public office he will have sought, he could or should have resisted – or resigned – to ensure responsibility rested where it should.

In the Bosnia–Serbia setting there was another very particular difficulty, as a recent and highly controversial ICTY Appeals Chamber judgment revealed. It was in the case of Momćilo Perišić, who was Chief of Staff of the Serbian / Yugoslavian Army (VJ) at a time when the prosecution had argued that Serbia / Yugoslavia was supporting the Bosnian Serbs in their genocide of the Bosnian Muslims, notably at Srebrenica, although Perišić was charged with crimes against humanity not with genocide.

The Appeals Chamber observed that the VRS (Bosnian Serb Army) was independent from the VJ and that the two armies were based in separate geographic regions. In addition, Perišić was not physically present when relevant criminal acts were planned or committed. In these circumstances evidence of Perišić giving *specific* directions to the VRS to commit criminal acts would have been required to establish guilt. The Appeals Chamber noted that previous judgments of the court had not provided extensive analysis of what evidence may prove specific direction, although a link would have to be shown between an accused – as aider and abettor – and crimes committed by principal perpetrators. The Appeals Chamber made clear that its inquiry focused solely on factors related to Perišić's individual criminal liability for the VRS crimes in Sarajevo and Srebrenica, not the potential liability of states, over which the tribunal had no jurisdiction.

The judgment went on to explain that specific direction is an analytically distinct element of *actus reus* – the thing(s) actually done by an accused to be contrasted with the mental state or *mens rea* – required for proof of guilt.

It found, among other things, that:

- Perišić served as the most senior officer of the VJ during the relevant period;
- Perišić was responsible for ensuring combat readiness and organisation of VJ operations;
- Perišić was subordinated to the President of the

Federal Republic of Yugoslavia;
- Operational priorities for the VJ rested with the Supreme Defence Council;
- SDC meetings were attended by many individuals, including Perišić;
- Final SDC decisions were taken by political leaders: the President of the Federal Republic of Yugoslavia and the Presidents of the Republics of Serbia and Montenegro;
- The decision to provide VJ assistance to the VRS was adopted by the SDC before Perišić was appointed Chief of the VJ General Staff;
- The SDC continued to support this policy during Perišić's tenure in this position;
- Perišić regularly attended and actively participated in meetings of the SDC;
- Perišić was delegated the legal authority by the SDC to administer assistance to the VRS;
- The SDC retained the power to review both particular requests for assistance and the general policy of providing aid to the VRS.

Despite findings adverse to the VRS and the revelation of Perišić's role in connecting the VRS to the SDC, Perišić was, to the astonishment of many, acquitted by the Appeals Chamber of all convictions recorded against him by the Trial Chamber, even of aiding and abetting.[17]

The test for 'aiding and abetting' these kinds of crimes has, seemingly, been raised very high. Some are saying that the beneficiaries of this ruling – apart from Perišić himself and Serbia – are the military around the world, who may be able more easily than formerly to rely on superior orders in defence of actions in war that are proved to be criminal.

The *latest* defined legal test of individual criminal responsibility, such as now from the Perišić case, will always be what has to be met for proof of war crimes by individuals. This may seem curious, especially to victims of any state-run criminal campaign who hear of high officers of government being freed from liability on the basis of what looks like an erroneous, or possibly politically driven, interpretation of the law.

THE NEW IDEALISM

The differences between prosecuting individuals and prosecuting states are considerable. Trying states in the form of governments, to the extent one can, is also intrinsically immensely problematic.

However successful the ICC and other tribunals may be or become as crime and punishment courts of individuals, their contribution to international peace and security will be as limited as are domestic crime and punishment systems to the functioning of a nation: in each case some individual criminals will be punished, some potential future offenders *may* be deterred – but crime will not be stopped.

Which brings me back to the public debate at the time of World War I. The sometimes idealistic dreams that had led to 19th- and early 20th-century reforms must surely have seemed further from reality then than similar dreams should seem today. The hope to *end* war and the desire to see international courts try war crimes may each have seemed unimaginably utopian.

How surprised would those dreamers be to see the judicially clean – if loaded – form of 'victor's justice' at Nuremberg, followed by the steps towards definition of previously undefined crimes – crimes against humanity and then genocide – and the establishment of a world court (ICJ) for treaty breaches and, later, an international criminal court (ICC) for international crimes?

If we are able now to generate similar optimistic positivism to what existed then, where might it lead us? Not, I think, to throwing all our efforts into a retributive justice system, however good the ICC may yet turn out to be.

The distinctions between individual criminal responsibility and state criminal responsibility and even government criminal responsibility are so significant that we need to think again about what Utopia we should be aiming at, given that our present starting point comes with knowledge of the way individual citizens become caught up in criminal wartime behaviour and an awareness that we have weapons capable of destroying us all.

As Cherif Bassiouni, one of today's leading international law scholars, suggests:

> The International Criminal Justice System will not likely occur as a result of planning and sound legal

> techniques but rather it will develop as a result of non-orderly processes in which fortuitous events and practical exigencies will incrementally enhance the goals intended to be attained.[18]

And perhaps it has done and is doing just that. If so, its processes should not be thought of as the exclusive preserve of lawyers and politicians.

With a legal system bolstered by the ability to try and punish the worst offenders, it should never have been possible for the true history of events leading up to Srebrenica to be hidden – as they are even now – in the interests of participating states and the international community, that has things it wishes not to be known. When the Iraq War was embarked upon we should not have had to wait to know how and why it happened through drawn-out processes in which individuals and governments have protested their right to hold information back. What we need as the next step in the development of the international process dealing with conflicts and wars is access to information from states showing what they, through their governments, have done. In some way, I believe, this may form part of the next idealism. It may fail now. Even if it does – as with the idealism of the late 19th century – it may come back, to serve a purpose.

Chapter 5

Regulation at Home, But not Everywhere

This chapter is about regulation as it operates for lawyers and judges. Regulation – like law itself – is a set of rules with sanctions for those who break them. But regulation is not just a question of forbidding things from being done. It also requires and encourages action.

Original lecture delivered on 8 May 2013.

We regulate professionals because we need to be able to trust them. Our own legal system has been regulated by judges controlling barristers since Edward I's time. For the last decade the Bar Standards Board has dealt with discipline and regulation.

More than 40 years ago when I came to the Bar it was a small profession of about 6,000 practitioners, mostly men and most working as self-employed referral barristers in cooperative organisations known as 'chambers'. I can recall nothing of formal education about regulatory rules – we mostly picked up ethics from our pupil-masters and 'on the job'. The profession is now much larger – 16,000 with 5,000 working as employed barristers for government departments, industry, solicitors' firms and so on.

When I started, much control of barrister and judicial conduct was informal – this is how it worked.

First, a profession of a few thousand barrister advocates in independent practice was gossipy. Make a mistake in Swansea today and tomorrow it could be the talk of the robing rooms in Norwich or Newcastle. Make an ethical blunder or do something perceived as dodgy or dishonest and your name could be muddied for life, with your career damaged or even destroyed. Barristers were aware of what would happen to their reputation if they put a foot out of line and, as they had only their reputations to sell, generally behaved well, simply in their own interest. Today's larger Bar may have made this mechanism less effective.

Second, there were and still are rules that allow a barrister in uncertainty or difficulty to check what he should be doing without fuss.

Third, we were – maybe still are – a form of elite (it should be noted there were few women and they often found it extremely hard to be treated as equals). This elite society, once entered, was not marked by wealth – earned or otherwise – or even merely by well-educated intelligence (although a disturbing percentage of public school and Oxbridge educations from 40-odd years ago still grace our judicial and advocate benches). Elite was defined by a particular ethos of the group that members would be ashamed not to honour. Pride at being members of an elite meant we had to honour its code if we were to be happy with ourselves.

HOW THE LAW HAS CHANGED

I should acknowledge that the legal system when I started did feel different from how it seems today. It was a masculine profession with many who had served in the war – robust, red-blooded, sexist often enough and racist – and with some real shockers on the bench along with very many decent judges.

The shockers might enjoy destroying counsel for sport or controlling a jury to be sure the defendant was convicted – 'potted'. In criminal courts there could be the sense that the judge and the prosecution were on the same side.

I have sat as a part-time judge for about 30 years in various capacities and have felt it change. All judges now go to residential training courses every year. And yet within the last 20 years at one such course a recently retired Lord Chief Justice repeated someone else's joke about a fictional rapist at Oxford or Cambridge in a mock sentencing exercise being given not five or six years but a 'blue'. I don't think he understood quite how the world had changed. But then one of his predecessors within my lifetime had written a report into Bloody Sunday that could generously be described as a greywash favourable to the army and adverse to the IRA that it took decades and millions of pounds to put right. The report itself led, some would say, to increases in terrorist recruitment and violence.[1]

Legal systems, even the best in the world, need time like large ships to change course and these bad things may now be largely of the past, and for a few reasons.

Selection, as well as training, of judges has become more professional and systematic, and judges with inappropriately reactionary, sexist, discriminatory or exclusionary views should be eliminated at detailed interviews by interviewing panels of lay and legal members.

Second, some of the motivation for getting defendants 'potted' was a belief that some procedures and some law benefited those who were, or may have been, guilty but who were acquitted under the 'proof beyond reasonable doubt' rule by reason of a technicality. Over time many of these procedures and laws have been abolished,[2] and there may be less of a sense of the legal system being loaded in favour of the guilty than once there was.

Third, jurors have become more willing to ask questions. Although judges are trained to discourage too many jury questions, judges are increasingly happy to leave verdicts fairly to jurors. In summing up cases to juries in England and Wales judges are expected to refer to, and to use or adapt, standard approved forms of words for particular offences or particular modes of liability. Judges are encouraged in all but the simplest of cases to provide a jury with directions, often part in writing, that constitute a logical route to a verdict, one way or another. These devices have rendered it harder for judges to 'pot' a defendant by a slanted summing up and have encouraged them to do their own job, not the jury's.

Professional culture

Effective regulation of a profession is not a simple question of having a rule book. In a way the rule book is the last force in line – the long stop. First in line should be the culture established by the body itself, maintained perhaps over centuries.

It would be a poor profession where instinct often went one way and the rules the other. The professional culture changes with time, as should the rule book. For the Bar at present there is much change, some of it imposed by the Legal Services Act. But the Bar – although probably not the main target when the reforming legislation was drafted – has never been that good at change.

When pressed to accept that publicly funded barristers need to be assessed and that that assessment had to be done by the judges in front of whom they appear (despite pretty obvious problems of conflict) barristers have resisted strongly. Quality assessment and even continuing professional development demands tend to draw strong negative reactions. How differently might the Bar be regarded now if its professional body had been actively pressing for methods of assessment – voluntary or compulsory – given that other professionals like doctors have to be assessed annually?

There is also the real difficulty with fees. At one end there are barristers taking millions of pounds every year and at the other very many serving the criminal and family courts doing publicly funded work at rates of pay barely sufficient to live on. It is hard to reconcile these groups or for them to find common ground from which to launch a defence of their current position or to establish a new and sustainable identity.

A CASE I PRESIDED OVER IN JERSEY

Developing procedures and changes in the cultures of the Bar and Bench in England were associated, in my thinking, with a shift from criminal trials being regarded simply as games to be played and won to being seen more as searches for truth. I may have been unwise to think other parts of the British Isles had been developing at the same rate and in the same direction.

I was appointed in 2006 as a Commissioner – temporary judge – to try a case in Jersey, *R. v Peter Michel and Simone Gallichan*. I was in several ways to find myself in a somewhat out of date legal culture, not something I appreciated immediately. The case lasted several weeks and ran smoothly enough – or so it seemed.

Jersey has a rather different system for trials in which two jurats – the island's most senior elected officials – sit with the judge. The jurats are effectively professional jurors who will have read the papers in advance. The judge deals with procedure and directs the jurats publicly about the law but then has to retire with the jurats while they consider their verdict. However, the judge has no part to play in the determination of any factual issue unless the two jurats are 'split' on their decision(s).

There was no complaint of my conduct of the case in a very intimate court where, had there been cause for concern, I would have expected it to be raised formally or informally. Michel was convicted – his co-accused, office manager Simone Gallichan, was acquitted. By the jurats, of course.

In the Court of Appeal – unknown to me – complaint was made about the number of questions I had asked and the tone or manner of my asking them. Sarcastic behaviour and all sorts of other things were alleged. The Court of Appeal had nothing to say about the allegations of offensive manner but said I had asked too many questions. They dismissed the appeal nevertheless.

The second stage of appeal was to the Privy Council, composed of some of the country's most senior Supreme Court judges – Lord Phillips, Lord Neuberger, Lord Brown, Lord Rodger and Baroness Hale. None of these judges knew me. They were addressed by two advocates, neither of whom had been in the trial court, one of whom was the attorney general of the island (for the prosecution). The allegation of offensive tone was revived. I cannot know what precisely was said because the

Privy Council declined to provide me with a transcript or a tape recording.

In its judgment, published in a newspaper without warning, I was condemned as the worst known form of judge and the appeal allowed. There was nothing I could do – for a time. The defendant had to be left to have his retrial. Eventually I discovered that he had pleaded guilty at his retrial and would not be in front of the Privy Council again. I wrote to the only person who might be able to offer a detached view, counsel for the co-accused. She had represented her client with industry, always prepared, always asking pertinent questions and being able to answer the questions asked of her by the court. She wrote back, clearly relieved at being approached. The case as described in the Privy Council judgment was unrecognisable as the case she had sat through. The judgment was a character assassination. She said quite a lot that could explain how it was that the jurats and I had been left to ask questions that could and should have been asked by counsel for the other parties. She explained that I had conducted the hearings with absolute courtesy from first to last. She was happy for her letter to go to the Privy Council and indeed to speak to them if asked. To which the reply from Lord Phillips was much as before, save that they acknowledged her view of the proceedings was much as mine. They did not acknowledge the possibility of error or identify a mechanism for putting error right.

I was able to circulate her letter to lawyers and judges known to me. Some of them, in very senior positions, were concerned and wrote to the Privy Council. After a long time they received an answer that procedures could not change but that if she (Caitriona Fogarty, the defence advocate) was right, they were wrong. That was the nearest they ever got to an acknowledgement of fallibility. Two of the senior lawyers then wrote an article published in *The Times* that corrected the history.[3]

I wrote once more setting out all the manifest errors revealed in the process to date and suggesting steps that might be taken, including referring the whole unhappy history for review to the Ministry of Justice. Lord Phillips eventually replied saying that he had consulted the other top judges in Scotland and Northern Ireland who did not think the finality of judgment of such courts as theirs should be subject to review.

There are many arguments about substance and procedure that can be advanced in criticism of the Privy Council's conduct. But the two most obvious are first that the Privy Council was prepared to leave unresolved a possible injustice without checking on the evidence available to them. Second, the Privy Council – just as the Supreme Court composed of the same judges for the most part – is regarded as infallible and beyond regulation of any kind.

Is this important apart from to me and to other judges consigned to outer darkness by incorrect judgments of this kind? Well, yes.

Supreme courts are very important places for their citizens – ours typically deals with vital issues of life, death, health, liberty of the subject and so on. They cannot expect to sit at the top of a machine that is subject to review and regulation in various ways without being in any way themselves exposed. To have them exempt is extraordinary, especially when they recognise their shortcomings in at least two ways. Baroness Hale, one of the judges, said of the Supreme Court (effectively the same for these purposes): 'We are not final because we are right – we are right because we are final' – in other words, they may make errors but those errors cannot be corrected. She also said in a speech that judges who have risen through the Bar, the Temples and other parts of the 'establishment' are not always ideally placed to cast judgment on the complexities of modern life, observing that,

> If the life-blood of the law is experience and common sense, then whose experience and common sense are we talking about? Surely it cannot only be the experience and common sense of the judges, many of whom have led such sheltered lives?[4]

In my case application of common sense would clearly have alerted the court as a minimum to their being at risk of being unfair. And, in another case concerning Jersey, the Privy Council itself observed that the written transcript of a trial – the only actual evidence to which the Council turned – is not necessarily something to be relied on.

There seem to me several steps that could be taken to avoid my particular misfortune happening to others. First, just as Lord Sumption was promoted straight from the ranks of the Bar to the Supreme Court, the Appointments Committee should encourage more applications from barristers and solicitors of diverse backgrounds, especially those with more radical approaches to the law. (Currently Baroness Hale is the only woman on the Supreme Court and it includes no one from an ethnic minority.) The Appointments Committee – at least the lay members of it – would probably be both astonished and delighted to find, say, a high-street solicitor – especially if with a non-white, non-Anglo-Saxon background – having the qualifications to sit as Supreme Court judge and able to bring common sense and an entirely different perspective to the major legal issues of the day. Another way to secure some form of control on the over-homogeneous bench might be to have lay assessors – not unlike jurors – sitting with them. Selection would be difficult and, of course, they would not be able to ask questions directly or to be involved in the writing of the legal judgment – but the lay view, with an ability to prod the justices into asking questions not asked by counsel, could be invaluable.

When my reputation was attacked by the Privy Council I had no doubt whatsoever that there was no alternative to finding the courage I needed not to jump from a bridge but to deal with these powerful people who knew me not at all. Sadly, the correspondence, which drew the attention of the justices to evidence of what actually happened, reveals that they were quite determined neither to face me nor to confront the evidence of courageous Caitriona Fogarty who put them right. Why not? They will not say.[5]

REGULATION OF INTERNATIONAL COURTS

As I turn from national to the new international criminal courts we may see similar problems appearing, but in different settings.

International criminal tribunals all have infallible courts that sit at the top of only two tiers of hearings, except for the ICJ, which has only a single unreviewable court of 15 judges. The individual-top-level courts of the Yugoslav, Rwanda and Sierra Leone proceedings are not subject to review on fact or law. As well as potentially giving rise to injustices this has possible consequences for the development of the relevant laws. Thus, for example, if one of these top courts renders a decision in law moderating a test of criminal liability the other courts are free to disagree.[6] And what if a top-tier court makes a decision in law because of local political pressure, as for example in the Perišić appeal decision dealt with in chapter 4? Should the rest of the world's international jurisprudence be affected by the local interest?

But other, perhaps greater problems exist that may need regulation. These courts are staffed on the basis of 'geographical spread', as the UN describes it. No two judges from the same country. Lawyers and other staff are all selected to ensure as many countries as possible have their nationals engaged at the court. On the bench, judges sit in threes, fours or fives, having no shared background and often no common first language. There have been many rumours of benches of judges being barely on speaking terms one with another, which is hardly surprising.

Most of the supporting lawyers will have relocated, often with families, perhaps from thousands of miles away. What is their response if, as happens, they are asked or pressed to do something improper or ethically wrong by their office superior? The independent lawyer may be tempted to yield but knows that if he does so he risks his one saleable item – his reputation – if caught out. For the employed lawyer different considerations apply: if pressure is applied through the boss, then the lawyer resists at his and his family's peril. It may not be surprising that, when ethical issues cropped up at the ICTY, the 'hired-gun' advocates from common law jurisdictions were more comfortable challenging the management – even at personal risk and suffering sanctions – than those from other backgrounds. But then we, in theory, could walk away to other work.

Let me tell you about the worst such problem I faced.

Seven days from the end of the prosecution's case in the Milošević trial it became clear that the presiding judge, Sir Richard May from England, had a serious medical problem. He was persuaded to go to the doctor and it was confirmed how ill he was. Indeed, sadly, he died shortly after. The ICTY's rules allowed a panel of judges to sit with one of its three members absent for up to five days *only if his absence was likely to be of short duration*, otherwise the hearings had to stop forthwith.

All three supposedly independent parts of the tribunal – judges, prosecution, registry – thought it would be a good idea to close the prosecution case by squeezing seven days' evidence into five without alerting Milošević to the gravity of Judge May's illness or, thus, to the illegality of the proceedings before only two judges. We all knew there was no possibility of Judge May's condition fitting in the 'short duration' category and the hearings simply had to stop immediately. But it was thought it would be a PR coup to get to the end of the prosecution case. Ironically, had Milošević been informed that the hearing might have to stop, he would probably have said he could not care less and the trial could carry on with two judges and some member of the animal kingdom, such was his attitude to the court.

I had no choice but to say that the plan was wrong. I was subject to extreme pressure to shut up. I declined. I was advised by another UK lawyer there to do what I knew was appropriate, namely to contact my own professional ethics body for a ruling. Unsurprisingly I was told by the Bar Council of England and Wales that I had to get off the case unless I could put things right. There was nowhere in the UN to turn to for assistance; nor is there an effective code of conduct for prosecution lawyers. I tracked down the Foreign Office's chief lawyer in Arusha (in Tanzania, where the Rwanda Tribunal was sitting), asking him somehow to persuade the court to behave in accordance with its own rules. I was told 'You're on your own.' Senior lawyers in the prosecutor's office were asked for written opinions. The majority were as clear as they dared to be in saying that what was planned was contrary to the rules and had to stop. There was a meeting of all lawyers. I was told that to seek advice from my professional body was blackmail – not a term I welcomed. I explained that I had no choice but to take particularly robust action to compel the tribunal to act in accordance with the law and left the room. No other lawyer had the courage to follow me. They could not possibly take the risk.

Although it was not possible to remove me from the case, I was detested for having put the law above short-term exigency. Such is the reality of working in frontier legal systems that are neither accountable nor regulated.

THE ARC OF REGULATION

Regulation – like law itself – is about getting people to behave well – to be 'good'. It is never easy to know who or what is good, but most have within us a personal sense of goodness from which we should not be separated. Clever law – and clever regulation – activates that sense of goodness to achieve what society wants, but not necessarily simply by having a law or a rule book. Rules are, after all, there to be broken.

It may be worth thinking of the way we regulate human interaction as an arc. At one end, the limited instances where there is almost no regulation of behaviour beyond what a nation's laws provides – queuing for buses, swimming in the sea, playing games in a park – circumstances where we feel we can trust each other. At the other end there is the fiercest of regulation, and I do not have in mind laws about murder or rape or crimes against humanity. More interesting are drink-drive laws. For decades we have known how dangerous it is to drive drunk. Tough laws have been introduced. We may now kid ourselves that a cultural shift has happened and that most people would not drive drunk. Wrong. Take the laws away tomorrow and we would return to the dangerous fool's confidence of driving with two or three pints of beer or half a bottle of wine swilling around our insides. The law has to be fierce, not just because of the damage caused by the drink-driving but because the citizen needs to be deterred from falling to temptation likely to be experienced as irresistible by many. It works – but it manifests distrust in ourselves and is probably never the best form of regulation.

We have a perfect example of regulation *not* working from which to learn. Hundreds of parliamentarians had their expense claims examined. The arc here starts with those confidently blameless because they made no claim or really only charged second-class rail tickets and cleaned their own moats.[7] At the other end were those knowing clearly that they were defrauding the public. In the middle? Worried parliamentarians seeing their images tarnished because they followed suggestions that, rather than vote themselves salary increases, they claim generous expenses – or when advised to do so by officials they thought it questionable but went ahead regardless.

Yet there was a simple way of regulating this problem. If it had been known from the beginning that all expenses claim forms were to be made publicly available, no one would have offended. The practice would either have frightened the claimants into good behaviour or played on their sense of goodness to persuade them to honour the public's trust. The outcome is what would have been required and our parliamentarians would have enjoyed enhanced respect. I am not sure that the lessons available from this category of behavioural control are recognised in today's regulatory world.

CONCLUSION

The Bar has had a difficult few decades, and barristers may now seem less than happy. It has lost its near-monopoly of rights of audience; it has seen Legal Aid work rise and more recently fall substantially in amount and in rates of pay; it has seen much of the work it used to do pass to institutions (like the Crown Prosecution Service [CPS]); it now finds itself obliged by the Legal Services Act to accommodate new systems of working that may never have been what the barrister when student contemplated.

However, being a barrister – any form of advocate – is to have the enormous privilege of representing another human being at a point of distress. It is a privilege shared with doctors and priests. It is a privilege that should reflect – by the conduct of the professionals and by the regulation to which the profession may have to be subject – that lawyers and judges work in the service of the citizen, not the other way round.

Chapter 6

The Russell Tribunal on Vietnam

Informal tribunals dealing with armed conflicts show how citizens are not to be denied judicial or quasi-judicial judgments about their suffering by atrocities committed in conflicts simply because the great international organisations decline – or fear – to act.

Original lecture delivered on 2 October 2013.

In focusing on the tribunal of Lord Russell on Vietnam I had expected to reach with ease a conclusion already in mind. But I didn't. Other questions intervened. There is no point in reserving them all for later – they are these: Is it always a good thing to examine whether war crimes were committed? May it sometimes be better to do nothing? Is there any evidence that confessions due from governments arising from the Vietnam conflict will serve any good? Are powerful countries like the US entitled to different standards of review by the international community from those we now apply to countries like the former Yugoslavia or Rwanda or, perhaps, Syria?

Intervention in Syria provided insight into how the world attempts to deal with humanitarian crises arising from armed conflicts and how the law does or does not feature at such times. Discussion about legality – in particular whether it could be legal to intervene without a supporting UN Security Council resolution – tends only to become relevant if the intervention is not a success or, at least, regarded as a success. Then – then only – are opponents of intervention able to beat governments with the legality argument.

Syria also reminds us how thin would seem the line between chemical weapons as defined by the Organisation for the Prohibition of Chemical Weapons (OPCW)[1] and other weapons used by the great powers that somehow avoid that definition, and how thin the line may be between conflict counted as unlawful when committed by countries *without* international power and very similar conduct in which the powerful have themselves engaged.

The Syria conflict has drawn us to the wonderland populated only by wicked bogeymen who are forever bad and demonstrated the potential for hypocrisy in those who wish to be seen as good. It is the way things are. Justice Jackson – whose words at Nuremberg were quoted at the start of the Russell Tribunal – said this:

> If certain acts and violations of treaties are crimes, they are crimes whether the United States does them or whether Germany does them. We are not prepared to lay down a rule of criminal conduct against others which we would not be willing to have invoked against us.

Yet, as I stated in chapter 1, Jackson also explained that in charging the Nazis with crimes against humanity a broader definition than the one the US was prepared to employ could have exposed the US to the same pursuit (under law) for things it had done in the past.

We subject the actions of the *bad* in any conflict to whatever the law may seem to be at the time, not just in the printed law but also by other instruments of almost no legal effect such as United Nations resolutions. But do we apply it to the powerful? Maybe we should face the fact that no individual, body, state or collection of states will ever own up properly to what it has done wrong if it has the power to do otherwise. Is this the fundamental problem to be faced, that covers all areas of life and that neither Parliament nor the courts nor any other system of inquiry has overcome?

RELEVANT LAW

The Vietnam War, a disaster and the second of two Indo-China conflicts, had a long history that started well after law-making for the conduct of war was under way. Bertrand Russell was born in 1872. He could not have recalled directly the Brussels Convention made two years later, but everything else relevant following that would have been in his active memory. It is sensible to attempt to cast his reactions to the Vietnam conflict that was to come at the end of his life in the setting of his own experience and (immense) knowledge.

The 1874 Brussels Convention prohibited the employment of poison or poisoned weapons and the use of arms, projectiles or material to cause unnecessary suffering. An agreement signed at The Hague in 1899 prohibited the use of projectiles filled with poison gas. The Hague Convention of 18 October 1907 denied belligerents unlimited choice for injuring an enemy and prohibited the use of arms deliberately destined to cause pointless suffering, along with attacks on towns, villages, dwellings or undefended buildings. The 1925 Geneva Protocol for the Prohibition of the Use of Asphyxiating, Poisonous or Other Gases, and Bacteriological Methods of Warfare banned the use of chemical and bacteriological (biological) weapons in war. The 1928 Pact of Paris, known as the Kellogg–Briand Pact, renounced the use of war and called for the peaceful settlement of disputes.

After World War II, Article 6 of the Charter of Nuremberg outlawed:

> CRIMES AGAINST PEACE: ... waging of a war of aggression, or a war in violation of international treaties, agreements or assurances ...
> WAR CRIMES including plunder of public or private property, wanton destruction of cities, towns or villages, or devastation not justified by military necessity ...
> CRIMES AGAINST HUMANITY: ... inhumane acts committed against any civilian population.

The Geneva Convention of 2 August 1949 prohibited attacks on civilian hospitals and private and collective property not rendered absolutely necessary by the conduct of the operations.

Also of relevance is the December 1960 United Nations resolution which decided that all peoples have fundamental rights to national independence, to sovereignty, to respect of the integrity of their territory, and that breaches of these fundamental rights may be regarded as crimes against the national existence of a people.[2]

THE FIRST INDO-CHINA WAR (1946–1954)

Following World War I, a Vietnamese patriot named Nguyen That Thanh, then in his late twenties, went to the Paris Peace Conference where American President Woodrow Wilson had promised 'self-determination' for all nations. Thanh hoped to see Vietnam freed from French rule. Like many other advocates of colonial independence who went to the Paris peace talks, Thanh was ignored. He returned to Vietnam, and later changed his name to Ho Chi Minh.

In 1945 Ho Chi Minh and his People's Congress created the National Liberation Committee of Vietnam – Vietminh – and declared independence. In 1946 negotiations between the French and the Vietminh failed and in December 1946 the First Indo-China War began; it was to last eight years. Early on, Ho Chi Minh told the French: 'You can kill ten of my men for every one I kill of yours, but even at those odds, you will lose and I will win.'

The war ended in 1954 with France's defeat in the Battle of Dien Bien Phu. A peace conference was held in Geneva to work out the future of Vietnam, Laos and Cambodia. In the same year US President Eisenhower coined the term 'domino theory' regarding

Southeast Asia: 'You have a row of dominoes set up, you knock over the first one, and what will happen to the last one is the certainty that it will go over very quickly.'[3] Eisenhower's administration, fearing communism, instructed US delegates to observe the proceedings but not to sign the Geneva Peace Accords. However, under Chinese and Soviet pressure, the Vietminh reached a compromise with the French that divided the country in half – *temporarily* – at the 17th parallel. Vietminh forces were to withdraw to the north of this line while French forces would withdraw to the south. Each side agreed not to sign military alliances or permit foreign bases on Vietnamese soil. Internationally supervised national elections were to be held in 1956 to unify the country.

The Geneva Accords were never fulfilled. The US initiated a military build-up and replaced the French puppet Bao Dai with Ngo Dinh Diem, a Christian anti-communist. Diem, fearing that communist leader Ho Chi Minh would easily win an open election, instead held a rigged referendum to legitimise his dictatorship. The French left Vietnam. The failure of the Geneva Accords can be viewed in hindsight as a lost opportunity, as the US became embroiled in the Second Indo-China War, one of the most destructive conflicts in modern history, and one that some historians mark as a key turning point in the decline of American hegemony.

The proxy war to come – fighting over a belief (if it was not recolonisation by another route) – was in the making. Looking back, we may think how odd it was to allow a war to develop largely premised on fear of an economic model. Extreme economic models all have something good about them and probably all moderate or modulate over time. What would an intelligent being from another galaxy have said had it been unwise enough to visit such a dangerous place as Planet Earth if it then found that we had destroyed ourselves altogether in a nuclear battle started by concern about an economic model of life – and President Nixon did consider the nuclear option.

THE VIETNAM WAR (1954–1975)

What was to come in deaths and horror overall we now know, although imprecisely (and the statistics are at best indicative). The Vietnamese government has said that there were over a million

North Vietnamese and Vietcong military deaths in the course of the war; more than 59,000 Americans were killed or remain missing, while the South Vietnamese forces had up to 250,000 dead. Civilian casualties are harder to enumerate but perhaps as many as 430,000 South Vietnamese civilians died in the war (at the hands of all sides), while North Vietnamese civilian losses included at least 50,000 killed by American bombing.

The US government spent more than $140 billion on the war but failed to achieve its objective of preserving an independent, non-communist state in South Vietnam.

Seven massacres were eventually confirmed by the American side as criminal. My Lai and My Khe claimed the largest number of victims with 420 and 90 respectively, and in five other places altogether about 100 civilians were executed.

As part of the US military's herbicidal warfare programme, Operation 'Ranch Hand', millions of gallons of Agent Orange (dioxin) were sprayed over about a tenth of the area of South Vietnam. The aim was to expose to view jungle roads and trails used by Vietcong and North Vietnamese forces and to destroy crops being grown to feed them. Vietnam's government has claimed that 400,000 people were killed or maimed at the time or later, and that half a million children have been born with birth defects; there has also been extensive environmental damage. There is no doubt that Agent Orange caused immense suffering – but it is not within the OPCW definition of what constitutes a chemical weapon. The moral outrage expressed recently by worthy governments over the use of chemical weapons in Syria may sound a little hollow.

Pretext for war

On 2 August 1964, three North Vietnamese patrol boats *allegedly* fired torpedoes at the USS *Maddox*, a destroyer located in the international waters of the Tonkin Gulf, some 30 miles off the coast of North Vietnam. A second, even more highly disputed attack was alleged to have taken place on 4 August. On 7 August 1964, President Lyndon Johnson secured almost unanimous consent from Congress for his Gulf of Tonkin Resolution that authorised him to 'take all necessary measures to repel any armed attack against forces of the United States and to prevent further aggression'. The resolution allowed Johnson to wage an all-out military campaign against North Vietnam without ever securing a formal declaration of war from Congress, and became the principal legislative basis for all subsequent American military deployments in Southeast Asia.

Using as a pretext a Vietcong attack on 7 February 1965 at Pleiku that killed eight American soldiers, Johnson ordered retaliatory bombing north of the Demilitarized Zone along the 17th parallel that divided North and South Vietnam. This Operation 'Rolling Thunder' became a gradually intensifying air bombardment of military bases, supply depots and infiltration routes in North Vietnam. The bombing continued for three years.

Legal challenges in the US

The first Vietnam legal case concerned US constitutional issues, not whether the conflict was itself unlawful.[4] In *United States v Mitchell* in December 1965, Mitchell asserted that, as war had not been declared, conscription was unlawful. He said that the US was committing war crimes and that other treaties binding the US were being breached. Mitchell's case became something of a model for many to follow in US federal courts during the war. Mitchell's conviction for refusing induction was upheld on grounds of lack of standing and because his contentions were 'wholly without merit … repeatedly and consistently rejected by the courts of the United States'. The court excluded evidence that US military operations in Vietnam violated treaties to which the US was committed by distinguishing between the power of Congress to provide armed forces by conscription and the use of such forces by the President and Congress.[5]

The Supreme Court – Justice Douglas dissenting – denied review in *Mitchell.* Justice Douglas believed that Mitchell's conviction and the defence he put forward, including his reliance on the 1945 Treaty of London, set out issues that should be reviewed.[6] The 'Juridical Memorandum on the Legality of the Participation of the United States in the Defence of Vietnam', submitted to the Senate Foreign Affairs Committee on 4 March 1966, argued that the American intervention in Vietnam merely constituted aid to the Saigon government against aggression from the North.

In *Mora* v. *McNamara* (February 1967), Mora and his fellow draftees filed suit to invalidate orders to go to Vietnam on grounds that military activity in Vietnam was 'illegal'. Justice Stewart observed that *Mora* presented 'questions of great magnitude':

> Is American military activity in Vietnam a 'war' within the meaning of the constitutional text granting to Congress the power to declare war? If so, may the President order these draftees to participate in this 'war' when Congress has not declared war? Of what relevance are present treaty obligations of the United States? Of what relevance is the Tonkin Gulf Resolution? Are Vietnam military operations within the terms of the resolution? If so, does the resolution represent an impermissible delegation of congressional war power to the unlimited discretion of the President?

Justice Stewart declared that the court should grant review: 'We cannot make these problems go away simply by refusing to hear the case of three obscure Army privates.'[7] There was at least some recognition of a legal duty to judge, apparently not recognised by the dissenting justice's colleagues.

In 1966 the Congress of Racial Equality issued a report claiming that the US military draft placed 'a heavy discriminatory burden on minority groups and the poor'.[8] I dare say it did. Was it an appropriate priority to consider the internal demographic unfairness of risk of loss of life in this way against the extraordinary loss of life being caused in Vietnam, the legality of which the courts declined to investigate?

Mens rea

In May 1964, US General Curtis LeMay stated: 'My solution to the problem would be to tell [the North Vietnamese] frankly that they've got to draw in their horns and stop their aggression or we're going to bomb them back into the Stone Ages.'[9] This was the sort of observation that would be very valuable to the prosecutor of a criminal trial for offences in conflict, were such a person as LeMay to be in the dock.

In a memo to President Johnson on 19 May 1967, US Secretary of Defense Robert McNamara warned:

> There may be a limit beyond which many Americans and much of the world will not permit the United States to go. The picture of the world's greatest superpower … trying to pound a tiny, backward nation into submission on an issue whose merits are hotly disputed, is not a

> pretty one. It could conceivably produce a costly distortion in the American national consciousness and in the world image of the United States.[10]

In criminal cases the lawyer looks for evidence of a criminal state of mind. This view of the Secretary of Defense with responsibility for the bombing of Vietnam might be thought a very good starting point for finding criminal culpability; it is hardly a ringing assertion of legality in what was being done.

THE AIMS OF THE RUSSELL TRIBUNAL

Bertrand Russell, in his early nineties by the time of the Vietnam War, was an active member of the Campaign for Nuclear Disarmament, and had been to prison as a result. He wrote this on the subject of civil disobedience:

> … this idea of weapons of mass extermination is utterly and absolutely horrible … and I will not pretend to obey a government which is organising the massacre of the whole of mankind. I will do anything I can to oppose such governments in any non-violent way that seems likely to be fruitful.[11]

The War Crimes Tribunal was Russell's idea and it was funded by him and others. As with the Comfort Women Tribunal discussed below, Russell's' motivation is made clear by the quotations reproduced here. He addressed the first meeting of members of his tribunal in London on 13 November 1966 in the following terms:

> Why is this war being fought in Vietnam? In whose interest is it being waged? We have, I am certain, an obligation to study these questions and to pronounce on them, after thorough investigation, for in doing so we can assist mankind in understanding why a small agrarian people have endured for more than twelve years the assault of the largest industrial power on earth, possessing the most developed and cruel military capacity … I believe that we are justified in concluding

> that it is necessary to convene a solemn tribunal, composed of men eminent not through their power, but through their intellectual and moral contribution to what we optimistically call 'human civilisation'.[12]

Looking back, who would now deny the humanity and wisdom of what he said? But Russell's elevated thinking would have to take account of the law.

What, according to modern scholarship, was the applicable law?[13] It included the Geneva Convention of 1949 that outlawed wilful killing, wilfully causing great suffering or serious injury to body or health, extensive destruction and appropriation of property, when not justified by military necessity. Violations included employment of poisonous weapons or other weapons calculated to cause unnecessary suffering; wanton destruction of cities, towns or villages; or devastation not justified by military necessity. With this law in their minds the tribunal of intellectuals of various kinds and others – including Bertrand Russell, Jean-Paul Sartre, A.J. Ayer, James Baldwin, Simone de Beauvoir, Stokely Carmichael, Lawrence Daly (General Secretary, National Union of Mineworkers) and Tariq Ali – set to work.

The aims of the tribunal were agreed at the constituting session in London on 15 November 1966:

> 1. Has the United States Government (and the Governments of Australia, New Zealand and South Korea) committed acts of aggression according to international law?
> 2. Has the American army made use of or experimented with new weapons or weapons forbidden by the laws of war?
> 3. Has there been bombardment of targets of a purely civilian character, for example hospitals, schools, sanatoria, dams, etc., and on what scale has this occurred?
> 4. Have Vietnamese prisoners been subjected to inhuman treatment forbidden by the laws of war and, in particular, to torture or mutilation? Have there been unjustified reprisals against the civilian population, in particular execution of hostages?

5. Have forced labour camps been created, has there been deportation of the population or other acts tending to the extermination of the population and which can be characterized juridically as acts of genocide?[14]

The first session of the tribunal was held in Stockholm, 2–10 May 1967. There were opening statements, a limited number of eyewitness accounts, expert reports (bombing, fragmentation bombs, significance of bombing dykes) and reports of those who had made specific inquiries for the tribunal. It was not, thus, a 'proper' court with evidence and cross-examination. That itself raises issues. Should we be bound only to attend to evidence presented in the way acceptable to Western criminal courts? I have presumed to doubt this. I raised with ICTY judges in The Hague the probability or certainty that they could reach the same conclusions they achieved after years of slow evidence by reading a range of well-informed books and journalism coupled with the live evidence that they might require. The tortoise of the common law criminal trial serves the bank balances of the lawyers and judges; it is less clear whether it really provides for better verdicts. It does, it is true, lay down a record of evidence meticulously chronicled and that record may serve later purposes. But does it equal the decision-making process that may be achieved by intelligent well-informed men and women making conscientious inquiry? I am not so sure.

The evidence presented to the tribunal merits detailed attention. Here are three samples:[15]

Gabriel Kolko, a left-wing American historian.
'Vietnam is essentially an American intervention against a nationalist, revolutionary agrarian movement which embodies social elements in incipient and similar forms of development in numerous other Third World nations … For the United States to fail in Vietnam … would be tantamount to a demotion of the United States from its present role as the world's dominant super-power.'

Do Van Ngoc, describing events when he was nine years old, in the village of Vinh Tuy.
'On the afternoon of 16 June 1966, I was looking after the oxen with my two friends, named Ha Khec and Do Van Giau, when three

American planes appeared from over the sea and dropped bombs on the place where we were. The bombs exploded and the flames reached the bodies of all three of us, causing us very serious burns. Since we could no longer bear the heat, we jumped into a flooded rice field; then the flames were put out and the heat lessened, but when we emerged from the water the flames broke out again on our bodies …

'That day the American bombs still set fire to the homes of our family and our neighbours. To my knowledge, apart from the three of us, Mr Du's family, while having their meal, lost six of its eight members, burned by bombs.'

Henrick Forss, on examinations of victims of US bombs.
'This is a simple report. It covers only a very small part of a subject of immense proportions: victims from bombings in North Vietnam … One [victim] was Nguyen Thi Nam, a 24-year-old woman from Nam Dinh … She was pregnant in her ninth month. Fragments of the CBU [cluster bomb unit] penetrated the intestines and the uterus, killing the foetus which had to be removed surgically … It is uncertain whether she can have any more children.'

At the conclusion of the Stockholm Session, Sartre recited the Kellogg–Briand Pact, Article 6 of the Statute of Nuremberg, Article 2 of the United Nations Charter and the United Nations resolution of December 1960, observing that the accession to independence and to national existence of the people of Vietnam dated back to 2 September 1945 but was called in question by the old colonial power. The war of national liberation – the First Indo-China War – then embarked upon ended with the victory of the Vietnam army. He went on:

> In defiance of the Geneva Agreements, the United States has, since 1954, introduced into Vietnam increasing quantities of military equipment and personnel and has set up bases there … the United States bears the responsibility for the use of force in Vietnam and that it has in consequence committed a crime of aggression against that country, a crime against peace … It should be added that states such as South Korea, Australia and New Zealand, which have in one form or another

Anti-Vietnam War protestors and police, Grosvenor Square, London, March 1968
All we could do to oppose the strategic and tactical crimes of the Vietnam War was protest. There was no cry to put Kissinger and Nixon on trial at an international court, because no such court existed. Pinochet's arrest in London in 1998, for a crime of universal jurisdiction in the UK, may have made Kissinger worry about where he could travel overseas. Yet it looks like he will never go on trial for the thousands of deaths for which many say he is guilty.

Norman Morrison and Thích Quảng Đức
Suicide was the response of people at the limit of what they could achieve by peaceful means. Buddhist monk Thích Quảng Đức, responding to religious oppression by the Vietnamese government, self-immolated in Saigon in 1963. Norman Morrison, a Quaker, set himself on fire outside the Pentagon in 1965 in protest against the Vietnam War. Modern suicide bombing can be traced to about 1981. Suicide bombers seek, often, to affect politics and to change opinion; as did the ethically driven Quảng Đức and Morrison.

Chinese 'Comfort Women' being interviewed after liberation, c. 1945
'Comfort Women' were obliged to 'serve' Japanese soldiers as sex slaves, suffering enormous physical and psychological damage, including being killed. The Tokyo trials took no account of their ordeal. It was only the work of a highly qualified panel of judges and others in an informal tribunal in 2000 that allowed the remaining survivors to make the history clear: namely that this was a crime for which, among others, the emperor himself was responsible.

Burmese Rohingya refugees, 1992
Note the date. The Rohingya Muslims remain at risk – even of genocide – today. For a time there was international enthusiasm to make Burma accountable for the grave human rights abuses perpetrated by the governing generals, but this dissipated once Aung San Suu Kyi was freed; now Burma is open to profitable mineral deals and is a popular holiday destination. What trust can the ordinary victim of war repose in international institutions, often staffed by 'here today, gone tomorrow' politicians and diplomats?

Bosnian Muslims holding a banner at the Srebrenica Genocide Memorial, Potočari, 2015
In July 2015 Nevenka Tromp and I took our law and genocide masterclass participants to an event commemorating the 20th anniversary of the Srebrenica massacre: an occasion attended by Clinton, Albright and every notable politician who had a hand in resolving the conflicts. When Aleksandar Vučić, Prime Minister of Serbia, appeared, this banner was unfurled, quoting a statement attributed to him during the conflict: 'For every killed Serb, we will kill 100 Bosniaks'.

20 years on, tensions continue to run high
As the column of dignitaries wound its way through graves and onlookers such as us, Vučić, centre, was stoned, had bottles thrown at him, and was verbally abused by the crowd. Surrounded by bodyguards, he had to flee to safety. We witnessed the multitude whipped to instant frenzy until the religious leader of all Bosnian Muslims demanded calm over the loudspeakers, quoting the Quran. Were we at a solemn memorial event, or an event where the warring parties could say it was not over?

The Separation Barrier, West Bank, 2009
If there are gods – and prophets and messiahs – is this how they would have wanted us to scar the land we have been given? Influential Zionist Ze'ev Jabotinsky used the metaphor of an 'iron wall' in 1923: 'Zionist colonization … [must be] carried out in defiance of the will of the native population…. under the protection of a force independent of the local population – an iron wall which the native population cannot break through'. Is this the physical manifestation of that wall? And on which side is Israel?

Palestinians in the remains of their home in the days after Operation 'Protective Edge', 2014
General Sir Nick Parker, Nevenka Tromp and I got into Gaza shortly after Operation 'Protective Edge' in 2014. The devastation of the Israeli attack made rational judgment hard; Nick's experience and wisdom leavened any emotional response. Where else would these people from Shejaia, east of Gaza City, go, but to the place once home? A similar family seated where their own home had been made us tea; this was hospitality in the face of unimaginable adversity.

> provided aid to the American aggression, have rendered themselves accomplices.

On the second question:

> The tribunal has been convinced that the aerial, naval and land bombardments of civil targets is of a massive, systematic and deliberate nature ... Its attention in particular has been drawn to the massive use of various kinds of anti-personnel bombs of the fragmentation type ... These devices [are] obviously intended to strike defenceless populations ... Because of their systematic employment with the object of destroying the fundamental rights of the people of Vietnam, their unity and their wish for peace, the crimes against humanity of which the government of the United States of America has rendered itself guilty, become a fundamental constituent part of the crime of aggression, a supreme crime which embraces all the others according to the Nuremberg verdict.

The second session of the Tribunal, held at Roskilde in Denmark, featured further expert reports, summaries from the region and questioning of US servicemen who had engaged in torture of Vietnamese or supervised the torturing of Vietnamese by South Vietnamese soldiers. It is difficult material to read, although there is no reason to doubt the accuracy of what the soldier witnesses described, including a beheading of a live man, gross torture of prisoners, throwing prisoners from helicopters and a policy of taking no prisoners. More of this would emerge later in the aftermath of the My Lai massacre that did get to court, but even at this early stage there was clear evidence of war crimes being committed by US servicemen and, if these witnesses were accurate, on a widespread basis.

Sartre wrote a paper on genocide that was adopted by the tribunal. In 1967 the Genocide Convention was nearly 20 years old and had another two decades to wait before it would be charged as a crime anywhere or be ratified by the US (the trial of Adolf Eichmann in Jerusalem in 1961 did not include genocide charges).

Accordingly it is unsurprising that Sartre, unassisted by jurisprudence developed since, might have found genocide established on a basis broader than might now be acceptable. His analysis is also, inevitably, informed by his own strongly held political beliefs. The paper merits reading in full. He distinguished between genocide committed against unequal force in the seizing of colonies from genocide committed as anti-guerrilla strategies that galvanise two peoples into total war. He observed that the US – unlike the departing French colonial power – had little real economic interest in Vietnam but could use genocide as a strategy as a warning to the guerrillas in the conflict and to those around the world who opposed American beliefs and values.

He concluded: 'The American government is guilty of having preferred a policy of war and aggression aimed at total genocide to a policy of peace.'

In the *Conclusions of the Second Session*, the tribunal detailed:

> The wholesale and indiscriminate use of napalm, which has been abundantly demonstrated before the tribunal …
>
> … the gases used in Vietnam… are used under conditions which make them always toxic and often deadly, especially when they are blown into the hideouts, shelters and underground tunnels where a large part of the Vietnamese population is forced to live. It is impossible to classify them as simple incapacitating gases; they must be classified as combat gases.
>
> The tribunal has studied the current practice of the American army consisting of spraying defoliating or herbicidal products over entire regions in Vietnam …
>
> Villages are entirely levelled, fields are devastated, livestock destroyed … Precise testimony and documents that have been put before the tribunal have reported the existence of free-fire zones, where everything that moves is considered hostile which amounts to saying that the entire population is taken as a target.

Russell's tribunal found the US guilty of treating civilians and prisoners in ways prohibited by law, and of genocide.

CONCLUSION

Some 50 years after this informal tribunal did its work there are significant – if anecdotal – conclusions that I draw. First, few people now know of the tribunal, its work or conclusions; and this is similar for other important informal tribunals that have taken place since, in particular the 'Comfort Women Tribunal' (see chapter 7). The contrast of the level of ignorance of the Russell Tribunal with knowledge of the Nuremberg Trials indelibly fixed in the minds of a very significant portion of the world's population – not least by the photographs of the men on trial – could not be greater. However, second, for those aware of the tribunal and its conclusions, it is extremely easy to argue in public – quoting the conclusions – that in Vietnam the US committed serious and sustained war crimes, and to do so because there is no official record to a contrary effect. Third, what seems to be the case with Russell's tribunal today may be even truer for all well-constructed informal tribunals that fill a 'gap' in official public recording of wars and of the crimes committed in wars in fifty, a hundred, two hundred years' time. Without any other record to turn to, such tribunals, however lost to memory in the short term, may become authoritative and beyond the ability of countries 'charged' with war crimes to challenge.

To the questions I asked at the start I have these comments. First, there was a serious shortcoming of the Russell Tribunal. Surprisingly, given the publicity attached to the Nuremberg Process being 'victor's justice', the tribunal declined to assess the conduct of the other side. Staughton Lynd had been chairman of the 1965 'March on Washington'. He was not willing to be a party to the tribunal's work if it would not consider the conduct of Ho Chi Minh's side.[16] David Horowitz, a member of the Bertrand Russell Peace Foundation, heard Sartre say that the North Vietnamese and National Liberation Front were *incapable* of committing war crimes, a comment he could not sustain were he ever to have had to confront a modern international criminal court approaching the conduct of all sides in an even-handed way. Of course the Vietcong *could* have been war criminals, however much they were an armed peasantry.[17] Sartre blinded himself to any possible genocide committed by the Vietcong and North Vietnamese Army even after the infamous Dak Son massacre and Hue massacre.

Second, however, the tribunal's conclusions were largely confirmed by evidence coming to light after it pronounced its verdict – the My Lai massacre, the Pentagon Papers, McNamara's expressed views.

Third, its conclusions adverse to the US would probably have been the same even if it had surveyed the actions of all sides to the conflict.

Fourth, it is not at all clear that this tribunal has *yet* made a difference because when a powerful body declines to engage – as through the Supreme Court the US declined to do over the legality of the war even with its own citizens – there is no way to make it do otherwise. And with the passage of time it may be inevitable that people will tend to forget. Only with total, public, visible defeat and public trial will public memory of what has been done be *certain* to remain strong.

And yet Russell's 'verdict' establishes *very clearly* that there was enough evidence to have the US inquired into for war crimes, as many Americans had effectively argued to the deaf ears of their own Supreme Court. The tribunal's potential value is immense but may have yet to be fully revealed.

Chapter 7

Japanese 'Comfort Women' and the Iran Tribunal

Informal tribunals provide many lessons for the citizen who is dissatisfied with the performance of bodies that may be reluctant to deal with politically difficult problems in faraway places. Two informal tribunals will be considered in this lecture. First, the Women's International War Crimes Tribunal for the Trial of Japanese Military Sexual Slavery, which investigated the experience of 'Comfort Women' abused by the Japanese armed forces in the 1930s and World War II. Second, the Iran Tribunal, which dealt with the atrocities of the regime of the ayatollahs in the 1980s.

With Shokoufeh Sakhi[1]

Original lecture delivered on 13 November 2013.

So far in this book I have asked to what extent the law can invade the arena of armed conflicts and whether law and the findings of legal and quasi-legal bodies about conflicts have real long-term value. Informal tribunals are filling an important role in modern society, most commonly when the law has failed the citizen. But, having no real power, these tribunals ultimately confront citizens with their inability to activate law without the engagement of national or international systems. These tribunals say they follow universal law that should be respected and applied, and the modern structure of international humanitarian law, that incorporates customary law, allows them to say just that. Despite that, as the use of law in all international tribunals shows, law remains a political tool. Does that limit informal tribunals to being political or social campaigns, having effect only on public opinion, if at all?

The conclusions of Lord Russell's tribunal on Vietnam (see chapter 6) were not unrealistic but of limited effect. Ask an American how they would characterise the US involvement in Vietnam, Cambodia and Laos and they are unlikely to say 'war crimes'. Had there been a formal international court making the same findings the position would inevitably be different. The Russell Tribunal has therefore not achieved much – yet – by way of lasting legacy. Must this be the same for all such tribunals?

JAPANESE 'COMFORT WOMEN'

We now know with certainty what the 'Comfort Women' suffered and, in a very short survey, can put things in chronological order. In the 1930s Japan increasingly sought domination of the Asia–Pacific region and perpetrated appalling atrocities on the populations it sought to subjugate. In 1932 Japan set up military-controlled 'comfort houses' in Shanghai. These were places for military personnel to have sexual pleasure. In 1937 Japan's taking of Nanking (now more usually Nanjing), in what is notoriously referred to as the 'Rape of Nanking', marked the beginning of the systematic establishment of military 'comfort stations' in China and elsewhere.

As many as 200,000 women from Japan, Korea, China, the Philippines, Burma, the Dutch East Indies, the Netherlands and Australia were forced to engage in sexual activity in Japanese-controlled territories in China, Manchuria, Taiwan, Borneo, the

Philippines, Singapore, Burma, Indonesia and Korea, as well as in Japan itself. The practice was so widespread that the way it worked could not be hidden and had to be documented. The 'comfort houses' institutionalised serial rape, not prostitution. The military leadership hoped that, by having government-run sex stations, sexually transmitted diseases could be controlled and the reputational damage that might follow if soldiers openly raped local women could be reduced.

There were some prostitutes who chose to work for the government and some young women who were sold into the work; but demand outstripped supply and led to abductions and kidnappings. Once rounded up, the women could be required to serve 60–70 men a day and the soldiers sometimes killed and commonly beat, stabbed and in other ways harmed the women. The authorities kept such victims from suicide by threatening to injure their families if they killed themselves. Soldier Yasuji Kaneko admitted many years later that the women 'cried out, but it didn't matter to us whether the women lived or died. We were the emperor's soldiers … we raped without reluctance.'[2]

This system ended only with Japan's defeat in 1945. The postwar trials of Japanese leaders – the International Criminal Tribunal for the Far East – were more controversial than the Nuremberg trials, not least for US General MacArthur's absolute determination to keep Emperor Hirohito from the dock. Verdicts were not unanimous. The tribunal had ample evidence of rape and sexual slavery in the so-called 'comfort system' but did not prosecute for it. After the war no effort was made by any country on behalf of its nationals to seek redress, while shame and stigma meant that the women mostly kept quiet.

Nevertheless, the story slowly emerged, and during the 1990s the Japanese government found itself under increasing pressure from individual victims and NGOs to stage an inquiry, make a formal apology and pay reparations. Initially the Japanese government argued that the system was the work of neither the Japanese government nor the military, but of private entrepreneurs; that Comfort Women were voluntary prostitutes; and that all claims had been settled under bilateral treaties and Japan was not required legally to pay compensation. The UN, where the matter was raised, did little, although in 1994 the UN Commission of Human Rights appointed Radhika Coomaraswamy as Special Rapporteur on

Violence Against Women, with a special brief to investigate crimes against Comfort Women.

THE JAPANESE 'COMFORT WOMEN' TRIBUNAL

Organised and funded by dedicated NGOs working around the world, this tribunal came into being in 2000. Its judges were leading jurists, and it claimed its authority in this way:

> The power of the Tribunal ... lies in its capacity to examine the evidence, develop an accurate historical record, and apply principles of international law to the facts as found. The Tribunal calls upon the government of Japan to realise that the greatest shame lies not in this recording of the truth about these crimes, but in its failure to accept full legal and moral responsibility for them.[3]

The tribunal traced its roots to the Russell and other informal tribunals, and its authority direct from the peoples of the Asia–Pacific and the lacuna left by states that could have acted but did not. It pronounced generally on the way women's rights were not respected.

After some days of evidence and reviewing of written material the tribunal pronounced unanimous guilty verdicts against the late Emperor Hirohito and others on the basis of individual responsibility for crimes of rape and sexual slavery as crimes against humanity. The tribunal also found that by the instigation and continuation of the Comfort Women system high-ranking Japanese military and government officials and thus the state of Japan had acted in violation of both its treaty obligations and its obligations under customary international law.

Its concluding paragraphs read:

> The crimes committed against these survivors remain one of the greatest unacknowledged and unremedied injustices of the Second World War ... Accordingly, through this Judgment, this Tribunal intends to honour all the women victimized by Japan's military sexual slavery system. The Judges recognize the great

> fortitude and dignity of the survivors who have toiled to survive and reconstruct their shattered lives and who have faced down fear and shame to tell their stories to the world.[4]

However – and this is the lesson from this tribunal – Japan has maintained its denial of responsibility, even if it has siphoned money anonymously to the Comfort Women. Those women who died after the late revelations and the findings of the tribunal may have gone to their graves with some sense of resolution. But it has not proved possible to exercise the law against the Japanese state or individual perpetrators in the absence of national or international will.

THE IRAN TRIBUNAL

The Iran Tribunal was the creation of the people of the Iranian diaspora, who sought a measure of justice for those imprisoned, tortured and executed by the revolutionary regime of the Ayatollah Khomeini in the 1980s. As with some other extraordinary violations of human rights, the international community has never felt able to investigate Iran's conduct in a public way.

The Iranian Revolution of 1979 produced profound change at great speed. A pro-Western monarchy was replaced by an anti-Western authoritarian theocracy in which the Supreme Leader was given unlimited powers as sole interpreter of God's laws. The Supreme Leader's commands effectively overrode the country's written laws.

Yet Iran was, and is, a party to the Charter of the United Nations, through which it has pledged to promote universal respect for, and observance of, human rights and fundamental freedoms for all, without distinction as to race, sex, language or religion, owing further specific international legal duties in respect of the rights of children and to protect people from enforced disappearance. Further, the rules of customary international law mean that Iran is legally responsible for acts of individuals and of the state itself when recognised as criminal according to international law.

Immediately after taking power in February 1979, the provisional government arrested many members of the previous regime, some of whom were brought before Islamic judges and swiftly executed without any due process. Thereafter, summary executions and the unchecked powers of the Islamic judges brought a reign of terror to Iran. Many Iranian political organisations openly challenged the Islamic regime soon after the revolution and were violently suppressed. Tens of thousands of their members were arrested, tortured and imprisoned.

The informal Iran Tribunal took evidence first as a Truth Commission in London and then as a tribunal in The Hague in 2012. I was initially asked to be part of the tribunal's Steering Committee and subsequently appeared to call some witnesses and make a closing argument in the Hague hearing. The Tribunal stated that its jurisdiction was 'given to it by the Campaign and the Legal Steering Committee on behalf of those who have suffered horrific pain and injuries, both mental and physical as a result of the crimes alleged'. Witness statements at the tribunal corroborated each other and the evidence provided by witnesses at the Truth Commission 'in the patterns of abuse and in the fine detail'.[5] The majority of arrests reported to the Truth Commission took place in the years 1981–83, most of these in 1981.

Physical and psychological torture

Physical torture was widely reported as being used to pressure detainees to inform on others, force confessions, extract information, or compel recantations of political beliefs. Children as well as adults were tortured. Methods included bastinado, in which the soles of a victim's feet are whipped with electric cables. Victims were often unable to walk afterwards. Other forms of torture included the squeezing of testicles, and burns inflicted with lighters, cigarettes or hot irons. Detainees were also flogged all over.

Many victims underwent *ghapani* during interrogation, being suspended in the air by their arms, one arm twisted behind the shoulder and the other wrenched behind their back, hands bound together with handcuffs and tied to a chain or rope from the ceiling. They would be left in this position for hours; permanent injuries were common. Prisoners were sometimes forced to stand still for up to 72 hours. Variations included standing on one leg or standing barefoot on ice. Prisoners were also made to sit or lie for hours in open boxes with the approximate dimension of coffins ('the Grave'). Prisoners were routinely consigned to solitary confinement for minor disobedience or for no reason at all; in some cases this lasted years.

Prisoners were sometimes subjected to mock executions. They were made to prepare for their deaths by saying their goodbyes and writing their wills. Sometimes blank cartridges were used. Other times there were mixed real and mock executions with prisoners blindfolded and those to be spared (unknown to them) having cards round their necks to identify them to those doing the shooting. Some of those condemned to death only learned of their sentences as they were led to execution.

Prisoners were frequently made to listen to or directly witness other prisoners being tortured. In one prison the sound of women being tortured was broadcast over loudspeakers. Several survivors testified that this experience was more painful than being tortured themselves. Infants detained with their mothers were sometimes present at their mothers' interrogations or in the next room so that while being tortured mothers were forced to listen to the sound of their children crying.

Sexual abuse

Sexual abuse of women prisoners was widespread. Many female prisoners were raped prior to being executed because executing virgin girls was not permitted under Islamic law as they would go to heaven. A number of witnesses testified that they had been raped by their interrogator or on his order to break their resistance. Rape of boys was also common.

Religious persecution

Religious and ethnic minorities were subject to persecution. Arabs, Kurds, Turkmen, Azeris, Lurs and Baluchis, who have lived in different regions of Iran for many centuries, were the subject of brutal attack. Bahá'ís were executed solely for belonging to the Bahá'í faith. One judge explained that the objective was the extermination of the Bahá'í people, saying, 'If we kill all the Bahá'ís collectively the whole world is going to protest, but we are going to take you [for execution] one by one ... so the international community will not object.'[6]

A religious judge, Khalkhali, responsible for show trials and countless executions, said in response to a complaint by an Arab prisoner that his right to counsel and a fair trial had not been respected, 'If you are innocent, then you will go to paradise.'[7]

The testimony of Shokoufeh Sakhi

Shokoufeh Sakhi was arrested on 12 August 1982 for being a supporter of a leftist group. Her trial was conducted at the Komitei Moshtarak detention facility in October or November 1982. Charged with offences concerning leftist groups, she rejected all charges and defended herself. She argued that all activities with these groups were legal prior to Khomeini's decrees. She told the judge that she was not religious, her family being Shi'ite Muslims. Finally, the judge Mobasheri asked if she was prepared to repent. She replied that she had not committed any crime, so there was no need to repent. The whole trial lasted no more than a few minutes. At first they issued a sentence of life imprisonment, but her sentence was later reduced to five years. She spent the next several years in one or other of Tehran's three major prisons.

On 1 September 1983, Haji Davood Rahmani, the warden of Ghezel-Hesar prison in Karaj, ordered Shokoufeh and others to put on blindfolds. The wardens beat her with a cable, yelled at her, and then dragged her into one of the small specially constructed 'coffins'. In the room where she was taken more than 30 of these box-shaped cells had been created. In each of these 'coffins' one female prisoner was held, forced at all times to wear a blindfold and a *chador*. They were constantly monitored, and every day the women had to sit for fourteen to fifteen hours facing the main wall. Anyone caught dozing off was punished. Punishable offences included speaking, standing up, laying down, coughing, sneezing, making noise while eating or asking to go to the bathroom.

This process of sensory deprivation/limitation was sometimes replaced by its opposite, sensory overload, as they were exposed to constant broadcasting of ideological, political and religious 'lessons', prayers and war propaganda, as well as having to hear other prisoners' lengthy public 'confessions', self-criticism and renunciations of beliefs and loyalties. More than 200 leftist female prisoners were subjected to these procedures. The whole saga went on for nine months. The purpose was to destroy the entire identity of the prisoners and render what remained a new breed of *tavaab* ('collaborator'). Rahmani, the warden, referred to the entire ensemble as his 'invented machinery' and '*tavaab* factory'. He used to tap on the wooden walls and say 'these are your graves'.

Although the majority of people subjected to the 'coffin' more or less broke down – some permanently changed their political stance, while many succumbed to deep depression and were psychologically damaged – there were a number who survived and remained defiant. Shokoufeh and others were able by unyielding will to maintain their characters intact and to learn a code to communicate.[8]

Executions

Many political prisoners were executed during the years 1980–88 all over Iran. The families were rarely informed of the process leading to the execution of their loved ones and representation by lawyers was not allowed. In most cases they were not told of the whereabouts of their loved ones until they were notified of their execution. Many prisoners were executed by firing squad. Many, however, were hanged, some from cranes or low ceilings in such a way that they slowly suffocated. Over 15,000 people were summarily executed between 1981 and 1988.

In 1988 'Death Commissions' were established in all prisons across Iran to investigate whether the political prisoners being held had (as ordered by Ayatollah Khomeini) repented their 'sins' or were to be condemned to death. Each Death Commission comprised a religious judge, the local prosecutor and a representative of the Ministry of Intelligence, along with other state officials. Prisoners were asked two or three questions over the space of a few minutes, regarding whether they believed in Islam, were willing to recant their views and would accept the Islamic Republic. Those whose answers displeased the Commission were taken out and executed. One witness testified that 'public heretics' (those who were not born to a Muslim father) were spared execution so that they might convert to Islam, on pain of death; those who refused were flogged. 'Innate heretics' (those born Muslims, who had left the faith) were executed, including those who agreed to return to Islam.

Prisoners were asked whether they would be willing to fight against Iraq or step on a landmine for Iran, and they were sentenced to death on refusing; others were asked whether they still sympathised with opposition groups and what they thought of the new regime; those who professed Marxist beliefs were invariably executed.

Death Commissions first dealt with members of the military wing of the left-wing *mujahedeen* of Iran in the summer of 1988. Later in the summer they focused on other leftist groups, including communists, and liquidated them as well. Thousands were executed throughout Iran during a period of three months, from July to September 1988.

The tribunal heard extensive evidence of executions performed as punishment for political charges, ordered without any basis in law and in the absence of any semblance of due process. Some executions were carried out in a space of minutes, hours or days after arrest; the use of firing squads was ubiquitous, and victims were finished off with *coups de grâce* if they survived the initial volleys. Disabled prisoners were taken to their executions on stretchers.

The tribunal heard harrowing evidence from a witness who had been pressured into collaborating with prison authorities by shooting other prisoners as a member of a firing squad. He described this pressure as 'psychological rape', adding: 'I was not myself, I was a puppet … It was not me who did this.'

TESTIMONY FROM THE INTERNATIONAL COMMUNITY

Professor Maurice Copithorne, a Canadian lawyer, testified to the tribunal about his experience as the United Nations Special Rapporteur on the human rights situation in Iran from 1995 to 2002, during which time he was consistently refused entry into Iran after his first visit. He testified that, as Special Rapporteur, he had heard only 'very general comments' about the abuses of the 1980s, for which the evidence available to the Truth Commission was 'much more complete' than the resources made available to him as an envoy of the United Nations.

Professor Copithorne stated that, in his experience, political pressures had meant that efforts for an official investigation into the abuses of the 1980s 'would not get through the full membership of the Human Rights Commission'. He explained that he saw no indication that a majority of states would support such an initiative. Professor Copithorne ended his testimony by recommending that the United Nations establish a formal commission of inquiry into the abuses of human rights in Iran in the 1980s.

Another witness, Ms Burley, confirmed that her report for Amnesty International, dated 1 February 1980, had revealed that the Islamic revolutionary courts established in the immediate aftermath of the Islamic Revolution 'frequently' passed death sentences and that detainees were not protected 'against threats to or violations of their physical security and integrity'. She testified that human rights abuses committed by the Islamic Republic bore some continuity with the earlier regime, noting that bastinado was 'very systematic' under the Shah. However, she noted that under the Islamic regime 'many more' people were killed and that violations were 'much more arbitrary ... [insofar as] anyone could find themselves arrested, ill treated and executed'. She observed that post-revolutionary human rights violations were at first performed in an 'anarchic' setting by independent revolutionary committees but that this became 'more clearly the responsibility of the central government' over time.

THE TRIBUNAL'S VERDICT

The prosecution charged the Islamic Republic of Iran with crimes against humanity. It was therefore the tribunal's mandate to determine:

- Whether the alleged violations of human rights had occurred;
- Whether these violations constituted crimes against humanity;
- Whether as a matter of international law the Islamic Republic of Iran had breached its international human rights obligations towards its citizens.

The verdict was as follows:

1. The Islamic Republic of Iran has committed crimes against humanity in the 1980–1989 period against its own citizens in violation of applicable international laws;
2. The Islamic Republic of Iran bears absolute responsibility for the gross violations of human rights against its citizens under the International Covenant of Civil and Political Rights; and,
3. Customary international law holds the Islamic Republic of Iran fully accountable for its systematic

> and widespread commission of crimes against humanity in Iran in the 1980–1989 period.

The tribunal had the courage to make that judgment, despite no official body having dared to investigate these events.

POSTSCRIPT: PRESENT-DAY IRAN

The current Iranian President, Hassan Rouhani, asked for the public execution of enemies of the state in a speech to Iran's parliament on 2 July 1980. He has been a member of the Supreme National Security Council since 1989. It is unlikely he was unaware of the extraordinarily grave crimes the regime committed.

Rouhani's Justice Minister is Mostafa Pour-Mohamadi, one of the three members of the province of Tehran's Death Commission during the 1988 mass execution of political prisoners. (Ironically – showing public understanding of reality – every audience I tell of one Death Commission member being a serving Iran minister guesses that it will be the Minister of Justice.) Iran's judiciary is said to be an 'independent' political institution, but its head is appointed by the Supreme Leader, Ayatollah Ali Khamenei.

CONCLUSION

These two informal tribunals were both very effective in settling some of the unresolved unhappiness of victims, yet they are little-known to the public at large. But their judgments may – along with the judgment of Russell's Vietnam Tribunal – come to be the only available evidence-based verdicts about criminal atrocities that powerful nations have sought to hide and keep from any judicial assessment. They may prove invaluable for the settling of historical uncertainties in the future.

Chapter 8

The Law as a New Religion

Law is everywhere providing answers to almost everything. Ever larger numbers of students want to be part of the legal mechanisms that control us, regulate us and take over from politicians when politicians sense their own incapability. In this chapter some of the issues dealt with by Professor Vernon Bogdanor in earlier years at Gresham College[1] *will be reviewed, as will the effect of Europe on our law.*

Original lecture delivered on 4 December 2013.

Professor Bogdanor asked questions about who rules us: the UK or Europe; the executive or the judges. One of the issues raised by Professor Bogdanor – human rights, European or home-grown – has featured in voting choices about UK withdrawal from the EU, and in the decision about Scotland separating or not from the UK. Making these choices wisely might ideally have required a bit more understanding of how the UK operates constitutionally than the non-lawyer citizen typically has.

What, in reality, does the educated non-lawyer citizen know of our constitution? In one clause, perhaps, 'that it is unwritten', and has to be derived from various sources. He may also know that Parliament is in some sense sovereign and can make any law it wants to. Our constitution is regularly contrasted with the Constitution of the US. It will never be possible for UK citizens to achieve an intimacy with our unwritten constitution of the kind Americans may have with theirs, because it is much more difficult to understand something derived from many sources – that may be changing unperceived over time – than it is to comprehend the US Constitution, which exists on a single piece of paper.

What is clear is that, however great or limited may be the UK citizen's understanding of his country's constitution, he and the politicians elected have been turning to the law for help or for control in ever more activities. Statistics show as much. The number of practising solicitors has more than tripled in just 30 years – there were 19,069 in 1960, 37,795 in 1980 and 125,011 in 2012.[2] In the last five or so years the number of barristers at the self-employed Bar, for which statistics are harder to find, has grown by about 6 per cent.[3]

I am not sure what this reveals about ourselves but have feared instinctively that it is unlikely to be healthy. By its ever increasing role in our lives has the law become a new religion? Are its practitioners and judges filling priestly functions whenever a problem with an ethical or moral component needs resolution? I confess to scepticism about lawyers, but I may simply be someone who (as George Bernard Shaw said) inevitably becomes a sceptic concerning his own profession.[4]

DON'T KILL ALL THE LAWYERS: SOME OF WHAT THEY DO IS GOOD

We must therefore ask what *good* reasons there may be for such an increase in lawyers. There are several, and it has not all been as a consequence of the generous grant of Legal Aid for criminal and civil cases that happened in the 1970s and 1980s. I offer a few examples.

First, it was not until 1964 that employment tribunals – now an established part of our legal life – were created (as industrial tribunals) leading to many lawyers specialising in the regulation of working practices. Before that the courts could and did deal with employment issues under the general law of contract, but there was nothing like the scope for pursuing employers over unfair dismissals, unequal treatment and so on that has developed since. Few would say *this* development – and the associated increase of work for lawyers – has been a bad thing.

Second, administrative law has expanded enormously, and generally for the public good. This may have been part of what Colm O'Cinneide says has been a slow transformation in how legal remedies ensure conformity with 'democratic constitutionalism'. He argues that

> The (re)emergence of much stronger regional identities in the 'Celtic Fringe', the impact of Europeanisation, [and] the existence of a growing disconnect from established political parties … have all helped to … create a demand for enhanced legal regulation of the exercise of state power … This shift in approach has resulted in a significant expansion of the role of the judiciary in the UK constitutional system … driven to a considerable extent by the influence of the ECHR [European Convention on Human Rights] and the incorporation of Convention rights into the UK legal system via the Human Rights Act 1998.[5]

Without checks, balances or judicial control, any government anywhere will be inclined to extend its powers. Our courts have, through judicial review, ensured restraint.

Once the courts started to require discretionary power, in particular the royal prerogative,[6] to be exercised in conformity with the rule of law, UK judges even dared to assert authority over the prerogative used in the area of foreign relations. For example, in the case of *R. (Abbassi) v Secretary of State for Foreign and Commonwealth Affairs* an order was made by a court requiring the UK Foreign Secretary to make representations to the US government to secure the release of British prisoners held in Guantanamo Bay. There are many other examples of judicial review of the exercise of executive powers that would formerly not have been touched by the courts.

The development of administrative law under our own unwritten constitution, affected as it is by the human rights law coming from Europe, may lead us again to glance enviously at the US where the written Constitution more readily allows courts to strike down a law as unconstitutional. We may also have in mind how the American Constitution was relied on for social change of great importance. In one of Professor Bogdanor's lectures he shared the platform with an American academic, Cristina Rodríguez. Her contribution provides a valuable antidote to the 'grass is greener' approach to the use of law.[7]

Rodríguez explained three interesting things: first, how the power of courts in the US to strike down unconstitutional laws can lead to the legislature passing laws it knows will be struck down and thus to being less responsible in the discharge of its legislating duties to the public. Second, the famous 1953 case of *Brown v Board of Education*, cited by those of liberal persuasion for its role in ending racial segregation, led, when delivered, to such discontent in the voting public that the decision was not implemented for years and then only when the Voting Rights Act of 1965 was enacted. Third, that the 1973 case of *Roe v Wade* that struck down a state law prohibiting abortion led to a backlash from the public, galvanising a certain segment of the American population and giving them a single issue around which to mobilise in support of the Republican Party. The history revealed that the Supreme Court intervened in a debate that was going on in the political process at far too early a stage; it was attempting to settle a controversy that the people themselves had not yet resolved. For Rodríguez, the American system is one in which the courts are in a developing dialogue with the legislature over topics such as discrimination and abortion.

MORE LAW TO PROTECT THE CITIZEN – AND BRING COMPENSATION

A further area of growth for lawyers has been in the regulation of professions and of trades. Regulation – of banks, lawyers, doctors, nurses, airline pilots, architects – has all developed enormously over the last few decades and some of that regulation needs lawyers. And then there has been the growth in personal injury litigation. As it happens, the Legal Aid system we used to have for civil claims was actually rather cost-effective. However, 'no win, no fee' arrangements have led to more accident litigation and to some claimant lawyers earning quite extravagant sums of money. The scheme is being scrapped and replaced by another, but the opportunities for lawyers in bringing claims for accident victims have had a significant effect in increasing the amount of work available for lawyers.

Lord Sumption, one of the Justices of the UK Supreme Court, has explained that the state, of which the courts are a part, has become 'the protector against misfortune of every kind'. This results in a more intrusive role for law. He went on:

> New criminal offences appear like mushrooms after every rainstorm. It has been estimated that in the decade from 1997 to 2007, more than 3,000 new criminal or regulatory offences were added to the statute-book of the United Kingdom … The role of social and religious sentiment, which was once so critical in the life of [Western] societies, has been largely taken over by law.[8]

But this is not the end of the list of reasons for lawyers becoming more numerous. How often do you hear of an inquiry being established into this, that or the other thing? Very often. Most inquiries involve lawyers. I would be only too pleased to work on or preside over an inquiry but, these days, I would have to wonder whether I was exercising, or being part of the exercise of, power that should not be in lawyers' hands. Many of these inquiries involve substantial policy decisions, and whereas it is understandable that lawyers might be used liberally to establish facts – on the assumption that their courtroom skills can enable them to do that – the policy recommendations that follow the factual findings should surely be for others.

If there have been far more public inquiries presided over and/or involving lawyers than there used to be, and if the conclusions that such inquiries are now being invited to reach are far more related to policy than they used to be,[9] then does this explain something about what lawyers may have become and what they might seek to be?

SOVEREIGN – STILL?

While Britain has been a member of the EU, the sovereignty of UK law and law-making has been preserved within a structure that includes the European Court of Human Rights (ECtHR), a product of the Council of Europe (Strasbourg) and EU law itself. For European Convention on Human Rights (ECHR) law, UK courts have been able to make a declaration of 'incompatibility' when a UK statute – or an act of a public authority – is incompatible with ECHR obligations incorporated into UK law by the 1998 Human Rights Act. After that a dialogue is expected and, save in exceptional circumstances, the UK has been required to change its laws to ensure compatibility with ECHR law. The structured way the UK has been obliged to negotiate with the European lawmakers may be somewhat similar to the way – very different in detail of course – that in the US system, a 'dialogue' happens when development of thought in the courts may be out of step with development of thinking on the same topics among the public or their elected representatives.

It must be harder for the UK newspaper-reading member of the public to grasp the concept of a 'declaration of incompatibility' and its slow consequences than it is for the US citizen to grasp the concept of a law being contrary to the provisions of the Constitution. And it may be worth suggesting that the best laws are those that are most easily understood, as they are more likely to win approval. Complicated laws and complex legal systems – such as binding but nonenforceable ECHR law pronounced on by the ECtHR, or enforceable law administered by the ECJ for laws *made* enforceable by the UK's ratifying of EU treaties – often fail to gather support, despite the good intentions of judges who run the systems; and they are vulnerable to populist, and certainly to popular, attack.

In his lecture on the Human Rights Act delivered on 25 January 2005 Professor Bogdanor discussed the December 2004 case of

A. v Secretary of State for the Home Department brought under the Anti-Terrorism, Crime and Security Act 2001. At issue was whether suspected terrorists who were not British citizens could be held indefinitely without trial and without charge if the Home Secretary believed that they were a threat to national security. The bill for the statute had been debated for only 16 hours in the House of Commons, though longer in the Lords, and received the Royal Assent in December 2001, just one month after being introduced into the Commons. Professor Bogdanor was concerned about whether the House of Commons was really scrutinising legislation bearing on human rights very effectively. He reminded us that the defence of rights is often the defence of the rights of very unpopular minorities – suspected terrorists, bogus asylum seekers, alleged paedophiles, prisoners – and asked whether Parliament, which should guarantee our rights, would do so when very unpopular minorities were in question?

In 'The Judges and the Constitution', delivered on 30 May 2006, Professor Bogdanor suggested said that the early 20th-century constitutional jurist A. V. Dicey was correct in saying that the roots of the idea of parliamentary sovereignty 'lie deep in the history of the English people and in the peculiar development of the English Constitution'. If this is correct, he suggested, then judges cannot alter this principle of the sovereignty of Parliament unless Parliament itself, and perhaps the people as well, in a referendum, agree.

In the third lecture, 'Judges or Legislators: Who Should Rule?', delivered on 16 March 2009, Professor Bogdanor reminded us that discretion remained with the government and Parliament to alter the law when a court had issued an ECtHR Declaration of Incompatibility – this was merely a statement of no legal effect, the law remaining as it had been, and it was up to Parliament to act and put things right. In fact, it was fair to say that it had done so in every case to that point. There had been some 20 Declarations, and on each occasion Parliament altered the law to fit.

Bogdanor gave as his own view that the Human Rights Act is of value primarily for small and unpopular minorities, who cannot use electoral and political processes effectively. Larger minorities, he thought, were better advised to use electoral and political processes, and, in general, members of ethnic minorities in Britain are able to use the political and electoral machinery to secure their rights when they are infringed. The philosophy of human rights, he suggested, is not wholly adequate to meet the kinds of challenges that we face in our multicultural society, and therefore judges should be given great power, but in very limited areas, when dealing with the rights of the minorities he identifies.

In the same lecture, Cristina Rodríguez explained how, across the US, people are highly supportive of the work of the courts, and much of what the courts do, as the public see things, is to hold the Legislature to account. So the main reason why judicial review in America was established early and has been reinforced often was because the written Constitution enshrined both a structure of government and a set of rights that were supposed to be beyond the sovereign will of the Legislature. That was, in part, a deliberate design to reject the British model. The American colonists, for a variety of reasons, did not believe that Parliament had done a very good job of protecting their rights. They thought it necessary to enshrine the individual liberties of citizens and to have them protected from the will of the Legislature. The US Constitution, Rodríguez said, is fundamental law, law that the Legislature cannot abrogate.

Two cases of ECtHR law affecting our own are of interest. In July 2011, in *Al-Skeini and Others v The United Kingdom*, the ECtHR was concerned with the applicability of UK human rights laws in Iraq where Iraqi civilians had been killed by security forces. The court held that all of the applicants were within the UK's Article 1 ECtHR jurisdiction and that, in consequence, the UK had to hold an Article 2-compliant investigation in five of the cases. For Baha Mousa, the sixth person to die, there was already a public inquiry under way.

The Supreme Court cases of *Chester* and *McGeoch* – heard together – concerned the rights of serving prisoners to vote. There had been a UK blanket ban, something seemingly popular with the electorate. There had already been ECtHR decisions – one involving the UK, one Spain – that determined that a blanket prohibition was by nature indiscriminate and incompatible with the European Convention on Human Rights that has been incorporated into UK law by the Human Rights Act and also into EU law. Appeals by both prisoners to the Supreme Court were rejected. Given that a declaration by the UK courts of incompatibility was already in place and awaiting resolution a further declaration would serve no purpose. The Supreme Court remained on proper respectful terms with the ECtHR judges so was not prepared to say that the previous decision of the ECtHR Grand Chamber was actually *wrong*; and it declined the Attorney General's 'combative' invitation to 'refuse to follow and apply the approach taken by the European Court of Human Rights in *Hirst (No. 2)* and *Scoppola*'. After all, the logic of the ECtHR's objection to a blanket ban on prisoners voting could be understood and the outstanding declaration of incompatibility was for Parliament to resolve.[10]

Do these cases really excite you? Upon reflection are they that important if the judgments represent attempts by courts to reach some understanding of where the law is? There have been several other cases exciting some popular misgiving, different from these two but probably similar in the level of public concern they have caused. Even if the judgments are subsequently found to be wrong or in need of reconsideration, is it better to have tried to reach enforced consensus and move ahead than to have 'drawn [English] stumps', withdrawn from the ECtHR and run the risk of becoming the outsider, the nasty man of Europe?

ENEMIES OF NO ONE – FRIENDS OF REASON

Recent lectures by two of the country's greatest authorities on constitutional issues, Lord Justice Laws and Lord Sumption, crystallise certain aspects of the present public debate.[11] Both speeches are beautifully scripted and easy to follow. I would recommend reading both.[12]

Lord Justice Laws referred to two of the common law's virtues: its 'catholicity', as he described the common law's ability to draw on law from any source, and its power of restraint. The restraint of which he spoke was, he thought, threatened by the phenomenon of human rights law. The law's quality of catholicity was threatened by *perceived* effects both of EU law and of the human rights law coming out of the European Court of Human Rights at Strasbourg.

The threat to the catholicity of the common law starts, he argued, from the fact that principles with a foreign ancestry, like any other principle of the common law, can only truly take their place and play their part if the law's users, its practitioners and its commentators, believe in their benign effects.[13] He went on to say that the political controversies and resentments concerning Europe may undermine the confidence which thinking people ought to have in the common law's catholicity.[14]

He challenged the traditional doctrine of sovereignty, saying that although it is not modified by the incorporation of external (EU) texts there is a category of statutes which may be called 'constitutional', such as the European Communities Act. Other examples are Magna Carta, the Bill of Rights 1689, the Acts of Union, the Reform Acts which distributed and enlarged the franchise, the Human Rights Act 1998, the Scotland Act 1998 and the Government of Wales Act 1998.

If we can make the law of human rights truly our own, he reckoned, perceived and rightly perceived as a construct of English law, we can protect the common law's catholicity, and at the same time control the proper place of human rights, and so protect the common law's power of restraint.

In some cases, arising from incompatibility, the debate is not only about the weight to be accorded to the Convention right on the merits. It is about the respective roles of government and judiciary. He considered that in this jurisdiction there remains a deep sense that matters of state policy are in essence the responsibility of the elected arms of government.

Lord Sumption took a slightly different view. He explained how the Convention was originally designed to save Europe from any repeat of what had happened under the German Reich and from what might come from the Soviet-dominated communist bloc. However, he explained, the interpretation of the Convention had led to recognition of a large number of new rights not expressly to be found in the language of the treaty. An example being Article 8, which

> protects private and family life, the privacy of the home and of personal correspondence. This perfectly straightforward provision was originally devised as a protection against the surveillance state by totalitarian governments. But in the hands of the Strasbourg court it has been extended ...[15]

Lord Sumption suggests that transferring legislative power to another body, as happened when legal decisions were put in the hands of judges of the Strasbourg court, was not a democratic action even though done by a sovereign, democratically elected parliament. He thought it odd 'to deny that this undermines the democratic process, simply because Parliament has done it'.

Citizens expect their politicians to be not just useful but attractive, he suggested. They demand principle, transparency and consistency from them. And when they do not get these things, they are inclined to turn to courts of law instead. Lord Sumption thought that there is, however, a price to be paid for these virtues. The *judicial* resolution of major policy issues undermines our ability to live together in harmony by depriving us of a method of mediating compromises among ourselves. Politics is a method of mediating compromises in which we can all participate, albeit indirectly, and Lord Sumption considered it to be one which we are more likely to recognise as legitimate.

CONCLUSION

I can hardly quote the views of others without giving my own. As suggested above, the debates that incompatibility arguments generate may have been worth more to the country than all the costs of being subject to European influence on our law.

I can understand how Professor Bogdanor considered human rights law may be more important for politically weak, unpopular minorities, but the system has to have a single method of operation.

Lord Justice Laws concluded that, applied through the mechanism of the common law, the Convention can be and should be a great force for good in this jurisdiction, 'put[ting] more teeth in the common law's mouth'. He reckoned that the constitutional balance between law and government is matured by the common law's process of continuous self-correction, which allows the refinement of principle over time, and the orderly development of state power. His conclusions are ones I hope to be correct.

Lord Sumption is concerned about the Convention being treated as a 'living instrument', so as to allow courts to interpret the Convention, in light of evolving social conceptions common to the democracies of Europe, to keep it up to date with conclusions in law that may never have been contemplated when the Convention was first drafted. His overall conclusion[16] that there may be a risk for societies that allow too much power to pass to the law-*making* courts is one I hope to be wrong.

To have been engaged on a journey with our nearest geographical neighbours where we sought to identify common principles for the good of all is unlikely to have been a bad thing. Compromises there may have had to be, but compromises a very, very long way from the sort of 'compromises' against which countries and their citizens were being protected when the Convention was created – compromises of the sort that Nazi Germany had demanded of people under its rule. We European Council, EU Europeans are not now going to be obliged to make concessions to racism or to arbitrary detention.

We have seen how, in a very different setting, dialogue within a country that has a settled constitution has been a necessary and effective step on the way to the very substantial positive reforms that America has achieved in the fundamental interests of its variegated people. We can, I believe, reasonably look forward to similar long-term benefits being derived from constructive engagement with Europe in the development of European human rights law.

Is law a new religion? Well not quite, even bearing in mind Lord Sumption's observation that the 'role of social and religious sentiment … has been largely taken over by law'. But without a Cold War to divide us ideologically and with increasing atheism in some countries such as the UK, human rights norms, as in the ECHR or the EU Charter, may become cross-boundary creeds on which citizens and the laws of different countries will focus. Even if 'Brits' quit Europe and lose the benefits as well as the burdens of the EU Charter they may cling to the ECHR when things go wrong at home and go to Strasbourg to seek redress at the ECtHR.[17] As long as there are judges and lawyers to enforce it – here and elsewhere – the law may indeed continue to do some of what had formerly been done by religions and priests.

Chapter 9

The Adversarial System and the Art of Advocacy

Is the adversarial legal system as good as we say it is? If it is, how should advocates be trained to do it? Are there some universal rules for advocates that should be followed?

Original lecture delivered on 5 March 2014.

More than 40 years ago, when I was called to the Bar, barristers had a near-complete monopoly of rights of audience in the higher courts of England and Wales. They received almost no training in advocacy, an art or skill it was assumed arrived in some osmotic way simply from being with someone who was then described as a 'pupil-master'. At Bar School there may have been one or two practical sessions with pretend witnesses, but no explanation of what advocacy was and certainly nothing remotely memorable about the skill we were to develop and by which we were to earn our livings for the rest of our lives.

On being called to the Bar in 1971 I was handed two slim volumes. The first book, published in 1933, spoke of the value to the public of the barrister's ability to sort out facts. On cross-examination, the exercise by which it is sometimes thought facts may be established, it said helpfully:

> I regard it as almost impossible to give much help or advice with regard to cross-examination ...

Observing, nevertheless, that:

> It is personality that counts; it is the personality of the advocate, having the material, which enables him the more readily to expose the untruthfulness of a witness.

The same book contains a passage advising barristers actually to see the client before the case started – it was still the practice of many advocates to refuse to see the client and to communicate with him, if at all, through his solicitor.

And finally:

> The greatest safeguard against revolution, riot and the like is that the public should have confidence in judicial tribunals and in their decisions.
>
> And let me remind you of the words of Lord Brougham: 'Conduct without eloquence is safer to trust to for success than eloquence without conduct.'[1]

The last point is worth remembering; but otherwise there was not much there to learn.

The later 1970 volume had nothing to say about advocacy beyond giving a few rules about what should *not* be asked in cross-examination – questions only intended to *annoy* the witness, for example. It referred to advocacy and advocates only in the context of behaviour and ethics; the business of *being* an advocate was otherwise rather taken for granted.[2] Those two books were what we received as training for advocacy.

I learned from my pupil-master[3] as he had learned from his. But he had little ability to explain what he was doing or why. I thought he was very good at what he did and imitated him. The system, however out of date it may sound, produced capable and, periodically, brilliant advocates as it had done since the adversarial system of law first came into being.

THE WINDS OF CHANGE

Twenty years later various influences had operated on the leaders of the Bar and on the Inns of Court of which barristers have to be members. They needed to be seen to be doing something for the profession they led, apart from teaching newcomers to eat and drink at Inn dinners and to wear tailor-made three-piece suits. From former colonies – Australia and the US – had come a disturbing suggestion: that advocacy was in fact a trainable skill.

For several years senior UK barristers, respected abroad for their courtroom skills but especially for that 'English accent', went to work to teach overseas advocacy courses. The barristers delighted in the free travel to Florida and elsewhere and pocketed the very modest stipends, but suppressed from their UK colleagues what they must have been learning. They allowed UK barristers to continue to believe they didn't need to be trained in what they obviously knew already. After a time that dam of arrogance broke and the leaders of the Bar of England and Wales became zealots in everything to do with advocacy training, as if they had invented it. I had the chance to go to Florida before this little revolution and was amazed at what attempted training of others could teach me about how wrong and, occasionally, right I had been in what I had been doing *un*trained.

Once advocacy training took flight, I trained advocacy a few weeks every year here and in America and in Africa for the next two decades. The four Inns of Court trained and trained, as did the circuits of the Bar and individual sets of chambers and everyone else, even solicitors. Judges or senior barristers, often with no flair for teaching or training, were pressed into becoming trainers. The remorseless training in little more than how to ask either a non-leading question or a leading one perhaps reflected the legal profession hoping, as Cicero said, that 'Constant practice devoted to one subject often outdoes both intelligence and skill.'

The very successful system adopted, known as the 'Hempel Method' after (retired) Australian Supreme Court of Victoria Judge George Hempel, QC, trains by breaking down such questions as are permitted in the adversarial system to elicit favourable, or to control unfavourable, testimony.

By last year I had had enough and decided to rest, partly because it was time for others to do what I had been doing, partly because I had begun to wonder whether what we were doing was enough, or appropriate, for a modern age. Partly, indeed, because I wondered whether well-intentioned, successful training in the Hempel Method we had borrowed from other jurisdictions might sometimes deprive the public of the brilliance some potential advocates might have displayed because they were *not* homogenised by such training. Partly – perhaps substantially – because I was not really sure the system of adversarial justice we export around the world is what any society should be wanting today.

ADVOCACY IN ANCIENT TIMES

It may be useful to consider how advocacy has been performed in different ages and places.

Legal systems have existed for at least some 3,800 years since the time of the Babylonian King Hammurabi,[4] whose laws were enforced by judges but without use, it seems, of the services of advocates. The sophists of ancient Athens were probably the first who existed as a class of people considered to be 'lawyers'. But Athenian law required citizens to plead their own cases and disallowed anyone from taking a fee to plead for someone else. Both rules restricted the use of advocates.

Socrates was, apparently, capable of great oratory and advocacy. It was said – to and of him – that

> When we listen to you, or to someone using your arguments, even if he's a hopeless speaker, we're overwhelmed and carried away ...[5]

When defending himself, however, in front of 500 fellow Athenians, many of whom were working men, he maintained the arrogant tone and superiority that was in part the subject of complaint. And although Socrates said something about himself and his family, he did not go as far as might have been *expected* of him by his fellow citizens in seeking a sympathetic decision based on personal circumstances. He thus overlooked a first basic rule for any advocate – to know your audience and to respect them. The men of Athens voted narrowly for conviction but by a substantial majority for death.

In the first century BCE, in the time of Julius Caesar, oratory was considered a great art in disseminating knowledge and promoting oneself at political elections. Cicero's rise to political office despite his relatively humble origins has been attributed to his brilliance as an orator in a society that *did* allow an advocate to represent others.

Cicero took on Quintus Hortensius Hortalus, who was known as the best lawyer in Rome, in the prosecution for corruption and maladministration in Sicily of its governor, Gaius Verres. Examples of his advocacy can be felt even in translation. One such example is found in the speech *In Verrem* I, in which he states: 'with you on this bench, gentlemen, with Marcus Acilius Glabrio as your president, I do not understand what Verres can hope to achieve'.[6]

Or in his address in *Pro Quinctio*:

> But if you, being the judge, shall appear to be no protection to a desolate and helpless condition against power and influence; if before this tribunal the cause is found to depend on interest, not on truth; then indeed there is nothing any longer holy and uncontaminated in the state, no hope that the firmness and virtue of the judge may counterbalance the lowly condition of any one. But undoubtedly before you and your colleagues truth will prevail, or else, if it be driven from this place

> by power and influence, it will not be able to find any place where it can stand.[7]

He was courageous and, as other records show, a master of detail. To be master of detail is a second basic rule of good advocacy.

Other advocates followed Cicero, and by the late fourth century in Rome a true legal profession had taken shape, dedicated to the study and practice of law, with regulations and standards in place for guidance.[8]

THE DEVELOPMENT OF THE ADVERSARIAL SYSTEM

But these historical examples should not allow an easy assumption that the English *adversarial* system is of long standing. It isn't, although those countries using it are keen to make it sound very old.

In England and Wales justice was for long enough in the hands of the local gentry who had immense power – including of life and death – that they did not want to lose. There were royal courts as well but no true centralisation of justice. There was no expectation that defendants would be represented by any advocate, and the prosecution in a criminal case had to be brought personally by the victim, if he could afford to, while the defendant was unrepresented; if innocent, it was assumed, the defendant's untutored answers would lead to acquittal. 'Trials' were confrontational, 'altercation' events which, by the 16th century, may have been little more than swearing matches between prosecutor and defender, often with backgrounds of blood feuds that were dangerous for the justness of any verdict. Truly draconian punishments followed.[9]

In the following century, in 1670, two rather important trials happened at the Old Bailey: the trial of William Penn and William Mead, and then the trial of the jurors who hadn't delivered the verdict the judge wanted. Article 39 of Magna Carta, that was to feature in the trials, can be regarded as the foundation of the modern concept of the right to a trial by jury[10] where it says:

> No free man shall be seized or imprisoned, or stripped of his rights or possessions, or outlawed or exiled, or deprived of his standing in any way, nor will we proceed with force against him, or send others to do so,

> except by the lawful judgment of his equals or by the law of the land.[11]

Penn[12] and Mead were Quakers. A memorial to them in London's Central Criminal Court (the Old Bailey) shows how they were tried for 'preaching to an unlawful assembly in London's Grace Church Street' at a time when religious assemblies of more than five people were illegal unless they had the authority of the Church of England. The jury convicted of the assembly but refused to add to their verdict the words 'to an unlawful/tumultuous assembly', as the judge wanted. The judge directed that 'you shall be locked up without meat, drink, fire, and tobacco ... We will have a verdict by the help of God or you will starve for it.' The jury stuck to their verdict, so the judge fined them for contempt and imprisoned them for non-payment of the fine.

Penn protested that this violated the laws of Magna Carta and was forcibly removed from the court, possibly bound and gagged. One of the jurors, Bushel, petitioned the Court of Common Pleas for a writ of *habeas corpus* and Chief Justice Vaughan delivered the opinion of the court 'which established the right of juries to give verdicts according to their consciences'.[13]

The principle of this trial – that juries have the right to give verdicts according to their convictions – has survived through all the developments to follow in many cases, including the 1985 Clive Ponting case in which a civil servant working in the Ministry of Defence saw documents showing the government of Mrs Thatcher may have lied about the sinking of the ship *General Belgrano* during the Falklands War. Ponting gave copies of these documents to an opposition MP so that the matter could be raised in Parliament and was charged under the Official Secrets Act. At his trial, and despite the judge's clear direction that Ponting's conduct *did* amount to an offence, the jury acquitted.

In Randle and Pottle in 1991 the defendants had assisted an infamous spy, George Blake, to escape from prison and wrote a book about the escape. They argued at their trial for assisting the escape that their actions were justified because of the severity of Blake's 42-year sentence. An unauthorised informal account of Randle's speech from the dock to the jury has him saying that: 'No judge, no prosecutor, no force on earth could stand between English jurors and their conscience.' He raised arguments about the morality of the

UK government's own use of spies and, it is reported, pointed to the steps leading from the dock to the cells, saying:

> They lead to a sewer called the British prison system. To send a man down them for 42 years is a death sentence. I have no apologies to make and no regrets.

The jury acquitted.[14]

So a third rule of advocacy, at least for our courts, is to be fearless when it may serve your purpose. However, it is rare in our country – perhaps because of the supremacy of Parliament and the fact that we have not had a revolution for a long time – for counsel to take *real* risk, unlike, simply by way of one example, someone like Juan Méndez of Argentina who early in his career became involved in representing political prisoners only to be arrested by the Argentinian military dictatorship and subjected to torture and administrative detention for 18 months.[15] Generally our adversarial system is adversarial in a formal way that allows the advocate to leave court without real blood being drawn.

FROM BUTCHERY BY THE COURTS TO SOMETHING DIFFERENT

Retracing our steps to the development of the normal jury trial, the Popish Plot of 1678 and Bloody Assizes of 1685, responsive to the end of the Monmouth rebellion at the battle of Sedgemoor, were instrumental in bringing about a 'bloody code' of punishments that were so severe that it needed moderating. The Glorious Revolution of 1688 that saw off James II and brought William and Mary to their thrones led to many allegations of treason, and then to the Treason Trial Act of 1696 that specifically allowed defendants in treason trials to have defence counsel.

For felony cases – unlike misdemeanour cases, surprisingly, and save for the provisions of the Treason Act of 1696 – defence counsel were not allowed until the mid-1730s. The justification for this prohibition was that it required 'no manner of skill to make a plain and honest defence' and the judges were thought capable of looking out for defendants' interests.

With the passage of time, use of counsel was encouraged by government practice. From the late 1690s there was funding of prosecutions for the most serious offences, such as cases of seditious words and libel, treason, coining and violent offences such as murder, rape and robbery. 'Once their presence [of counsel] as government prosecutors had been accepted, their services were gradually exploited by prosecutors in other cases.'[16]

An upward 'zigzag' in representation followed, with more defence lawyers being allowed for fairness or balance, particularly in difficult cases – blood-money cases being one example. Judges also wanted lawyers to assist with points of law, and a couple of statutes meant that prosecutors even for modest cases could be paid from court funds. Thus, by 1834, the use of prosecution counsel was widespread.[17]

It may also be the case that once the French and American revolutions were done there was a gap left in various democratic states by the reduction in the power of monarchs that allowed more room, and created a need for determination of disputes by lawyers and courts. Lawyers started to be seen as serving the essential democratic concept of all citizens being equal before the law. Defence lawyers were, nevertheless, rarely used until the late 18th century and not allowed to address juries until the following century, in 1836.[18]

Various practices – rewarding 'thief takers' when a conviction was secured, for example, or being granted immunity for giving evidence against an accomplice – allowed defence counsel to hone their cross-examination skills as motivation of prosecution witnesses could be impugned. Apart from justifying increasing use of lawyers, this also allowed scepticism to creep in where hearsay was concerned and to the expectation of there being corroboration of accomplice evidence. Eventually, defendants – who were allowed to speak but not to give evidence on oath until 1898[19] – enjoyed the privilege of remaining silent with counsel speaking for them and this helped shift the burden of proof onto the prosecution.[20]

The over-prescription of capital punishment – rising from 50 to 200 offences between the 17th century and the start of the 19th – saw juries convicting only of lesser offences than those charged and judges often granting reprieves from capital sentences.

Thus, it was from all these different strands that the modern adversarial trial developed, for criminal and also for some civil cases, over roughly 200–300 years, not such a long time considering that legal systems have existed for nearly 4,000 years.

Of note today, when all aspects of society are subject to 'evidence-based' analysis, this developing system, that was not created in any properly considered way, has never been reviewed seriously against alternative trial models. It has rarely, if at all, been considered even by informal press analysis in terms of whether it is a good or less good system; it developed and it is as it is. It is easy to find lurid newspaper stories about murder trials from the last couple of hundred years but harder to find critical accounts in those newspapers of the performance of advocates in the developing adversarial legal system. Their skills seem to have earned little fame or notoriety until late Victorian times, when someone like Edward Marshall-Hall, KC, *did* become a great celebrity, applying techniques appropriate for his age not ours, and doing nothing that validates our present system. His most famous plea to an all-male jury, apparently a last-minute thought, defending a pathetic prostitute on a charge of murder, was to point to the woman and, with a sob in his voice say: 'Look at her. God never gave her a chance. Won't you?' The jury did and acquitted of murder, convicting of manslaughter. It must be doubtful whether a jury today would be so easily affected, susceptible though they still may appear to be to 'political' arguments such as in the Ponting or Randle cases.[21]

IS ADVOCACY NOW SOMETHING WE ALL DO?

'Advocacy' as a word covers more functions than it used to. Not only does it describe the work of barristers and solicitors who have rights of audience in courts and tribunals and who are referred to as advocates, but businesses and NGOs have 'advocates' or 'advocacy officers'. Is this advocacy the same activity as that of the courtroom advocate? Has the use of the word become imprecise? Or has the business of advocacy actually expanded?

What, for example, of John Humphrys and Jeremy Paxman – are they doing something that almost merits the term advocacy, advocacy for the sceptical citizen? Subjecting society's leaders to a non-reverential interview probably developed from no earlier than Robin Day's interview with Prime Minister Macmillan in 1958 and did not reach its present shape until a couple of decades later. The citizen is exposed to much more of this type of advocacy than of any other kind. A rapid survey of the last 50 years of styles shows that the most effective advocacy can be brief, usually courteous and not too confrontational. These modern media tribunes are experts who, in a standard three-minute interview, usually manage to make a point or two and to elicit detail all in one go. Courtroom advocates will undoubtedly have been affected by listening to how the public discourse is helped or hindered by the skill of the masters of radio and TV. They would be foolish not to understand those skills and to appreciate how Cicero's approach or Marshall-Hall's would no longer work well to persuade a modern audience: too much of Cicero's emotions and life in his advocacy; too much of emotions of all kinds in Marshall-Hall's. Modern audiences are alive to many tricks of the advocate's trade and those tricks need to be avoided.[22]

CONCLUSION

The adversarial trial is simply not that ancient. And it did not come into being by reason but by chance and, to some degree, by the need to control the carnage being enacted on the citizenry by a code of punishment that was extreme. It is not an investigation into truth but into proof. Its use has never been shown to be more effective than European civil systems where the judge takes charge of investigating in order to discover the truth. It may be more effective; who knows. If I may be excused an over-used phrase: 'the jury is out'.

My tentative answers to the question I asked at the beginning are as follows.

Is the adversarial legal system as good as we say it is?

We have, first, to be very careful about how any and every institution of government has built-in and powerful methods of self-protection. The legal system is part of government. It needs to justify what it does. That means that it selects from history what it wants the citizen to hear. From a long history going back to Magna Carta it selects those events that justify maintenance of the *status quo.* It overlooks, forgets, brushes aside the other bits of history that are less convenient, such as the real reason why we have the present adversarial system at all. It was never designed to establish truth but always reflective of criminal courts as settings for battles of *proof*. Many miscarriages of justice known to have occurred under our system, such as in IRA and other cases not so very long ago, were brought about largely by failures to disclose evidence to the defence.[23] But once these were dealt with, the system itself that permitted such miscarriages is rapidly resealed against further criticism and 'stamped' as the world's best.

Perhaps quite as important over the years is how the established legal system has, in its self-interest, had to disregard or minimise all those occasions when victims – typically of sex attacks or offences against children – have seen their cases dismissed by judges or juries for unnecessary requirements of corroboration. Those requirements were rooted in the very adversarial system we still praise and that, in the course of 'unsuccessful' trials, had exposed the victims to terrible cross-examination (finally officially deprecated), without juries knowing anything of how those subject to such attacks are likely to behave.

It is with embarrassment that I can recall how in the 1990s I both prosecuted and defended in sex and children cases where the results – either way, guilty or not guilty – were substantially the products of procedures and laws now regarded as having been simply wrong. Some reason for self-praise may be found in the recent change from a system that allowed brutal, or simply inappropriate questioning of 'vulnerable witnesses' under the adversarial system to mandatory questioning processes for such witness that are more likely to establish some form of truth.[24] Anecdotally – by which I mean from training sessions of judges and part-time judges dealing with vulnerable witnesses – I have seen hardened traditional lawyers and judges acknowledging how these gentler forms of questioning might be better not just for vulnerable witnesses but for *all* witnesses.[25]

Second, the system has been extremely good – subject to the sort of exceptions already cited – at not convicting too many innocent people, but at the expense, it is said, of letting many guilty people escape.

Third, the stylised combat in court brings out some very good qualities of loyalty, industry and determination in the advocates representing clients in court.

Fourth, the game of the law – and it is a game – is immensely enjoyable to those who enjoy the form of advocacy required.

Fifth, the game is great public entertainment and, in a curious way, its entertainment value may feed back to justify the system's very existence – there are, it seems, fewer examples of courtroom dramas as a form of entertainment in other European countries.

But, sixth, the system is actually quite recent and came into existence largely by chance to deal with problems we no longer have.

Seventh, it is time-consuming and sometimes very expensive of a state's resources.

Eighth, it is not shown to have any effect on reconciling unhappiness in a national community (much as similar systems bring little reconciliation to war-torn states where applied in war crimes tribunals).

Ninth, it may not deter future crime any more efficiently than other systems.

If the system is good – or at least worth preserving for the time being – how should advocates be trained to do it?

This question needs to be addressed because the present legal system will almost certainly only change, if at all, slowly and incrementally. I wonder how much more society gets by narrowing the barrister's presentation by trained rules of questioning when, for many people, advocacy is a natural response to a situation, *provided* you know the facts and the law and are determined to do right by the client you represent. The present training technique is not unhelpful. But now that we know so much more about how and why some advocates are *really* bad in how they ask questions, should we not look again within ourselves? We may be able to supplement instinctive skill – that comes from within – with something derived somewhat more intellectually from considerations of duty and function and aided by a spirit of inquiry. If we do this we *may* be able to adjust the legal system a bit to what is really wanted or needed in a modern world; it is unlikely to be a simple adversarial system rooted in medieval combat. Nor is the law likely to be best served by a training method that regiments the individual too much in how he can or cannot ask questions. The advocate for a modern age may need to apply the desire he has to represent others in resolution of their difficulties by *instinct assisted by method* not by *method that can crush instinct.*

Are there some universal rules for advocates that should be followed?
Back in the 1970s John Mortimer, QC, wrote the TV series *Rumpole of the Bailey*. He showed the realities of professional life of a fearless but non-establishment barrister whose brain was filled with poetry and other learning, and whose instinctive advocacy could hardly be further away from the 'skill-based' techniques we now offer our students.[26] My sensing *now* that relying on instinct – as Rumpole did – may be better than focusing on some oral equivalent of a 'good forehand drive' at tennis or a 'perfect parallel turn' in skiing reveals either that I am simply out of date or possibly ahead of my time, with a return to earlier practices yet to come.

The fictional Rumpole, just like all the best advocates I have known, always follows the one truly universal rule binding any advocate: to be 'in his client's shoes' from first to last, in court or out. The rule is binding, however accurate may be the private, and sometimes confidentially expressed opinions held by the advocate about that client and his case. This rule should surely apply to advocates in every well-functioning legal system with whatever procedural rules.

It may be a rule harder to apply in any country that has governments of extreme persuasion that wish advocates to 'toe the line'; then it requires real courage, as persecuted lawyers around the world can attest. The duty to fill the client's shoes comes with a recognition of the *privilege* of representing anyone – absolutely anyone – at a time of inevitable stress and often personal distress. And even if corporate clients or governments represented have no individual *personal* distress – often they actually do in the individuals in charge – they are in a state of stress in court actions with real interests to protect.

It is the privilege of representing others that makes people want to become advocates, or so at least I have always hoped. It is because it is such a privilege that I have become weary of advocates who seem to have 'monetised' their professional calling and try to tell you how much they earn, rather like judges who 'let on' how much they grossed before they became judges. People inclined to such vanities should step aside for those better suited – as advocates or judges – to the real privilege of trying to sort out the problems of others.[27] Once this universal rule is followed the advocacy itself is – and probably always has been – best when it comes with fullest knowledge of relevant facts and law and respect for all others, especially witnesses, in a process of genuinely attempting to show a factual truth or the accuracy of a theory that will help the decision maker. Nothing more and rarely anything less. Easy to say; fun to try; hard to do.

Chapter 10

Burma and North Korea: Avoid the Law Unless Convenient

Conflicts in both these countries show the real limits of international law when there are powerful neighbours and geopolitical interests to worry about. Both conflicts show how easy it is without international legal intervention for such conflicts to stay little-known. In this chapter the history of these conflicts, and the atrocities known to have been committed in each, will be summarised and set beside legal actions that have been attempted but have failed.

Original lecture delivered on 2 April 2014.

There is not very much law in this chapter – and that is the point. Law should be universal in reach within whatever global or local universe it operates. International legal institutions do not come down with equal force on every international criminal outrage against humanity because there are *political* reasons to justify treating them differently. Should the citizen care?

BURMA

We know of Aung San Suu Kyi and possibly recall something of the massacre of the Buddhist monks and their Saffron Revolution in 2007 but maybe little else – apart from having heard it is a great new holiday destination. Is there more?

In fact, Burma has been the scene of appalling human rights violations, state-sponsored many would say, for decades. Since at least the 1990s there has been forced labour, the recruitment of tens of thousands of child soldiers, widespread sexual violence, extra-judicial killings and torture; more than a million people have been forcibly displaced; over 3,000 villages with ethnic populations regarded as hostile by the government have been burned to the ground. The ruling Burma military junta and its leaders have avoided justice and accountability and look set to continue to do so.

It would be easy enough to give descriptions of some of the crimes committed in the period spoken of – but better to do what the Harvard Law School's International Human Rights Clinic Report of May 2009[1] did and to rely on authorised documents of the UN itself in order to explain what happened.

The UN Special Rapporteur for Burma/Myanmar has listed human rights violations in every year between 1993 and 2008: forced displacement (every year); sexual violence (every year except 2001); extra-judicial killing (every year except 2001); torture (every year except 2001); arbitrary detention (every year). The UN Commission on Human Rights and the Human Rights Council has listed human rights violations for each of those offences every year between 1992 and 2008, except for 2006 and 2007. General Assembly resolutions listed these violations – all of them – for every one of the same years except for 2007 and 2008 (where one or two categories were not identified).

In consequence, human rights abuses committed by Burma's military regime, *and already documented by the United Nations*, include human rights violations listed under Article 7 of the Rome Statute as 'crimes against humanity' including murder, enslavement, torture, rape, sexual slavery, enforced prostitution and others, along with human rights abuses listed under Article 8 of the Rome Statute, Section 2 (c) and (e) as 'war crimes': mutilation, cruel treatment and torture; intentionally directing attacks against the civilian population; conscripting or enlisting children under the age of 15 years.

The Harvard report concluded that Burma has lived under autocratic and repressive military rule for more than four decades. Yet for too many years, as the commissioners of the report observed, the world had done little to address these human rights abuses. The commissioners explained that, each of them having dealt directly with severe human rights abuses in the international system *and* having seen the painful consequences of inaction:

> We have seen how severe human rights abuses are not simply condemnable acts, but require concerted efforts to achieve some semblance of accountability and justice ... We have been struck by the finding that for years the United Nations (UN) has been on notice of severe, indeed widespread and systematic abuses that appear to rise to the level of state policy ... we call on the UN Security Council urgently to establish a Commission of Inquiry to investigate and report on crimes against humanity and war crimes in Burma. The world cannot wait while the military regime continues its atrocities against the people of Burma. The day may come for a referral of the situation in Burma to the International Criminal Court or the establishment of a special tribunal to deal with Burma.

Was a commission of inquiry established? Certainly not. Such commissions may require further action and what happens can be unpredictable. What did the lawyers and the law do instead to safeguard the interests of all those victims? There was, in fact, little they could do if the UN did not act. But let there be no doubt there have been thousands and thousands of victims of crimes, some dead, many still alive.

What happened next?
The Burma Campaign UK, a focused expert NGO, has reported month by month on events in Burma. A review of those reports shows what happens when the interest of victims may become inconvenient. Extracts from some of their monthly reports showed how over time:

- Thousands of refugees fled to China;
- Thousands of people were internally displaced;
- The Burmese military burned homes and caused people to flee.

All this happened despite the UN General Assembly condemning human rights abuses against civilians.

The UN Special Rapporteur on Human Rights in Burma, Tomás Ojea Quintana, also recommended that the UN consider establishing a commission of inquiry into war crimes and crimes against humanity in Burma stating that the 'gross and systematic nature of the abuses and the lack of action to stop them indicates a state policy that involves authorities in the executive, military and judiciary at all levels'.[2]

Following the release of Aung San Suu Kyi from house arrest and with modest reforms in train, Western countries changed their approach from maintaining sanctions and supporting UN condemnation to dealing amicably with the government and sending business delegations. They did this notwithstanding the well-known record of human rights abuses in general and in particular the suffering of the Muslim Rohingya people, which has attracted increasing international concern since at least 2102. The military junta's former head, Than Shwe, was always acutely fearful of international punitive action – believed to be a key reason why he began reforms. Western leaders now actively court the government, probably largely for economic reasons and to dilute China's regional standing. They may also fear that any mention of the International Criminal Court, to which Burma might have been referred by the Security Council, would affect these budding relations. Perhaps a silent agreement was made that if the government pushed ahead with the transition then the international community generally would pull back from earlier threats to engage the ICC, such as that made by the European Parliament in 2008.

Aung San Suu Kyi, who never agreed with an ICC referral, is clearly calling all the shots for Western action on Burma – the chance of anything of this magnitude being done without her approval is slim. She has chosen to take a role in government and work with the military, rather than remaining in opposition to them; her language is about moving on and working together. There has been international concern about the plight of the Rohingya people but it seems the majority of Burmese are hostile towards Rohingya and a very significant part of her support base would feel betrayed were she to speak out in their defence.

The international community has stopped calling for a commission of inquiry or a referral to the ICC.

What other legal remedies are there? Some devoted lawyers working pro bono make applications to the United Nations Working Group on Arbitrary Detention where they plead – always successfully, I believe – that their clients have suffered breaches of the UN Declaration of Human Rights, namely breach of basic rights: right to freedom of thought, freedom of association, freedom of conscience, right not to be discriminated against, and so on.[3] But once Aung San Suu Kyi was released from house detention and the governments of the world chose to treat the generals' new regime as worthy of attention and some respect it became hard for NGOs and individuals to do much. There is a sense of palpable disenchantment, almost disillusion, among well-intentioned, well-informed activists.

As a result of the new enthusiasm for Burma as a place to make money and as a tourist centre it begins to look as though all those arguments in favour of having a commission of inquiry or of referring the regime leaders to the ICC will come to nothing. This is more unfortunate and more important than politicians might think. Putting past violations on one side is leaving the victims without a champion, without even the prospect, however remote, of seeing accountability. They will have their history written by the enemy or by no one at all.

We will never know how much better or worse things would have been had the international community had the nerve to keep the human rights and legal interests of victims in Burma at the top of its agenda, by having a formal inquiry and a referral to the ICC. We – or future generations – may discover whether leaving these issues of accountability unresolved for now will, as on occasions elsewhere, bring them back with a vengeance this year, next year, sometime or – as those deaf and blind to victims may hope – never.

NORTH KOREA

Citizens of the Democratic People's Republic of Korea, a single-party state, suffer violations of human rights almost impossible to comprehend. Since its foundation in 1948 by Kim Il-sung, grandfather of the present leader, Kim Jong-un, North Korea has been subject to the dictatorship of one family that controls the party, the state and the military. The regime is protected from collapse by 'ideological' beliefs, roughly premised on Marxist-Leninist theory. Little information about what goes on inside the borders of North Korea filters through to the outside world, but what does emerge – especially about the practice of guilt by familial association for up to three generations and the use of prisoners and their offspring in what are life-long slave camps – strains understanding and even the belief of those who live in totally different cultures.

There has not been a comprehensive peace treaty between North and South Korea since the cessation of the Korean War (1950–53). On both sides of the border the fear of invasion and infiltration remains. In North Korea this fear has 'justified' maintaining a state of emergency, allowing the harshest of totalitarian rule and widespread and grave human rights violations.

From as early as the 1950s the Kim dynasty established a cult of personality with a 'Supreme [and infallible] Leader' that achieved the tightest possible control over its people with purges by executions and detention in huge, remote prison camps for opponents, together with a ban on movement internally and abroad. Class status – with associated levels of access to food, education, freedom to move and other privileges – is fixed by reference to political allegiance; food was used to maintain control, on occasion leading to mass starvation as with the famine occurring between 1996 and 1999, when it is estimated that between 450,000 and 2 million people starved to death.[4]

As with Burma, various bodies, NGOs and individuals were concerned to do what they could. There was pressure for a UN commission of inquiry, perhaps with little expectation that one would be forthcoming. To the surprise of many, the UN Human

Rights Council instituted such a commission in 2013 under the chairmanship of Justice Kirby of Australia. Evidence hearings took place in Seoul, London, Tokyo and Washington, held in public to the maximum extent possible. The findings were published in 2014.[5]

Kirby's commission found that the regime violates freedom of thought, expression and religion on a widespread scale, subjecting its citizens to almost complete denial of freedoms, even of the freedom to think. Freedom of opinion, expression, information and association, as well as of conscience and religion, are comprehensively denied. An all-encompassing indoctrination machine achieves absolute obedience. The state monitors the people and dictates their daily activities with surveillance permeating the private lives of all citizens.[6]

The commission also detailed violations of the right to food and related aspects of the right to life and explained how military spending and the nuclear programme have been prioritised, even during periods of mass starvation. Starvation of its own citizens has, indeed, been used by the state as a means of control and punishment, with hundreds of thousands of people dying or suffering permanent physical and psychological injuries as a consequence.[7]

Turning to the matter of arbitrary detention, torture, executions and prison camps:

> Gross human rights violations … involving detention, executions and disappearances are characterized by a high degree of centralized coordination between different parts of the extensive security apparatus … The use of torture is an established feature of the interrogation process … Persons who are found to have engaged in major political crimes are 'disappeared', without trial or judicial order, to political prison camps (*kwanliso*). There … the inmate population has been gradually eliminated through deliberate starvation, forced labour, executions, torture, rape and the denial of reproductive rights enforced through punishment, forced abortion and infanticide. The commission estimates that hundreds of thousands of political prisoners have perished in these camps over the past five decades. The unspeakable atrocities that are being committed

> against inmates of the *kwanliso* political prison camps resemble the horrors of camps that totalitarian states established during the twentieth century.[8]

There were also extensive findings about abductions and enforced disappearances from other countries.[9]

The commission made many recommendations for North Korea – and for China, which has for long resisted international intervention and done much to allow North Korea to maintain its grip on its citizens, for example by returning to North Korea those who escape across the China border. For the international community, among a number of proposals to assist the development of North Korea, the commission urged the Security Council to refer the situation in North Korea to the International Criminal Court and to adopt targeted sanctions against those who appear to be most responsible for crimes against humanity.

CONCLUSION

The Burma government leaders may be seen to have been clever and the outside world somewhat naïve. Those in country or who cross from Thailand with medical supplies or education services for those denied these things by the Burma government all despair at the reality behind the reforms that they suspect are skin deep at best. Perhaps, as one commentator suggested to me, the government leaders see that half of the world is run by dictators who are tolerated by the other democratic half and all they desire is to move from pariah dictatorship to ordinary dictatorship, dressed as something else.

What is difficult for the active diaspora and for activists is to go to governments where in recent years the officials' eyes were warm with regard when a commission of inquiry or a justice mechanism was proposed, but where now they glaze over if such things are mentioned, looking patronisingly and condescendingly at those whose efforts they once encouraged.

Whatever their motivation, the victims remain victims. Their suffering has not diminished and many new victims are being created every day. Their story – their entitlement to have their story known – is less important than the right of businessmen to trade with Burma at considerable profit or the right of holidaymakers to enjoy new resorts in a country where the best must be made of its recent progress if planes are to continue flying the tourists in. The international community has no interest in recording their suffering, only in burying the memory of it.

We will never know what would have happened if the outside world had stood firm with Burma and given no encouragement. Had the approach been tougher would the generals have retreated to more violence or would they have given real not phoney ground?

In contrast the citizens of North Korea, who have made only very limited recent gains, may be better poised, ultimately, both to see an end to their suffering and to have what has happened since the Kim dynasty took power properly recorded in a formal way. This is for two reasons. First, the regime has not (yet) seen how to play the West and win and may not do so until it is too late, when 'defeat' will be as total as defeat was, for example, for the Nazi leadership. Second, the outside world has stood firm in its resolve thus far and the Commission of Inquiry report may bring the UN to action. The present regime will fall even if we cannot predict how. When it does, if its then leaders have not shown the guile of the Burmese leaders they might have a one-way ticket to a court in The Hague or elsewhere as a parting gift from the people they have so abused. At such a court, as with the Nazi leaders, trials and punishment of individuals will serve also to record the comprehensive wickedness of the state itself.

But will the politicians recognise that they now live in an age in which the works of activists and failed-state diaspora are not irritants to be brushed aside, as powerful countries hoped to do with public protests in earlier times, but increasingly significant creators of reliable records of terrible events, and the enforcers (sometimes) of real political change?

And so the victims in Burma and the bereaved of those killed by crimes of the state may now have a reduced or even no prospect of seeing a proper record left of their suffering, whereas the victims of the regime in North Korea may have to wait longer but may ultimately have the benefits of public accountability.

Chapter 11

Cases I Have Known

I must find in my 40-odd years at the Bar of England and Wales something more than the merely amusing or interesting. What can be inferred from cases I have done that informs us about the law, its development and related changes in society? As in other professions, I only learned from what went wrong, rarely from whatever successes I may have had.

Original lecture delivered on 4 March 2015.

The relevant biography can be dealt with swiftly. I was brought up in South London and my family had no connections of any kind with the law. But I was immensely privileged, not in the sense of our having much money – my father was in the print and my mother was a primary school mistress and my first teacher. My privilege was in excellent parents who knew how to encourage and not to force a weedy, lazy child so he could pass from good junior school to excellent local direct grant school, privileged in that school having a disproportionately good hold on the university to which I went in the slip-stream of my brother, privileged in the best universities giving the best prospects of getting a reasonable job and all on a welfare state that made it possible to finish education with no debt. Better still, Lewisham Council gave me a grant to cover fees at Law School when, after a couple of other jobs, I decided to go to the Bar. Privileged yet more in entering the Bar when Legal Aid had expanded dramatically the money available for the enlarged categories of cases for which Legal Aid was granted. I was launched at a favourable time into a career I chose almost by chance.

A START

Luck, too, played its part. A neighbour and friend, John Leech, noted I had no connections for my chosen profession so he secretly created a summer job in the legal department of the Commonwealth Development Corporation and recruited me; a lawyer there, Michael Konstam, saw I had no legal contacts and sent me to the head of a set of chambers he knew. Now for the hard bit, the interview to get a pupillage, an exercise today in which only a small percentage ever succeed and then after anxious rounds of interviews and reams of application forms completed in triplicate.

I entered the head of chambers' room – he was a tall patrician figure about to become a judge. 'Have a cigarette? Konstam thinks you're OK, when would you like to start? September?' That was that.

My interview by his successor a year later was very different. After the first six months observing and learning and the second six months of the year as a novice 'on his feet', chambers felt obliged to take me on, perhaps because a solicitor had negligently entrusted me already with a two-week rape case in the Old Bailey and the other tenants thought I might contribute satisfactorily to chambers' income. I am not sure what my client the rapist thought of his solicitor having chosen me over more experienced counsel – but he had five years of seclusion to think about it. Two pupils were taken on at that time. The new head of chambers, a man soon to go on the High Court Bench but not beyond and not missed much when he left chambers or the bench, observed: 'The other pupil is clearly the much nicer man but we have decided to offer you a tenancy.' He then said something about my flared trousers (tailor-made though they were) but the detail of what he said was lost in the confusion caused by the chill of his overall welcome.

EARLY DAYS

Once practice started in earnest it was roughly like this. Get up really early. Set off maybe by train (fewer tubes, buses and trains then so not necessarily that easy) or 'old banger' on a two- or three-hour drive to a county town or city (Norwich, or Wisbech in the Fens, or Canterbury, or Lewes). Arrive by 09.30 latest – see clients. Open to the judge a couple of pleas of guilty for the prosecution; blend those with mitigation on behalf of others pleading guilty. Rush up and down the cell steps to see your client, bumping into one you had just prosecuted. Maybe followed by a trial. If it was in front of a High Court judge on the equivalent of Assize (and I heard the very last Commission of Assize read in Maidstone) then maybe lunch with the county set as guest of the High Sherriff or carted away in the judicial Daimler with the judge – robed in the back escorted by an outrider – to his lodgings for a quick but formal lunch.

When that day – or stint – was all over, back to chambers to collect briefs wrapped in red tape for more of the same – perhaps civil cases this time – often for overnight preparation to be in court the following day. We learned very fast and only hoped our clients did not suffer too much.

MORE LUCK

Some chambers liked to squeeze as much as possible from the system and would have their man in Stratford, East London, at 10.00

and Ealing, West London, at 14.00. This was great if it worked, but what if the morning case overran or the buses and trains did not quite do their job? My chambers – Farrar's Building – were run by a traditional senior clerk, Arthur Hathaway, and George Hales his number 2, and they did not take this kind of risk. One day the chambers next door had taken the risk and it hadn't worked. Their man would miss a 14.00 Barking case. I was free. It came to me even though I was not approved Metropolitan Police counsel. And there followed weekly appearances in this case, which was for a particularly powerful in-house police solicitor, Clive Winston. He saw that we had been loyal to him and he repaid the compliment. First with trade union picketing cases one of which, with me sitting behind a QC, went to the House of Lords, while another had me prosecuting a present-day shadow minister.

I was then promoted to sex cases. From there it was a short hop to prostitutes and escort agencies, matters taken very seriously by the CPS, as the prosecuting authority was now called, and 'leaders' – QCs – were taken in to lead me. I worked with a few significant leaders and here's a story of one of these trials.

John Marriage, QC, was an extremely skilful advocate with true animal attraction to all jurors. He was nearly a toff but of a rakish style. He had a racehorse trainer's licence and was a member of the Horse Race Betting Levy Board. The case he led me in was about an escort agency – Nina Spitzer's Agency – where Nina's 'nice gals' accompanied only the best class of gentlemen and engaged in conversation at, and presumably in the interval at, the theatre, but nowhere else. Or perhaps not.

The trial was in a room immediately opposite the back door of Harrods, and the trial judge, a very nice man from my chambers, Munroe Davies, QC, smoked and liked his morning breaks. So every morning at about 11.45 the judge rose for a couple of cigarettes and John and I popped across the road for a double G&T, or perhaps two, in the Harrods basement bar.

There were four female defendants and they all gave evidence on their own behalf. Nina Spitzer was a glorious target – John destroyed her in cross-examination. No. 2 had written lots of documents and it is documents that make for the best cross-examination often enough. John disposed of her in short order. Next one for the tumbril? But John was away the following day at a Levy Board meeting. 'You can cross-examine,' he said, 'I'll be back the day after.'

There were no documents against Defendant No. 3. I was hopeless, absolutely hopeless. Back for Defendant 4 John was on tip-top form and he had her spinning with absolutely silly answers, but kept her too long in the box because he was enjoying himself. Then closing addresses, summing-up and verdict. Another Betting Levy Board meeting loomed so I was all alone after John's closing speech. Counsel for No. 3 enjoyed himself. When he ran out of good things to say about his client he had a go at me for my palpable incompetence. I shrank, and just when I thought it was over he had another swipe. The jury verdict – the inevitable final humiliation was bound to be guilty, guilty, not guilty, guilty. But no. Bless the jury. It was guilty, guilty, guilty (for No. 3) and not guilty (for No. 4)! A reasonable interpretation of the verdicts was that the jury would not have me bullied so mercilessly by No. 3's counsel and punished poor No. 3 (who really had the best prospects of an acquittal) but would not convict No. 4 after her being treated with quite such relish by John.

Perfect result for me. John was as happy as could be. Counsel for No. 3 still looks surprised when we speak of the case.

John was also my route to the part-time bench as a recorder, a job I have enjoyed for some six weeks a year for over 30 years. These days the application form takes about a week to complete and competition is so fierce that many highly qualified potential judges simply do not bother to apply. At lunch John noted that someone from the Lord Chancellor's Department had asked for names of those suitable to be assistant recorders. 'Phone this number,' he said, 'and say John Marriage says you're suitable.' I did and was on the training course in a few weeks.

DOING BATTLE

The adversarial system requires the barrister to do battle on behalf of his client. But the battle is stylised and the barrister should never be exposed to great embarrassment provided he has read his papers and the relevant law and knows what his case is. The odds are stacked in favour of the barrister getting out reasonably honourably, whatever befalls the client. But outside court the barrister does have to fight without protection, for example when bargaining in civil cases or in criminal cases over some procedural issue or about pleas to be accepted, and can find himself in difficult personal conflicts with other counsel in multi-party cases where interests do not coincide. One way and another the experienced barrister will have had personal battles and for many, I think, the time comes when they have had enough and want an easier life. And for some the bench can be a comfortably different place – so do not believe those silly judges who say they went to the bench for Queen and Country – they may well have run out of battle steam and found the pay more than sufficient (whatever they say pretending to earnings they may not have received) and the pension very attractive.

I learned about the need to fight from two unappealing judges, each of whom wanted to harm me by publicly condemning what I had said in mitigation. In each case they said that, but for what I had said on behalf of my clients, they would have been more lenient. The first, a high court judge, criticised me heavily for providing him with a probation or social services report on the woman of very limited intellect for whom I was appearing. I was trying to flesh out detail of her limitations to help the judge and was clearly acting conscientiously. Whether my poor client realised our relationship of client and lawyer had been intentionally destroyed in public by a deeply unpleasant man I do not know. Protracted insomnia followed. The second, a mere circuit judge, was known for his delight at hurting counsel; after I had pleaded in mitigation for three men of previous good character, whose crimes were bound to take them straight to jail according to then guidelines, he started his sentencing ,'When I read the papers I thought all three of you should receive suspended prison sentences but having heard Mr Nice I am nearly persuaded you should serve immediate terms of imprisonment.' These three chaps *did* understand what he had done and the post-sentence celebration was awkward. But I was not going to leave it at insomnia this time. The judge needed to learn the error of his ways and to apologise. And he did. I realised that the superficially civilised world of the English legal system is a jungle in which there are some nasty beasts against whom the advocate must be ready to fight personally once he has done all he can for his clients. It is a lesson that has served me since, has made me tougher and that has in turn made it easier to protect clients in the courtroom.

Leave no stone unturned

Cases – civil and criminal – arising from deaths become a significant part of the common lawyer's practice and provide many lessons. One memorable case concerned a railway man who was found dead on busy tracks in Croydon with his head close to but not touching a part of a train that had just come to rest. Had he died of a heart attack or been hit by the train? The British Rail investigation was inconclusive – two trains could have been involved and just possibly a third. But no explanation made sense. The widow could not recover damages. I just about kept the case alive but my solicitor was negligent and the case was about to expire for want of his action. We were all sacked by the client, the dead man's widow. New trial counsel did what we had not thought to do and sent an inquiry agent to the home of the train driver of the remotely possible third train. He opened the door and confessed. The widow recovered compensation. Lessons: never take anything for granted, always ask questions, and allow for the unexpected.

IN SILK

In 1990 I 'took silk' – became a Queen's Counsel – and thereafter always had the good fortune to appear with a junior to assist.

Barrett v Ministry of Defence

A naval airman died on his 30th birthday at a UK naval base at Bardufoss, Norway. The base had a culture of extreme use of alcohol. In the days before his birthday the deceased was justifiably concerned – as he wrote to his wife, the mother of his young son – about what 'they' would do to him on the night. He passed through officers' mess, NCOs' mess and his own mess by which time – perhaps having drink poured down his throat and possibly being thrown in the snow – he was paralytic. He was carried to his bunk where he was left with inadequate supervision in the coma position to die in his vomit. Barrett's widow blamed the MoD for her husband's death.

I had a great junior, Anthony Seys Llewellyn,[1] who knew the law and was highly conscientious. A kindly high court judge – Popplewell J – compelled the MoD to hand over its inquiry report into the death, something it was then reluctant to do. We later compelled production of another equally substantial report into the death that the MoD had completely overlooked – all useful material. We dared to call as a witness the base's on-duty chief petty officer who was willing to tell the truth of the regime on the night. All was going swimmingly. Brian Leveson[2] defended extremely well, but the terrific circuit judge Phelan, sitting as a high court judge for these purposes, found in our favour and made a modest reduction for what is called contributory negligence, as my junior and I had recognised he would.

Our advice to the widow when Brian Leveson had made an offer to settle was vindicated. Alas the Court of Appeal, presided over by an expert in defamation law, had a common law judge sitting with him conversant with the Navy. He delivered the judgment[3] and started with a passage from a book on life in the Georgian Navy, *The Wooden World*, that said:

> Everybody knew that drink was a factor in crime, most often the chief factor, but it was virtually impossible to do much about it ... the midshipmen of the watch were to 'see all men they find far gone in drink, put in their hammacoes [hammocks]'. If riotous they were to be confined until sober and then punished. Drinking as such was not a crime.[4]

Apportion of liability was reversed. The deceased was now said to be the principal cause of his own death. The offer Leveson had cleverly made exceeded what the widow had recovered so she had to pay every penny awarded to her for the MoD's costs. Mrs Barrett was absolutely resolute. She was not going to allow her son Liam to go through life believing his mother had conceded that his father was author of his own untimely death and the money was unimportant – she was entirely happy to have fought for what she knew was right. I am almost certain this case would be decided quite differently today in Mrs Barrett's favour.

WAR CRIMES TRIALS

In 1998 I started as a prosecutor at the UN's International Criminal Tribunal for the former Yugoslavia (ICTY) in The Hague, maintaining my UK practice but letting it sleep. I applied for the UN job because it seemed interesting, not to save the world. It pretty well changed my career for good. After over six years prosecuting there I have remained in practice but normally work on war crimes-related issues, usually advising governments and some individuals at risk of prosecutions or those who want to bring actions arising from conflicts but can't (victim groups or representatives of interests in North Korea, Burma or Iran, for example).

What did I need from my previous experience to work successfully at the UN? Making war crimes cases is enormously hard work – it was no problem for me to do it seven days a week and literally every possible working hour because it was fascinating work and because there was always more to read, more to learn, more to research and put together. Twenty-seven years of having done the same helped.

The court was political on various occasions and posed ethical problems that needed personal fight if I was not to surrender standards and compromise a fair trial. It was never difficult to fight because the independent barrister knows that yielding once to temptation or weakness in the face of pressure can destroy the self-employed reputation for good.[5]

My team varied in size for the Milošević case but could be a dozen lawyers and up to 100 people altogether, not all full-time. I remember, as one of my more successful management actions, a day when we had lost badly some procedural issue in court. The following morning there was a team meeting of about 15–20 people, mostly lawyers, all with long faces and in a sombre mood. I told them they were the luckiest lawyers in the world. They looked confused. I reminded them that the case they were working on made them the envy of all their lawyer friends who would give various parts of their anatomy to be on the case. Their faces did not lighten. I explained that the lawyer does his job because he cannot do a proper job like farming or manufacturing and is lucky to be allowed to fiddle with decisions of others. They remained confused. I suggested that being a lawyer – judge or advocate – is to be involved in solving problems. Dim acceptance. And that as problem solvers nothing could be more satisfying than having a hard problem to solve and solving it. Nothing could be more boring than having an over-simple problem. Accordingly, I reasoned, the setback of the previous day simply made their jobs more enjoyable as the judges had made our work more difficult.

The lawyer is never happier than when in the middle of something difficult and uncertain of result.

One example of this concerned the infamous and historically significant massacre at Račak. Unhappily we were in possession of – but had overlooked although we had provided it to Milošević – a stack of material apparently showing it was not a massacre at all but a fight between the Serb military and the violent Kosovo Liberation Army (KLA). We did not believe this material but had to deal with it, although many in the office wanted to avoid embarrassment and drop the charge – impossible and in any case wrong. No one wanted to take responsibility for getting out of the mess and the problem was, in any case, mine. I loved it. 'Confront it without fear', I said, 'and we will see what comes out.' We all went down to Kosovo and got on with the problem, starting at the very beginning. Little by little the falsity of bad evidence became clear – its creation manifestly fraudulent, or at least very arguably fraudulent – and we were able to strengthen our previous case by the fact that the Serbs had felt the need, as we were able to demonstrate, to create the mass of false material that we had failed even to read before handing it to the defendant.

The Skorpions video

Let me recite one of the best things I did – one of the things you would do in an ordinary case, but writ large. There was a paramilitary group called the Skorpions who were filmed by one of their own number killing six very young men from Srebrenica. The film was of critical value as the paramilitary group was from Serbia, not Bosnia, and thus was under the command of the government of which Milošević was president. It could link Serbia directly to the genocidal Srebrenica massacre, and this link was what Milošević was determined to obscure.

The film was sensationally good as it had all members of the Skorpions face to camera at the start when they were blessed by a priest – with these 'mug shots' every member of the group, including the particular killers of the young men, could be identified by anyone who saw the film. By great good fortune, at the very moment when it became possible for me to use the film (when the safety of the provider of the film had been secured) there was in the witness box a defence witness, Serbian Police General Obrad Stevanović, to whom, ultimately, this unit might report. But I knew if I attempted to introduce the 1¾ hour-long film there would be objections for almost any reason and either it would never be shown or it would take forever to overcome obstacles thrown in my way.

Also, I could not rely on the prosecutor's office not to block me as, at the very top, there were curious forces at work that seemed keen to favour Serbia. I laid a careful plan and had the necessary minimum extracts from the film prepared so that I could reduce to a couple of minutes the amount of film that had to be shown to make my point – and had to play the excerpts before objections stalled my progress.

The witness gave evidence for Milošević for 15 days altogether, and my cross-examination started on the eighth day and lasted about five days. There were many other matters to deal with. How should I deal with the Skorpions video? I knew that I had to get as much done as possible before anyone realised what was afoot and that I had to lull the witness – despite all the other nasty suggestions I put to him – into cooperation. Very early I asked the general:

> **Q.** You've taken the solemn declaration. Are you prepared to help this Chamber if I give you that opportunity a little later? Are you prepared to help them? Or are you here to help the accused?
> **A.** I have already said that I am here to answer questions both put to me by the defence and the prosecution, and I will answer them by telling the truth.[6]

As the days of my cross-examination passed I returned regularly enough to the theme – usually by reference to some detail on which I sought his help although I did not really need it. He was conditioned to think he was helping and being treated seriously. When the time was right I turned to the Skorpions.[7]

> **Q.** I'm going to show you some extracts from a video. The video lasts about two hours, but it will only be a few minutes of it that we will show in order to give its context.

I asked a few questions based on the opening of the film which simply showed the members of the unit being blessed. Then:

Q. This video, which is potentially distressing viewing and I'm only going to play very small parts of it, reveals, Mr Stevanović, if the evidence is in due course admitted, and that's why I want your assistance, reveals that men were brought from Srebrenica in batches to this group of Skorpions to be executed and they were executed, and what you see here is a lorry load of six young men. This is the same truck with the men in the back. And you can see the red berets.
A. Yes, I see that, but I don't see or, rather, I haven't seen any Skorpion insignia so far.
Q. You'd recognise the Skorpion insignia, would you, if you saw it?
A. Well, I think it would be clear. I don't know exactly what it looks like, but I assume that there's a picture of a scorpion.
Q. You just guessed that, did you?
A. As I said, in Erdut I had occasion to see several members of this unit. I think they were in uniform and had insignia.

[Videotape played]

Mr Nice: The lorry leaves. The men are eventually taken up into the hills … Here they are taken up into the surrounding countryside. Two remaining not shot are untied … They're untied, they move the four bodies, and then they are themselves shot, and I'll leave it there.
Judge Robinson: Mr Nice, can you tell us about that film?
Mr Nice: Yes, to a degree I will. But if I can just deal with –
Mr Kay [Court-imposed counsel for Milošević]: We haven't established any foundation for this. To my mind, this looks like sensationalism. There are no questions directed to the witness on the content of that film in a way that he can deal with it … It's not cross-examination.
Judge Robinson: Mr Nice, there is some merit in that … Who made it, in what circumstances, and what questions are you putting to the witness in relation to it? …

Q. I'm suggesting this film shows Skorpions executing prisoners from Srebrenica.
A. I am upset, I have to say that this is one of the most monstrous images I have ever seen … Of course I have never seen anything like this in [real life]. I am astonished that you have played this video in connection with my testimony because you know full well that this has nothing to do with me or the units I commanded.
Judge Robinson: Do you agree with the Prosecutor's suggestion or proposition that this is a film that shows Skorpions executing prisoners from Srebrenica?
The Witness: Of course I do not intend to cast doubt on what the Prosecutor is saying, but I have not seen a single person I know here, and I have seen no evidence that this is the unit in question.
Q. I want your assistance, please, now or later, with the identification of and with the function of the people we can identify from this film. The first one, the leader … is Slobodan Medić, and there are two photographs of him. Do you recognise that man?
A. I recall only the nickname. The nickname Boca is familiar, but I cannot recall his face. I think I saw a man with this nickname in Erdut in 1995 on two or three occasions, but he did not come to see me. I saw him, if I recall rightly, at Mr Milanović's place.
Q. And he was the man who headed the Skorpions … Is that the man?
A. I saw him on two or three occasions, I told you where, but I had nothing to do with him.
Judge Bonomy: Well, I'm not clear about that answer. Are you acknowledging, General, that that is Boca?
The Witness: No, I'm not acknowledging that because I can't recall his face. All I recall is the nickname Boca.

Had the court been conditioned and the witness manipulated into being an unwilling helper? By dealing with it quickly, and knowing where we were going with the material, Stevanović actually confessed to knowing Boca, the head of this unit.

This is a question asked shortly after by Judge Bonomy:

> **Judge Bonomy:** I think the question was asked because in relation to some of the earlier documents you made the comment that you could make inquiries. Now, is that not something that can be done in relation to the material that's now been presented to you in this video?
> **The Witness:** Along those lines, of course, I think I can. I don't know what the response will be from the organs involved, but if you give me a list of names at the end of my testimony, I could check it out and see whether they were members of the MUP [Serbian Ministry of Internal Affairs] or not.

The film was never formally admitted as evidence, but it ended up having a much broader impact. Playing it in court led to the whole film being shown on Serbian prime-time TV that same day, lifting the fog of propaganda and sparking a sea change in attitudes towards the war. Rather than continuing in a state of denial, the majority of Serbs and their government from that moment on accepted that the Srebrenica massacre – the genocide – had actually happened.

CLOSING THOUGHTS

Legal decisions in our system, but probably in all systems, often turn on a word here, or an answer there or a whim of a judge or a mistake by counsel. Is the 'justice' in justice systems self-defining: he who wins achieves a just result?

What is clear to me, as I explained to the lawyers in The Hague, is that the lawyer who spends his time solving problems within justice systems has an enjoyable job. As to the worth of what lawyers do, compare lawyers with natural scientists, intergalactic explorers or engineers. They for the most part solve problems set by the laws and realities of nature that may reflect the goodness of the gods. We lawyers seek to solve problems set by the badness of man.

Chapter 12

Srebrenica: Genocide and Trial

The killings at Srebrenica in Bosnia were the worst atrocity committed in Europe since World War II. Two courts have found these killings to be genocide. With the 20th anniversary of this atrocity now past, through what lens should we look at Srebrenica? Must it always be through the lenses of law and legal process?

Original lecture delivered on 1 April 2015.

In the break-up of Yugoslavia, Serbs in Bosnia – 'Bosnian Serbs' – formed their own entity, Republika Srpska, that had its own government and army. It wanted to gain independence from Bosnia and join Serbia to form a contiguous state. To achieve this, it needed to take corridors of land, some parts of which did not have natural Serb majorities, and it took them by force. Three enclaves of non-Serbs – Srebrenica, Žepa and Goražde – were protected by the UN from 1993 until 1995 when Srebrenica and Žepa fell. Serbia proper was actively involved with the Bosnian Serb Army, which it supported; it paid and pensioned the officers of the army at 'overtime' rates (up to three times normal pay and pension) for participating in this war in which Serbia always maintained it was not engaged. When Srebrenica fell to Serb forces in July 1995 some 8,000 men and boys were killed, without reason, by Serb forces.

The bereaved of the Srebrenica massacre think and speak of it as a genocide, a definition found as established against the army of Republika Srpska and its officers by the International Court of Justice (ICJ) in a case brought by Bosnia against Serbia proper and as against its officers in the International Criminal Tribunal for the former Yugoslavia (ICTY).

Those still alive and suffering – personally or for those who died – are unable to accept the judgment of the International Court of Justice that said that Serbia itself was not responsible for genocide, only for not having done more to stop the genocide once it was under way.

Twenty years after the killings, there have been many 'never again' expressions of hope and many apologies or near-apologies from those whose conduct cannot altogether be overlooked. Again there has been the disappointment in judicial processes and the law itself of those who mourn the 8,000 fathers, husbands, brothers and sons who perished.

THE EVOLUTION OF GENOCIDE AS A CONCEPT

Genocide became a crime that could be charged in indictments against 'war criminals' almost by accident. Its role in our lives may be much broader than simply as a defined crime. Rather than weary the reader too much with detail about genocide law, I will argue that genocide is a concept – invaluable to us all – that is owned by the *people* not the lawyers. A consequence of this is that what the law provides for crimes such as happened at Srebrenica may rarely satisfy the people whose interests articulation of the crimes was supposed to serve.

Raphael Lemkin coined the term 'genocide' in the 1940s. He was a Polish Jew and almost 50 of his family members died in the Holocaust. His concern with control of conflict by law was apparent from an early stage of his pre-war career as a Polish state prosecutor, a position from which he had to resign when, in 1933, he started a public campaign to establish the crime of 'barbarism / vandalism', terms he later changed to 'genocide'. His campaigning was driven by his study of the Armenian Genocide (as now described) that started in 1915, the Assyrians murdered in Iraq during the 1933 Simele massacre and the starvation of Ukrainians by the Soviet Union occurring at about the same time.

Although his concern was to institute legal instruments which could outlaw certain acts commonly performed by states, he saw things somewhat differently from how genocidal acts are construed today. In particular he proposed a definition of genocide that embraced non-physical means of destruction of communities, not just the immediate *violent* destruction of a nation or part of a nation by mass killings. He conceived of genocide as signifying:

> ... different actions aiming at the destruction of essential foundations of the life of national groups, with the aim of annihilating the groups themselves ... disintegration of the political and social institutions, of culture, language, national feelings, religion, and the economic existence of national groups, and the destruction of the personal security, liberty, health, dignity, and even the lives of the individuals belonging to such groups.[1]

He conceived of genocide as directed against a national group as an entity, where the actions involved are directed against individuals, not in their individual capacity, but as members of the national group.

He thought of the crime as having two phases:

> ... one, destruction of the national pattern of the oppressed group; the other, the imposition of the

> national pattern of the oppressor. This imposition, in turn, may be made upon the oppressed population which is allowed to remain or upon the territory alone, after removal of the population and the colonization by the oppressor's own nationals.[2]

The account of his determination after World War II to have a Genocide Convention passed and ratified should be inspiring. He lobbied country after country to get the convention accepted by the General Assembly, working tirelessly in his shabby, stained suit, not eating properly and seemingly with few real friends – for only seven attended his funeral when he died of a heart attack in 1959 aged 59. But it is worth recognising that this somewhat tragic man has changed the way every reasonably educated man and woman on the planet thinks and speaks about the heart of darkness that lies within us once we become packs not people. Our language has been enriched by understanding *in one word* what from well before the Armenian massacre had been the experience of countless victims of a crime without a name.[3] He had the citizen's hope to end war.

Another man who followed in the footsteps of Lemkin, Benjamin Ferencz, is the last surviving prosecutor from the Nuremberg trials. Ferencz prosecuted not the main trial but one of follow-on trials of personnel of the *Einsatzgruppen*, mobile death squads of the Nazi SS, operating behind the front line in occupied Eastern Europe. From 1941 to 1943 alone, they murdered more than one million Jews and tens of thousands of 'partisans', Romani, disabled persons, political commissars and others. The 24 defendants in this trial were all officers of these *Einsatzgruppen* and faced mass-murder charges.

In his opening speech to the judges Ferencz used the term 'genocide', although it was not yet an identified crime.

Ferencz was for many years a tireless proponent of the International Criminal Court and of the inclusion in the Statute of that court of a provision outlawing 'aggression'. That law is on its way to full enactment, although a conference of the ICC States Parties in The Hague in 2016 attended by the author saw the matter effectively put on hold until at the earliest the next conference at the end of 2017. Ferencz has also argued – more controversially – that: 'Any person responsible for the illegal use of armed force in violation of the United Nations Charter, which unavoidably and

Milošević with the Red Berets at Kula Camp
Milošević attended this 1997 celebration of his founding of the elite Serbian Red Berets unit in 1991, a unit that went on to commit war crimes in Croatia and Bosnia despite Serbia not being technically at war. The video showed Milošević saying he had read reports from the unit and being shown the various theatres of war where they had been engaged. This video was perhaps the best single piece of evidence in the case as forming a military unit to commit war crimes showed Milošević had a criminal state of mind.

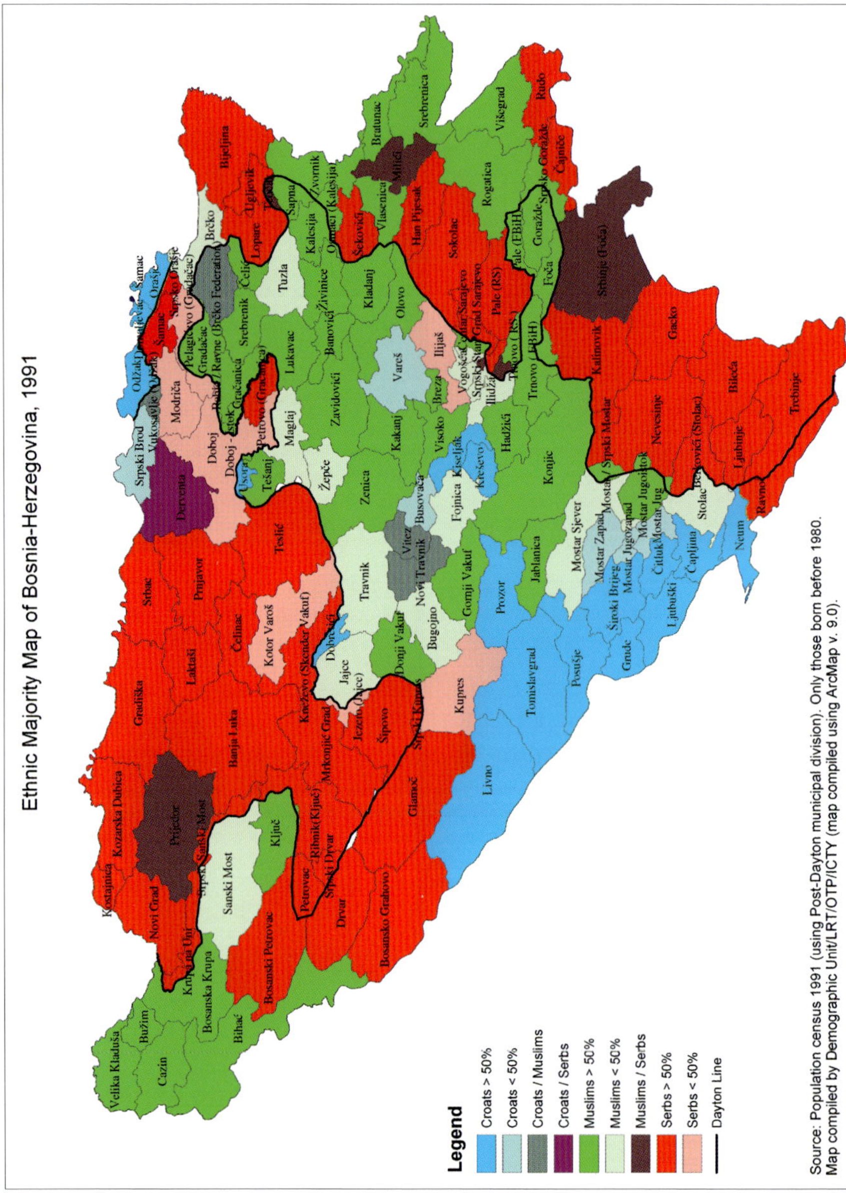

Demographers' maps speak

The 1991 map shows an ethnic mix, rather of the kind to be approved in multi-ethnic Northern Europe but unhelpful to the Serb cause of having a Serb state for all Serbs. The worst Serb crimes, including genocide – evidenced and charged against Milošević – were committed in the non-red municipalities that had no Serb majority, thereby creating what is shown in the 1997 map (Croat crimes turned some municipalities blue). The red Serb-majority municipalities in the 1997 map depict Republika Srpska, the Serb component of Bosnia–Herzegovina established by the 1995 Dayton Accords. Its near-contiguous territory – broken only by the linking district of Brčko at the apex of Republika Srpska, still

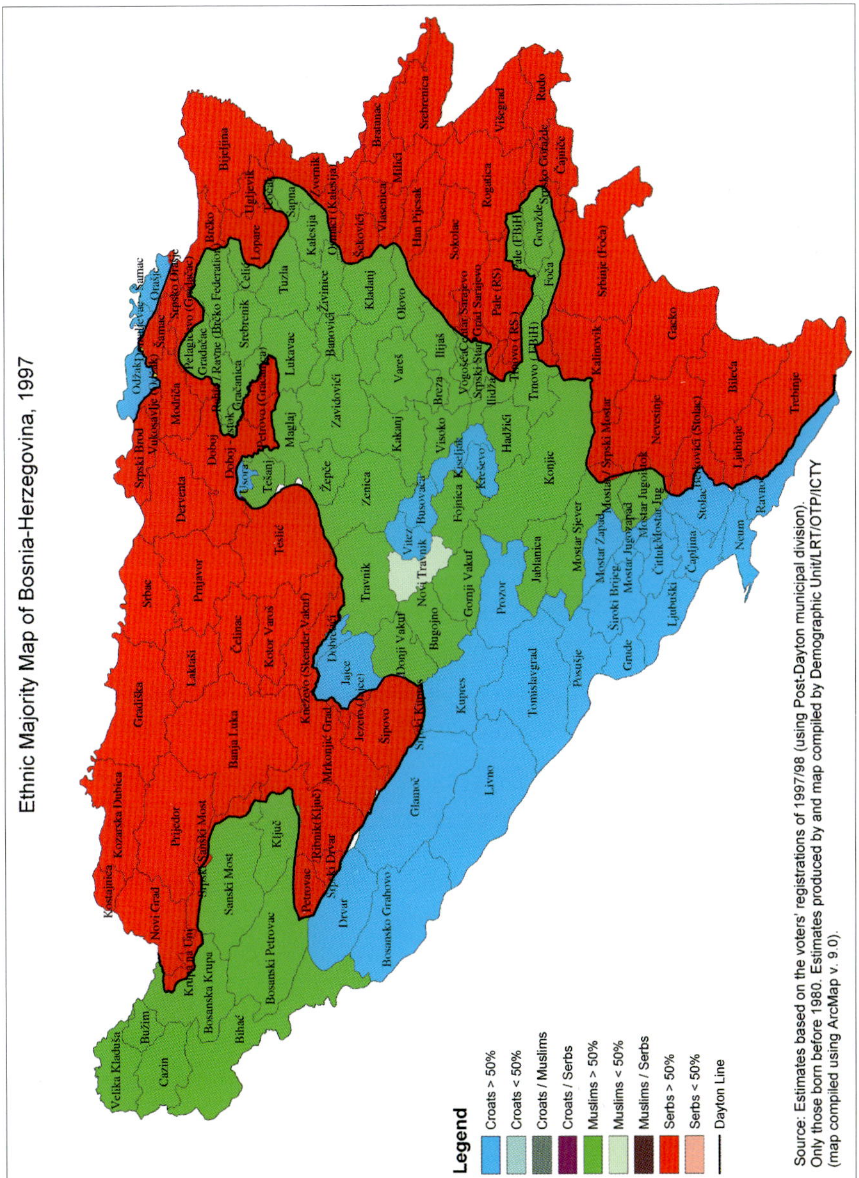

under international control – could be joined along its 300-kilometre eastern border to Serbia proper. Curiously, all international 'peace' agreements sought resolution by ethnic separation, encouraging creation of ethnically homogeneous areas and thus arguably encouraging terrible crimes to be committed, one of which turned out to be genocide. The Serb project survives for another leader to merge Republika Srpska with Serbia, thereby establishing a state for all Serbs and perhaps hegemony for Serbs in the region; something that will have been obtained by releasing the wickedness inherent in man to commit evil acts, such as genocide for a political cause.

Captured in the act of killing
Multi-ethnic Brčko had to be changed to a Serb majority if contiguous Serb territory was to be created (see previous pages, 'Demographers' maps speak'). To this end, Bosnian Muslims and Croats were killed and these killings were horrific. Goran Jelisić – styled or self-styled as the 'Serbian Adolf' – is here shown killing someone, probably from the Muslim leadership of Brčko, after a short police interview. Such photographs often have hidden depths. Note the bodies at the end of the street, previously shot by Jelisić, all due for a form of regular 'milk round' truck collection. Jelisić had been recruited only a few days before and had no background of being anti-Muslim. He was given a gun and a police uniform, and that was enough to make him a mass killer. Immediately after he was put in charge of a warehouse full of detained Muslims, whom he selected to kill at will.

The Skorpions video

To many Serbs the Srebrenica massacre was pure fiction/propaganda – but if not, then a crime of Republika Srpska, not of Serbia itself. The prosecution asserted Serbia was directly responsible by charging Milošević as President of Serbia with genocide at Srebrenica and elsewhere. These horrifying images are from an extract of a long video taken by and of the Skorpions, a Serbian paramilitary unit. They show members of that unit killing very young men – mere boys, in reality – from Srebrenica.

By extraordinary good fortune I was able to play the extract in court during my cross-examination of Obrad Stevanović (a Serbian Police General who should have known of this unit's activities), an exercise requiring meticulous planning to ensure I would not be stopped from showing it. This led to the whole tape being played immediately on Serbian television, reversing overnight Serb opinion about the Srebrenica massacre being a Western lie and demonstrating direct Serbian responsibility.

Mass graves at Brčko
To make Brčko a majority Serb community the district was first isolated from Croatia, its neighbour across the river Sava, by blowing the connecting bridges, killing maybe 100 people. Expulsion and dreadful killings of Croats and Bosniaks followed. These pictures of one of the mass graves may be even more revealing than that of the Jelisić execution (see previous page, 'Captured in the act of killing'). All ethnicities in Brčko, no doubt, had dignified funeral ceremonies; yet these images show bodies of the dead – individuals unknown to the truck drivers who dumped them in the mass graves – dehumanised in death as at the moment they were killed.

Exhumation of the bodies

The mass graves – a short distance from a petrol station and within sight of blocks of flats – were dug, filled with bodies and then had the masonry of mosques – representative of the faith of those killed – dumped on top. Yet when investigators sought to find the graves no one would say where they were. Investigators found them by searching for the tell-tale markers (trees and lampposts) shown in the photographs. The conflict had silenced all inhabitants of this cultured town into coadjutors of mass crime.

Examining the Račak massacre evidence
The Serb massacre of 45 civilians in Račak in Kosovo on 15 January 1999 led to NATO bombing Serbia, Serbia withdrawing from Kosovo and, later, to Kosovo gaining independence. Milošević argued that those killed were Kosovo Liberation Army (KLA) fighters. We had many signed witness statements dated *before* the massacre saying the victims were indeed KLA.

This diagram shows one feature of our analysis. Račak villagers had been herded by Serbs into two houses and then driven to a gully to be killed. But all occupants from Drita Emini's house escaped. Those said to be KLA (green highlight) covered the 22 from Sadik Osmani's house who *were* killed, and only two others. The policeman, Dragan Jasović, forgot that he should have made up statements for all villagers from both houses.

inevitably results in the death of large numbers of civilians, should be subject to punishment for crimes against humanity.'[4]

This radical development would require some states to adapt their respective legislation to this effect, and/or the prosecutors and judges – domestic or international – to adopt such an interpretation of the definition of crimes against humanity.

Ferencz says:

> The precise character of 'other inhumane acts' as crimes against humanity was left to interpretation by courts and judges. The door was deliberately left open to possible inclusion of other unforeseeable major inhumanities that might otherwise have escaped judicial scrutiny. Nuremberg correctly condemned aggression as 'the supreme international crime' because it included all the other crimes. Even if the appellation 'aggression' is not used, the consequences of the illegal use of armed force may be equally reprehensible and should not be allowed to escape criminalization because of nomenclature.[5]

Ferencz approaches the problem of illegal war from two different angles: ratification of the law against aggression and the expansion of the concept of crimes against humanity, each directed at bringing closer the outlawing of war itself, something that always starts with unlawful violence.

On this matter my view has changed over time. The public will label events as genocide that may not match the legal definition and that may never be found to be genocide in courts under the present law. The public can sense or feel a genocide when they experience it or learn about it. They are, I now think, fully entitled to fix the label even if the consequences are sometimes unfortunate. In the long run the view of the public – supported or not by detailed law – may be more important.

THE LAW AND SREBRENICA

This background brings us to the law that applies to Srebrenica. The relevant modern law, from the ICC Statute, includes:

> For the purpose of this Statute, 'crime of aggression' means the planning, preparation, initiation or execution, by a person in a position effectively to exercise control over or to direct the political or military action of a State, of an act of aggression which, by its character, gravity and scale, constitutes a manifest violation of the Charter of the United Nations.[6]

The words of such statutes can be argued over by lawyers and judges. But the broad and essential contours are very clear. For *any* crime you have to know what you are doing and what the likely outcome may be. For genocide that additional element, the 'intent to destroy, in whole or in part, a national, ethnical, racial or religious group, as such', has to be proved.

Intention features regularly enough in countries like ours and in terms to similar effect in the laws of countries subject to other criminal codes. In the UK, for example, rungs on the ladder of assault crimes from 'common assault' to 'assault occasioning actual bodily harm' to 'wounding' to 'wounding with intent to wound or cause serious bodily harm' each require different mental states. At the top, for example, the intent to be proved is that the defendant really intended to wound or cause serious bodily harm. These distinctions are not difficult to understand.

In genocide, once the concept and the intent are understood, complexities of all kinds can be imagined. President A of country X leads Field Marshal B, General C and General D, brigadiers, colonels, majors, captains, lieutenants, NCOs and privates. In their conduct of a battle against the armed force of country Y they might all obey the laws of war and take care of prisoners and civilians. Or they might all be fuelled with genocidal intent and slaughter the wholly innocent. But what if A and B want to conduct the war properly as does General C but General D is filled with genocidal intent toward citizens of Y? Does his intention – reflected in orders he may issue – characterise his part of the battle? What about if people further down the chain of command have genocidal intent and he does nothing to stop them? What about if the worthy General C has subordinates who harbour genocidal intent and he does nothing about it? And suppose an international body hints to A that blind eyes will be turned to whatever is done in the interests of seeing the conflict over and some controversial map sorted out.[7]

Suppose A tells B who thinks things will be over quicker with D in charge (A guessing and B knowing or believing D has genocidal intent that will speed the process) and sends C on leave, who reckons he is being got out of the way for D to do his worst. May A, B or C now be caught?

Identifying who bears criminal responsibility for Srebrenica has taken a very long time, partly because it has been necessary – in trial after trial – to explore the intent of individuals and of the state of Serbia and to unravel exactly this kind of difficulty. This would not have happened to the same extent had it only been possible to charge events as crimes against humanity or war crimes. The time taken to explore genocide at many trials may not have served the victims well, but if the victim and the bystander are entitled – as I believe they are – to say or have said on their behalf 'this was a genocide' then such a consequence will follow and may have to be accepted.

Establishing proof

The facts about Srebrenica were known very early. I found an article printed in the *New York Times* on 29 October 1995[8] – 3½ months after the start of the killing – and like other papers and news media it was able to set out in great detail what had happened. How much more evidence of barbarity / vandalism / genocide does one need? What should we have done when a full story was available so soon after the event was over? Unhappily, court processes do not allow sensible short cuts through use of contemporaneous journalism, reliable though it may be. The proof process had to start afresh; evidence had to be gathered to prove this difficult and perhaps problematic crime.

As Nevenka Tromp explained[9] there are some eight steps to proof of genocide – as articulated by Gregory H. Stenton – which are very helpful for understanding the genocidal process:

1. Classification,
2. Symbolisation,
3. Dehumanisation,
4. Organisation,
5. Polarisation,
6. Preparation,
7. Extermination,
8. Denial.[10]

It was important to make a distinction between the evidence of genocidal process before, during and after the Srebrenica take-over and there was, as we discovered, evidence of each of these eight stages for the Srebrenica massacre.[11]

Investigating in accordance with norms of a legal process led us to evidence from many sources: large parts of the evidence came from the open sources; some evidence was created for the purposes of the trial from primary source material (by the ICTY's Office of the Prosecutor's [OTP's] demographic unit, for example, that researched electoral rolls and censuses to confirm or establish ethnic cleansing); some documents were seized by the OTP's investigators from state archives; some documents were received from states, notably Serbia, following requests or 'compulsory' court process. Regrettably for the value of ICTY trials as overall components of a reliable history of this massacre, and to be contrasted with the Nuremberg trials, many critically important documents have not yet surfaced despite certainty as to their existence. At Nuremberg the prosecutors had keys to all the cupboards of documents, which allowed the trials to be efficient and short, and even boring – for much of the time the Nuremberg public gallery was half empty.

Nevertheless, there was a mass of available, significant evidence. All of it fitted a picture of genocide. None of it detracted from that picture. As but one detail, there was no Serb general rising from a table to dissociate himself from an unlawful attack, although there was *some* evidence of disaffection of officers being paid by Serbia for what they were asked to do. The genocidal process initiated at the very top that always needs to carry subordinates with it had worked. The 8,000 dead from Srebrenica died from a killing machine that was turned to a purpose. To very many people the purpose was absolutely clear.[12]

The plight of victims

The Mothers of Srebrenica and other victim groups have received almost no compensation for the loss of their fathers, husbands, brothers or sons, even if they were financially dependent on them at the time they were killed. The UN has no compensation fund for them despite the President of the ICTY (Judge Robinson) pleading for one. Individual offenders have never been pursued for compensation. One political entity that *should* be held responsible – the Republika Srpska – is part of the Bosniaks' own state of Bosnia–Herzegovina (of which they are a component group along with Serbs and Croats) by dint of the Dayton Accords and, therefore, cannot be pursued.

Reaction by victims was initially positive to those ICTY judgments, including to the findings of genocide. Over time they became negative about the length of trials and about 'excessive' rights of accused where there seemed to be no parallel rights for victims. The pomp of Western-style justice was initially accepted, but probably no longer. Several witnesses have told me in recent years that they would not now be willing to give evidence. Convicted prisoners of early trials being freed to live cheek by jowl with victims before the tribunal finished its trials of Karadžić and Mladić was unacceptable to many. The 2004 deadline date for indictments, meaning that offenders not charged by then have nothing to fear from the tribunal and can act in their home environment with apparent impunity, causes bitterness and distress.

THE SERBIAN STATE ESCAPING A FINDING OF RESPONSIBILITY

Most disappointing of all for victims and bereaved was the case brought against Serbia proper at the International Court of Justice that resulted in a judgment that Serbia was *not* directly responsible for the genocide – accepted as having happened – and could only be held responsible for failing to stop the genocide after a certain late date in the killing and for failing to hand Mladić over to the ICTY.

The ICJ concluded that the acts committed at Srebrenica falling within Article II (a) and (b) of the Genocide Convention were committed with the specific intent to destroy in part the group of Muslims of Bosnia–Herzegovina as such and accordingly that these were acts of genocide, committed by members of the Bosnian Serb army – the VRS – in and around Srebrenica from about 13 July 1995. However, the VRS was found to be operating separately from the army of Serbia proper.

The finding, so disappointing to Bosniaks in Bosnia and to many others, turned on the failure of Bosnia to prove that Serbia was sufficiently in control of the VRS, despite paying and pensioning its officers at two or three times the standard rate because they were fighting in the war in Bosnia. The Skorpion paramilitary group, videoed in the very act of killing Srebrenica victims and answerable to Belgrade, was – said the court – not shown to be an 'organ' of Serbia as defined. And when it came to compensation for the proven failure to do enough to stop genocide and the failure to hand over Mladić[13] there would be no compensation because it was only so late in the day that Serbia's limited culpability was established.

However, the then vice-president of that court, Judge Awn Shawkat Al-Khasawneh, dissented on the grounds that Serbia's involvement, as a principal actor or accomplice, in the genocide that took place in Srebrenica, was supported by massive and compelling evidence. He disagreed with the Court's methodology for appreciating the facts and drawing inferences therefrom:

> … the Court has refused to infer genocidal intent from the consistent pattern of conduct in Bosnia and Herzegovina. In its reasoning, the Court relies heavily on several arguments, each of which is inadequate for the purpose, and contradictory to the consistent jurisprudence of the international criminal tribunals.[14]

Marlise Simons of the *New York Times*, a seasoned reporter on the ICTY, has explained how confidentiality rules to protect 'national security interests' have often been invoked at the tribunal.[15] In the Bosnia–Serbia case, as Judge Al-Khasawneh made clear, the court's failure to obtain the best evidence on confidentiality grounds was a matter of profound criticism. Another judge of the court, Ahmed Mahiou of Algeria, joined Al-Khasawneh to an extent in expressing his concern that in failing to obtain best evidence the majority of the court demonstrated a fear of being seen to 'take sides' or to intrude on the sovereignty of a state.

Simons suggested from her researches that had documents seen by the ICJ been freed from the redactions imposed at the ICTY they might have demonstrated that VRS forces were indeed agents of Serbia; she also reported that Nataša Kandić, the director of the Humanitarian Law Centre in Belgrade, said, 'It was well known in the Serbian government that the archives spelled out the responsibility of the state.'

With the vice-president of the world's court at complete odds with the majority and with another member unable to understand why the court declined to seek available evidence for fear of causing itself embarrassment, why should the victims respect the law that much, why should they not follow their own judgment in their use of the word Lemkin made available to them?

When I delivered my lecture in 2015 I drew the following conclusions:

> If they do apply the term 'genocide' and if they want the term to 'stick', other responsibilities follow because, as I explained [previously], law can be used and abused to write or rewrite history. It remains possible – just – for a successor Bosnian government to seek revision of the unsatisfactory judgment that causes Bosniaks so much dissatisfaction and unhappiness. If the Bosnian government does not even try then the words of the majority of the judges, however wrong, may prevail, impossible ever to correct, even by future historians. Today's Bosnians should not seek reasons *not* to try to put the ICJ judgment right – for example, because both Serbia and Croatia failed in their tit-for-tat applications to the same court for genocide verdicts against each other. They should recognise that the Bosnian case for genocide against Serbia is perhaps the strongest of any genocide allegations arising from the conflicts in the former Yugoslavia,[16] and that it should honour its dead and its living by seeking to correct a record that may be wrong.

This is where my lecture ended. Unfortunately subsequent events proved disappointing.

Eventually, far too late in the day for anything to be achieved, Bosnia sought in February 2017 to make an application for revision of the judgment. It was rejected almost immediately on procedural grounds. There is little or no prospect of the 2007 judgment ever now being revisited by the ICJ.[17]

The near certainty that there is no prospect of the ICJ judgment *ever* being revised, despite many being firmly of the view that it should have been, shows how court processes that do not work satisfactorily bring risks – unintended consequences, maybe – that can harm the very people laws and legal systems are established to protect. In this case, the victims of Srebrenica are going to feel disappointed with the law until the ends of their lives. But those – either now, or in decades or centuries to come – who may wish to manipulate the historical record in favour of a Serb narrative detached from the truth in order to achieve some as yet unforeseen political objective have little or nothing from the judges of the world's top court standing in their way.

Chapter 13

Gaza–Israel: The Legal and the Military View

Commentators have usually assumed the Israel–Palestine armed conflict might be lawful, but may the conflict lack legality altogether? The 2014 Israeli–Gaza conflict that lasted some 52 days allows a way to explore some of the underlying issues of the overall conflict. Were war crimes committed by either side?

With General Sir Nick Parker

Original lecture delivered on 7 October 2015.

In 52 days of the summer of 2014 there was an armed conflict – a war – between Israel and the Palestinians of Gaza, known by Israel as Operation 'Protective Edge'. The death toll was estimated at 67 Israeli military and 6 Israeli civilians; the Gaza total was some 2,251 dead, of whom 1,462 have been identified as civilians, including 551 children.[1]

When Operation 'Protective Edge' was under way I was asked if I could make a presentation about war crimes committed in the conflict. I assembled a multidisciplinary team[2] to investigate how the issue would be approached. Three of us got into Gaza later in the year to see for ourselves what there was of the conflict left to see. One of our number had been in Jerusalem as the conflict was in progress. All of us bar one were newcomers to this particular conflict and brought, we hoped, eyes and ears unaffected by emotion, prejudice, predisposition and so on. The historian Professor Avi Shlaim had well-formed views about the question, and for that reason we turned to him for matters of history but tried to form our own opinions on war crimes independently of his. To do our task properly required expertise in law, political science and military matters, but not to any especially great level of sophistication for our purposes: laws by which we regulate ourselves need to be understandable by the reasonably well-informed citizen.

HISTORY

Some knowledge of relevant history is crucial to an understanding of how any armed conflict arose and of the mental state of possible offenders; but the history cannot alone excuse criminality on either side. Once in a conflict, lawfulness of military actions is judged objectively according to the then present reality. By analogy, two men may get into a fistfight because one has wronged the other dreadfully and for a very long time. Once in the fight this 'victim' is subject to the law and has no excuse for a criminal assault, for manslaughter or murder. His being wronged cannot save him from the force of law. It is much the same for states at war.

Thousands of years of expulsion, oppression and persecution of the Jewish people led to the formation of a Jewish diaspora that enabled Jews to maintain their identity. At the end of the 19th century the vision of a state where Jews could be the majority took hold in many Jewish communities. Creation of Israel as a state was supported by the British government in the Balfour Declaration of 1918, which quoted the decision of a British Cabinet meeting of 31 October 1917:

> His Majesty's Government view with favour the establishment in Palestine of a national home for the Jewish people, and will use their best endeavours to facilitate the achievement of this object, it being clearly understood that nothing shall be done which may prejudice the civil and religious rights of existing non-Jewish communities in Palestine …

The declaration was accepted by the League of Nations in 1922 and embodied in the mandate that gave Great Britain temporary administrative control of Palestine, which lasted from 1922 until 1948.

Professor Avi Shlaim explains how Ze'ev Jabotinsky demanded that the mainstream Zionist movement recognise as its stated objective the establishment of a Jewish state on both banks of the Jordan River. In 1923 Jabotinsky published an article 'On the Iron Wall (We and the Arabs)' in which he argued that no nation in history ever agreed voluntarily to make way for another people to come and create a state on its land, and that Palestinian resistance to a Jewish state was an inescapable fact. The only way to realise the Zionist project of an independent Jewish state in Palestine was unilaterally and by military force. The Arabs would eventually give up any hope of overpowering the Zionists, and only then would the time come for stage two, negotiating with the leaders of the Palestine Arabs about their rights and status. Professor Shlaim suggests, as his personal opinion, that Jabotinsky was the spiritual father of the Israeli right whose influence continues until today, and that the 'Iron Wall' became the national strategy for dealing with the Arabs from the 1930s onwards.

In 1947 the United Nations proposed a partition. In 1948 David Ben-Gurion proclaimed the establishment of the State of Israel and the US recognised the new nation the same day. Israel as a state was thus imposed on and within Palestine in 1948 starting, as Dr Nevenka Tromp suggests, an as yet unfinished state project because the territorial ambitions of Israel were not satisfied. Wars with Arab neighbours followed, all of which Israel won comprehensively until the second Lebanon War of 2006. Maps show what offers of territory Palestinian Arabs refused in succession as they lost wars while Israel grew in size.

The Gaza Strip is 40 km long and 10 km wide and is home to more than 1.5 million Palestinians. The shape of the territory was defined by the armistice line that followed the creation of Israel in 1948 and the subsequent war between the Israeli and Arab armies. Egypt administered the Strip for the first 19 years, but Israel captured it during the 1967 Arab–Israeli War, when it took the Sinai Peninsula, the West Bank and the Golan Heights. The 1967 War encouraged a revival of the idea of a 'Greater Israel', envisaged by the founder of Zionism, Theodor Herzl, as extending 'from the Brook of Egypt to the Euphrates'.[3] After 1967 Israel ruled the Palestinian territories as an occupying and colonial power. The main objective was to keep the occupied territories under control and to expand the Jewish population to the occupying territories by establishing settlements. The 'Greater Israel' ideology excluded any possibility of national self-determination of the Palestinian nation, and in peace negotiations from 1967 to 1993 a two-state solution never featured as an option for the Israeli side.

Between 1993 and 2000 the Oslo Peace Process reflected Israeli Prime Minister Yitzhak Rabin's initiative in moving on the Palestinian front from stage one, the building of military power, to stage two, serious negotiations. Critical to the architecture of Oslo, Professor Shlaim notes, was the notion of gradualism. The Oslo text did not address any of the key issues in this dispute: Jerusalem; the right of return of the 1948 Palestinian refugees; the status of the Jewish settlements built on occupied Palestinian land; or the borders of the Palestinian entity. All these 'permanent status' issues were deferred for negotiation towards the end of the five-year transition period. Basically, this was a modest experiment in Palestinian self-government. The text did not promise or even mention an independent Palestinian state at the end of the transition period. The Palestinians believed that in return for giving up their claim to 78 per cent of Mandated Palestine, they would gain an independent state in the remaining 22 per cent with a capital city in Jerusalem. They were to be bitterly disappointed.

In 1995 Rabin was assassinated by a Jewish fanatic at a peace rally and in 2000 the Oslo peace process broke down following the failure of the Camp David summit and the outbreak of the second *intifada*. Israelis claim that the Palestinians were responsible for the breakdown of the peace process because they made a choice to return to violence and, consequently, there was no Palestinian partner for peace. Palestinian violence was indeed a contributory factor to the breakdown but not, according to Professor Shlaim, the main cause. The fundamental reason, he maintains, was that Israel reneged on its side of the deal following Rabin's assassination.[4]

GREATER ISRAEL IDEOLOGY AND BENJAMIN NETANYAHU

Benjamin Netanyahu, prime minister during 'Protective Edge' and now, was elected leader of the Likud Party in 1993. In the same year he published a book seemingly inspired by the teaching both of Jabotinsky and Netanyahu's father, the historian Benzion Netanyahu, who had been an adviser to Jabotinsky. The central element in Benjamin Netanyahu's worldview was the right of the Jewish people to the whole Land of Israel. In his book he denied that the Palestinians had a right to national self-determination.[5] Netanyahu and his even more extreme religious–nationalist partners believe that only Jews have historical rights over what they call 'Judea and Samaria'. Their policy is the expansion of Jewish settlements on the West Bank and the accelerated Judaisation of East Jerusalem. Likud is an ideological party which upholds the right of the Jewish people to the whole 'Land of Israel'.[6] In line with this view, it is opposed to partition and explicitly rejects the idea of an independent Palestinian state alongside Israel.[7]

HAMAS

With the collapse of the Oslo peace process and Israel's determination to keep Palestinians outside any power-sharing schemes, Hamas, the Islamic resistance movement, emerged as a new political force. Hamas conducted an effective campaign to drive the Israelis out of Gaza. In August 2005 a Likud government headed by Ariel Sharon effected a unilateral Israeli pull-out from Gaza, withdrawing all 8,000 settlers and destroying the houses that they had left behind. The withdrawal was a victory for Hamas and a humiliation for the

Israel Defense Forces (IDF). Sharon presented the move as a contribution to peace based on a two-state solution. In the year after the withdrawal, however, another 12,000 Israelis settled on the West Bank, further reducing the scope for an independent and territorially contiguous Palestinian state.

In January 2006 elections were held in the West Bank and Gaza, and Hamas unexpectedly won a decisive victory over Fatah. Numerous international observers confirmed that the elections had been both peaceful and orderly.[8] Israel refused to recognise the new government; the US and the European Union followed Israel's lead. Israel resorted to withholding tax revenues while its Western allies suspended direct aid to the Hamas-led Palestinian Authority (PA).

The 'Palestine Papers', a cache of 1,600 diplomatic documents of the Israel–PA negotiations leaked to the Al Jazeera news agency, revealed how Israel and America armed and trained the security forces of President Mahmoud Abbas with the aim of overthrowing Hamas.[9] American neoconservatives participated in a plot to instigate a Palestinian civil war. Hamas pre-empted a Fatah coup with a violent seizure of power in Gaza in June 2007. At this point the Palestinian national movement became fractured, with Fatah ruling the West Bank and Hamas ruling the Gaza Strip.

Israel responded to the Hamas move by declaring the Gaza Strip a 'hostile territory'. It enacted a series of social, economic and military measures designed to isolate and undermine Hamas. By far the most significant of these measures was the imposition in 2007 of a blockade. The stated purpose of the blockade was to stop the transfer of weapons and military equipment to Hamas but it also restricted the flow of food, fuel and medical supplies to the civilian population.

Punitive expeditions in Gaza

From February 2008 there were four major attacks on Gaza, military incursions reflecting the new Israeli government policy of containment of Gaza – some would say by creating an 'open prison'.

On 27 December 2008 the IDF launched a massive air attack on Gaza, followed by a ground invasion on 3 January 2009. In the 22 days of Operation 'Cast Lead' Israel suffered 13 dead and the Gazans 1,417 dead, including 313 children, and more than 5,500 wounded. The UN Human Rights Council established a commission under Richard Goldstone. In the opinion of Goldstone and his colleagues, the grave breaches of the Fourth Geneva Convention committed by the Israeli armed forces in Gaza gave rise to individual criminal responsibility. They recommended that the UN Human Rights Council should formally submit their report to the Prosecutor of the International Criminal Court. But joint Israeli–American pressure on the Palestinian Authority and at the UN ensured that no further action was taken.

In March 2009 Netanyahu returned as prime minister at the first elections held after 'Cast Lead'. Professor Shlaim concludes that violence is the defining characteristic of the Netanyahu government's approach to Hamas. Like its predecessors it shunned diplomacy and relied heavily on brute military force. In doing so it missed one opportunity after another to end the cycle of violence.

Israel broke the informal ceasefire to launch Operation 'Pillar of Defence', its second major military operation against Gaza following disengagement. In eight days of intense aerial bombardment in December 2012, 132 Palestinians were killed. The operation ended with a ceasefire brokered by Egypt. This specified that Israel and the Palestinian factions would stop all hostilities and that Israel would open the border crossings to allow the movement of people and the transfer of goods.

The sequel is described by Nathan Thrall of the International Crisis Group:

> During the three months that followed the ceasefire, Shin Bet [the Israeli security service] recorded only a single attack ... Israeli officials were impressed. But they convinced themselves that the quiet on Gaza's border was primarily the result of Israeli deterrence and Palestinian self-interest. Israel therefore saw little incentive in upholding its end of the deal ... The end of the closure never came. Crossings were repeatedly shut ... Imports declined, exports were blocked, and fewer Gazans were given exit permits to Israel and the West Bank ... The lesson for Hamas was clear. Even if an agreement was brokered by the US and Egypt, Israel could still fail to honour it.[10]

THE BEGINNINGS OF OPERATION 'PROTECTIVE EDGE'

One of the important factors in Israeli politics was to keep Fatah and Hamas hostile to each other. In April 2014 a breakthrough happened between Fatah and Hamas and they formed a unity government. The unity government was remarkably moderate both in its composition and in its policies. To escape isolation and bankruptcy, Hamas handed over power to the Fatah-dominated, pro-Western Palestinian Authority in West Bank Ramallah. The unity government explicitly accepted the three conditions of the Quartet (the US, Russia, the UN and the EU) for receiving Western aid: recognition of Israel; respect for past agreements; and renunciation of violence.

Israel showed nervousness at this new unity by hostile propaganda that was then followed by economic measures and a military assault on Gaza on 8 July 2014. It seems that Netanyahu's government may have been waiting for an excuse to start a punitive expedition, and the opportunity came with the abduction of three Israeli teenagers in the West Bank. Netanyahu stated that Hamas was responsible,[11] but was not able to produce any evidence. The murder was possibly / probably committed by a lone cell without the knowledge of the Hamas leadership. The Israeli authorities knew that the teenagers were killed soon after their abduction but they did not announce the death until 18 days later.

The intervening period was used to launch a powerful, worldwide propaganda offensive to denounce Hamas. At the same time, the IDF initiated Operation 'Brother's Keeper', ostensibly to search for the teenagers but in reality to deal a body blow to Hamas. Some 350 Palestinians were arrested, including nearly all of Hamas's leaders on the West Bank. Netanyahu seemed to see an opportunity to destabilise the newly established unity government and to undermine President Mahmoud Abbas. Rising to the challenge, perhaps reluctantly, Hamas responded with rockets.[12] The sequence of events clearly suggests that the terrible and wickedly criminal murder of the three Israeli teenagers became the pretext, but may not have been the cause, for the next onslaught on Gaza.

Covert and overt war aims

There was then a desire to punish the people of Gaza for electing Hamas and for continuing to support it in defiance of Israel's repeated warnings. Related to this was the irresistible urge to display

Israel's raw military power.[13] The overriding aim, however, was to defeat the struggle for Palestinian independence, to maintain the colonial *status quo*, and to preserve Israel's position as the imperial overlord. Israel portrayed the attack as an act of self-defence in response to Hamas rockets launched against its civilian population.

Professor Shlaim notes how official war aims for 'Protective Edge' kept changing. First, the stated aim was to halt the rocket and mortar attacks from Gaza; then it was to destroy the 'terror tunnels' that Hamas had dug under the border to launch raids inside Israeli territory; and subsequently it was said that war would continue until Hamas was completely disarmed.[14]

INTERNATIONAL HUMANITARIAN LAW AND DEFENCE OF A STATE

Rodney Dixon[15] explains that whether or not an armed conflict is lawful, it must be conducted in accordance with international humanitarian law. For Israel's attack on Gaza these issues need to be considered:

- Were there legitimate military objectives (rockets, tunnels, etc.)?
- Were civilians directly targeted?
- Were the military operations excessive and disproportionate in the circumstances?
- Could other methods have been used?

The terms 'proportionate' and 'disproportionate' regularly feature in discourse on war crimes. These terms do not appear in the Conventions or Protocols but in the authoritative International Committee of the Red Cross (ICRC) Commentaries drawn from Protocols Additional to the Geneva Convention of 1949. Protocol 1, Article 51, on Indiscriminate Attacks includes its definition of an unlawful indiscriminate attack:

> … an attack which may be expected to cause incidental loss of civilian life, injury to civilians, damage to civilian objects, or a combination thereof, which would be excessive in relation to the concrete and direct military advantage anticipated.

Protocol 1, Article 57, on Precautions in Attack states:

> 1. In the conduct of military operations, constant care shall be taken to spare the civilian population, civilians and civilian objects …
>
> 2b. … an attack shall be cancelled or suspended if it becomes apparent that the objective is not a military one or is subject to special protection or that the attack may be expected to cause incidental loss of civilian life, injury to civilians, damage to civilian objects, or a combination thereof, which would be excessive in relation to the concrete and direct military advantage anticipated.

Thus, when 'proportionality' is invoked, the test to be considered is whether civilian loss of all kinds is excessive in relation to concrete and direct military advantage. Further, at each level of command – strategic, operational, tactical – the combatant authority has to take all reasonable and necessary steps to prevent crimes and make sure they do not reoccur.

Dixon explains the basic position in law about defence of a state:

> A State is entitled, in general, to use force in self-defence if it is attacked … The State under attack must establish that its use of force is 'necessary' in order to defend itself from the attack and the actions taken must be 'proportionate' in repelling the attack. The International Court of Justice has held that in considering these requirements a State cannot rely on its subjective assessment … the State concerned must also comply with the laws applicable to the conduct of hostilities, in particular the clear protections afforded civilians.[16]

Whether a state's actions in purporting to defend itself against the threat or use of force are lawful will turn on an objective assessment of whether these actions were strictly necessary and proportionate to repel the threat. Even if the threat was absolutely genuine, it would still need to be established that the defensive measures were necessary to counter the threat and were appropriately tailored specifically to address this threat and no more. In the event that the threat was not genuine, but the state nevertheless believed it was under attack, this belief alone would not be a sufficient basis to find that the state had acted lawfully in self-defence.

If the legal requirements for self-defence are not met, the whole attack is rendered unlawful, making the state and those who planned and directed the attack responsible for breaching the UN Charter and international law. Such action could be regarded as an illegitimate use of force or an aggressive war that amounts to a crime under international law. Crimes against peace were described by the Nuremberg Tribunal as 'the supreme international crime'.

SIX INCIDENTS

As Operation 'Protective Edge' was under way an investigator in Gaza was able to inquire into some incidents, selected in discussion with me for specific consideration. We were able to begin to think how the law *might* apply to these incidents. The incidents were as follows, described with the assistance of General Sir Nick Parker.

Boys on the beach

On 16 July 2014 Ahed Bakr lost a son, a grandson and two nephews to precision missile strikes fired by the IDF. The dead children ranged from nine to twelve years of age and had been playing on the beach when a first missile struck, killing one boy. The remaining boys fled in the direction of a nearby cafe. After just a few moments a second missile struck, killing three more young boys, injuring two others and partially eviscerating a young man who had gone to their aid.

The IDF initially stated they had fired upon a Hamas target and then at fleeing fighters. They then retracted this account, announcing that a criminal investigation had been ordered. It is difficult to assess the validity of the target without knowing precisely what surveillance systems were being employed and what deductions were made at the time. This has all the hallmarks of a tragic mistake. It was not unintentional, however, since at least two rounds were fired at separate but related targets.

In June 2015 an internal IDF investigation was terminated, without any charges brought, on grounds that the beach on which the boys were playing had been used by Hamas fighters to launch rockets at Israel and that the attack was not, *according to the assessment of the operational entities*, expected to result in any collateral damage to civilians or to civilian property.[17]

Khuza'a white flag shooting

This incident took place during the close combat phase of the ground offensive. A civilian waving a white flag exposed himself to ground troops and was shot and killed. Members of his family were then used to gather tactical intelligence and provide protection to the attackers.

The Alwafa hospital

The Alwafa hospital was Gaza's only rehabilitation hospital caring for the long-term sick. On 11 July the hospital's upper floors were hit by four or five heavy weapon rounds. The director had already evacuated the top floors, moving patients to lower floors. On 18 July the hospital received telephone calls from the IDF and ICRC informing them that they must evacuate. Staff and patients were subjected to artillery bombardment throughout the evacuation. Fortunately, no one was injured or killed.

On 22 July the hospital was razed to the ground by a number of airstrikes. The IDF released a video claiming that small-arms fire was coming from the hospital, and that tunnel entrances existed nearby. It was alleged that Hamas fighters were using it as a firing position and a store for missiles. The hospital did occupy a dominating position which directly overlooks the border. It was ideally placed as a defensive position, and it does seem likely that it would be used by Hamas to engage the IDF with small arms, and that as the IDF advanced it would have become increasingly threatening to the attacker.

But the subsequent level of destruction applied to the hospital is significantly greater than any of the buildings around it – all of which offered equally effective firing positions. The initial attack took place six days before the IDF land assault, indicating that the hospital was on the high-level target list. Its systematic destruction seems to have been a deliberate attempt to limit any further use for any purpose without considerable reconstruction effort. A number of other hospitals were targeted during the operation and it is possible that this points to a deliberate policy of reducing the medical capacity within the Strip.

'Knock on the roof' at Jabaliya

In the early hours of 24 July 2014 the Abu Aita family at their home in Tal al-Zaatar in the Jabaliya area of Gaza City were awoken by the crashing of an inert projectile onto the roof of a house immediately behind theirs. The family knew that this was the first of the IDF's 'knock on the roof' warnings, a harbinger of a highly destructive strike to follow a few minutes later.

The family fled to a ground-floor room. A second warning missile struck the house behind them. No more than five minutes after the first warning a third missile struck, destroying the house behind. The blast wave ripped across the narrow street dividing the houses and smashed its way through the Abu Aitas' rear wall. Five family members were killed and nine injured; Mrs Aita was decapitated by the blast.

No one in the target house was harmed. The mission was successful but resulted in 'accidental' collateral damage. It would normally qualify – as with the previous incident – as a tragic mistake if the target was sufficiently important. But in this case the target was a residential building with no apparent military use. The occupants were warned so that they could flee. Any collateral damage, particularly killing innocent civilians, must have been considered. If this practice is intended to deter, some form of assessment should have been made of the risk/benefit between successful engagement of the target and civilian casualties. If the desired effect is not to kill the target it seems odd that any collateral casualties are accepted.

The timing of the attack and its location suggest that it was not an integral part of the main attack's supporting fire-plan. It is likely to have been authorised at a higher level than the tactical battle and delivered by guided missile. It does appear that the principal outcome of this type of attack is intended to be psychological, not physical. The 'knock on the roof' as warning was condemned by the Goldstone report, which examined similar methods used during 'Cast Lead'.

The power station

Over a period of days, IDF missiles targeted the Gaza power-generating plant, gradually degrading its output capability until it was incapable of any form of power generation. Responsible for meeting 40 per cent of Gaza's power needs and normally capable of supplying just under a million people, the power plant was Gaza's only power source, other than domestic generators, not under Israeli control. The destruction of the power plant left Gaza absolutely reliant on power piped into Gaza from Israel.

Brigadier General Yaron Rosen said it was possible the plant had been hit by Israel by mistake. Yet it is hard to concede that a series of carefully targeted attacks was accidental; the authority for targeting will have been at the highest level, as this was not in an area of any interest to the ground troops. This is a tactic that affords Israel greater control over the inhabitants of Gaza; it is presumably part of a higher-level plan to maintain a stranglehold on the area. Since 2007, when Israel initiated the blockade, it has used the supply of gas and electricity as a 'lever' to retaliate against rockets.[18]

UNRWA school

The United Nations Relief and Works Agency (UNRWA) school is a UN complex in the Jabaliya district. Following the IDF assault on the Beit Hanoun area, several thousand displaced people descended upon the complex seeking shelter and safety. In the early hours of 30 July 2014 an extensive artillery bombardment started to strike the area, and a number of rounds hit the school. Within a short time 15 people had been killed and in the region of 140 people injured. The IDF claimed that mortar bombs had been fired from the compound. Witnesses in the compound dispute this vehemently.

The school was behind the front lines and did not overlook them. It would not have been used by snipers, though the playground might have been a convenient site to fire mortars from. However, at the time of the engagement the buildings and open spaces were full of refugees, and this would have been visible to aerial surveillance. The detonations on the school were inside buildings and therefore cannot have been intended to destroy any active mortar positions. This suggests that the authority for engagement was at a higher level than the attacking brigades. There is also evidence of the use of 155-mm artillery ammunition on this target, indicating a complete disregard of the risk of civilian casualties.

***

General Sir Nick Parker's Presentation

THE MILITARY VIEW

My study of tactics used by the IDF during Operation 'Protective Edge' has allowed me to draw conclusions on their legitimacy from a military perspective. Initially the focus was around six incidents (summarised above) and which it was felt should be examined to identify possible illegal military activity. I am not going to go into the detail of the incidents because, even though my comments have been informed by this investigation, I have concentrated on the broader deductions. You should also note that I have had no access to secret material and my account has only been informed by open-source material.

It is important when assessing why military actions are taken to examine the facts at a number of levels. There will be a grand strategic 'narrative' which has considerable influence. It will clearly set the baseline for the development of a national security strategy, but it will also work its way into doctrine, be discussed in training colleges and play its part in establishing the cultural approach of the armed forces. Inside a military organisation the 'chain of command' will exercise influence through the general tenor and conduct of leaders, through the detailed direction given by policy and through the tone of specific orders given to complete tasks. And then at the coal face instinctive reactions will be conditioned by perceptions of the threat and the amount of freedom given to act.

THE STRATEGIC CONTEXT

There is a considerable weight of evidence to indicate that the Israeli state considers itself to be constantly under a military threat. There have been many statements from Israeli political and military leaders expressing the view that the defence of Israel is a matter of national survival, with threats from every neighbour, from hostile states with the capacity to fire missiles, from a possible Iranian nuclear capability and from global terrorism. There is also evidence to show that Israel does not believe that it has the capacity to 'defend in depth', where the defender can choose ground that is most suitable for defence, lure the attacker in and then use secondary manoeuvre to outflank and defeat the incursion. It is therefore understandable from a military perspective why Israel's defensive posture appears to be to pre-empt and/or deter since it cannot afford to yield ground. Indeed, this may also lead to Israeli tactical military objectives favouring the proactive seizure of land in order to provide a strong political bargaining position.

Contemporary statements that reflect this approach include Benjamin Netanyahu's address to the 2014 UN General Assembly. In this he emphasised the threats to his country from anti-Semitism, militant Islam and Iranian nuclear power, and he highlighted his responsibility as prime minister of Israel in a very uncompromising tone that has clearly had an impact on the attitudes of military leaders and on the behaviour of individual soldiers.

Focusing on Gaza for a moment, it might be concluded that there is a deliberate Israeli policy to encourage the vilification of the Palestinians living there. The expansion of settlements, such as Sderot, close to the border, sustained by a new railway on which local residents can travel for free, suggests that the government encourages its people to live under the threat of rockets. They clearly recognise that the Hamas capability is very limited, their counter-measures are effective, and the risk to the population is very low. But the external message is very different.

THE PALESTINIAN PERSPECTIVE

The Palestinians are restricted to a narrow strip of land that cannot sustain its large population[19] and relies on life support through Israel. The flow of fuel, food, medicines and machinery are all regulated. Only 40 per cent of electricity can be generated within the Strip, and only a proportion of their food consumption. All fuel has to be imported. People are concentrated into small areas, and the population density in Gaza City is rated as the fifth-highest in the world. There are also constraints from the sea: the fishing limit has been reduced incrementally and is now 3 miles.

The capacity to generate military capability within the Gaza Strip is limited, although motivation is high. There are a number of armed groups, loosely referred to as Hamas although they are not all controlled by a single chain of command. Their main offensive weapons are rockets, which have deadly capability although they are unsophisticated and have limited range and guidance systems. The threat they pose will have an impact on the lives of those living in Israel within range, although the evidence on the ground was that it was not materially significant. The armed groups have a capacity to make limited incursions into Israel on foot, using tunnels; it is possible that this could result in kidnap, small-arms attacks or suicide bombs. To defend Gaza the principal weapons in use are small arms and mines/improvised explosive devices. There are rudimentary and fluid command and control systems, and it is hard to identify well-established command and control locations.

The operations in Gaza have to be considered in the context of its historical importance. The territory occupied by Palestinians after the 1967 War was largely a home for refugees displaced from other parts of the Holy Land.[20] Since its withdrawal from Gaza in 2005, Israel's approach to security has had to be based on containment rather than internal security. But Israel still bears the responsibilities of an occupying power, controlling all borders bar one, and all resources entering the area. Perceptions within Israel are that Hamas is not just resisting the siege, but also has the objective of the destruction of Israel.

THE ISRAEL DEFENSE FORCES

The IDF is a standing force designed to protect the Israeli state.[21] It is the sixth-highest global military spender with 176,500 active and 445,000 reserve personnel, and has the second-highest spending per capita after the US. It depends on reserves to conduct operations, and this means that there will be a planning lead time for any major engagement. Its mission is to 'defend the existence, territorial integrity and sovereignty of the state of Israel' and to 'protect the inhabitants of Israel and to combat all forms of terrorism which threaten daily life'.[22] The overarching ethics of the IDF are consistent with the requirements of any military force, although there is an emphasis on the defence of the state and the traditions of the Jewish people.

Operational planning and execution

There is no credible tactical, territorial military threat to Israel from Gaza. Armed groups are restricted to the use of rockets that are manufactured within the Strip, or possibly smuggled through tunnels, and the deployment of lightly armed infantry who have the capacity for limited infiltration. These are largely contained by border and movement control, although Hamas has constructed military tunnels to enable communications and conduct raids. The rocket threat from Gaza has triggered extensive defensive measures within Israel and an effective anti-missile defence system ('Iron Dome'). The rocket attacks' impact is psychological.

Hamas and other fighters are hard to distinguish from the civilian population, in part because they choose to be, and in part because the area is so densely populated that it is impossible to delineate a 'combat' zone. The normal distinction between front lines and the 'rear area' where civilians and support functions can exist in relative safely is not evident in Gaza; the whole area is a battle zone. In these circumstances, where there is so little tactical depth, it is almost impossible for Hamas not to appear to use civilians as a shield. The size of Hamas's military capability is difficult to determine, but may amount to around 10,000 fighters.

THE FOUR STAGES OF OPERATION 'PROTECTIVE EDGE'

The IDF occupies the key terrain, particularly over the northern half of the Strip where Israeli positions overlook Gaza City. It also has surveillance systems that will give a clear picture of activity in depth. It is safe to assume that it has a very high level of *situational awareness* which allows it to plan operations in great detail. In the case of Operation 'Protective Edge', it appears that the overall plan was executed in four stages.

Preparations

During the period from April to July a detailed plan will have been developed. This was not a spontaneous reaction to a single incident. In order to generate the required capability some of the units involved had to be mobilised from other parts of Israel. A key milestone in the planning will have been the decision to call up reserves.

Phase 1
The air operation began on 7 July; it would be normal military practice for this phase of the operation to be designed to destroy command and control nodes in depth and any other targets that can be pre-empted. As the start time for the land engagement drew closer there will have been an increasing concentration on the areas where ground troops were to attack. It is unlikely that ceasefire negotiations at this stage were credible, since the operational objectives required a land incursion to destroy tunnels, 'dominate' the terrain, intimidate any aggressors and provide a bargaining position for further political action.

Phase 2
The main land attack took place from 17 July to 10 August, with withdrawal starting on 3 August. The main objectives are likely to have been achieved by 3 August, including the destruction of the tunnels and sufficient offensive action to overpower the opposition.

Phase 3
Consolidation followed from 10 to 26 August. Interestingly there seems to have been a significant Hamas rocket and mortar bombardment during 22–26 August, which did not provoke a commensurate retaliation by the IDF, suggesting that the Israeli objectives did not include the complete eradication of Hamas capability, but domination. On 26 August an open-ended ceasefire was declared.

IDF tactics
There are four particular aspects of IDF tactics that were evident during the operation and deserve reflection.

The *Hannibal protocol* is the IDF drill for reacting to the kidnapping or capture of one or more of its soldiers. This may have been activated twice during this operation, in particular on 1 August, by the Givati Brigade commander Colonel Winter in the Rafah area where there are reports of the use of disproportionate force. It appears that the authority for the execution of Hannibal was given by the Chief of the Israeli General Staff. It is difficult to understand why the response needs the sanction of the Chief of Staff and the level of force required appears to result in a dramatic increase in fire, including artillery fire in depth; it seems as if time is sacrificed to seek authority from the very highest level to apply a huge weight of fire on the target area, with a high likelihood that captives and captors will be killed.

Dahyia tactics are the systematic and deliberate application of disproportionate force, including inflicting civilian suffering, to deter and alienate the fighters from the population. They are also designed, in ground combat, to minimise the risk to the IDF. Providing effective covering fire is a necessary requirement when ground troops are manoeuvring. Ideally this will be precisely aimed at the enemy, but, particularly in a built-up area, it is hard to pinpoint enemy firing positions. In an area like Shuja'iyya it is almost inevitable that the use of tank, mortar and 155-mm artillery fire will cause civilian casualties. And, given the population density in Gaza, operations such as 'Protective Edge' will always cause civilian suffering and intimidation.

'Mowing the grass' is a term used by the IDF to imply that every so often there will be a need to attack an area in order to dominate it, reduce enemy capacity and deter further action. It is also accepted that over time the enemy military capability will be refreshed and further attack will be necessary.

'Knock on the roof'. At first sight the idea of the 'knock on the roof' seems sensible, but in the case of Gaza it is illogical. It does not make sense to warn the occupants of a house that it is to be attacked and allow them to escape unless it is known that they are innocent and the target is hiding military capability. Since the Hamas command and control mechanisms are not dependent on infrastructure it can only be assumed that this tactic is designed to intimidate by the destruction of residential buildings.

CONCLUSIONS

There are three particular areas that emerge from this analysis which are worth highlighting.

The link between tactical, operational and strategic actions

It seems likely that Operation 'Protective Edge' was a deliberate plan constructed over a number of months/weeks and that it was therefore cleared at the very highest levels of government. The overall scheme of manoeuvre will have been understood and authorised at the political level. There is evidence to support targeting decisions being taken at the very highest level, which makes it difficult to judge how much was actually delegated to senior commanders. It is also assumed that there were political briefings at key stages in the campaign: on all these occasions a sufficient level of military detail will have been required for the political decision to be made.

The purpose of seizing ground

The incursions seized certain areas of ground; these may have had tunnels in them, or rocket stores, but they were almost certainly not the only areas in Gaza to have defensive construction. It is difficult to see why the areas were chosen other than to have an impact on the population, to provide a bargaining chip for ceasefire negotiations and to destroy industrial and agricultural capacity in furtherance of the 'mowing the grass' policy. Ground was not taken to provide a tactical military advantage but to intimidate and to achieve the best possible bargaining position with the time and resources available.

The management of refugees

Normally it would be expected that there would be a plan for the management of refugees, since innocent civilians will always be displaced by fighting. In the case of Gaza, since there is no escape route for refugees, it should be anticipated that there are declared safe areas for civilians. But there is no evidence of such a plan in the IDF orders. In fact, attacks on the UN school and the 'knock on the roof' incidents give the appearance of a deliberate attempt to demonstrate that 'nowhere is safe'.

***

Military expertise inevitably affected any untutored views I and others may have formed about whether what we saw could require consideration as war crimes. At this stage it became helpful to add another category of material researched by Dr Tromp.

Dr Tromp and her team examined aspects of Operation 'Protective Edge' not specifically covered by General Parker or Avi Shlaim, including what was said of relevance by Israeli public figures *before, during and after* the Israeli attack.

She explained, for example, how retired Major General Giora Eiland, the former head of Israel's National Security Council, claimed that there is no such thing as 'innocent civilians' in Gaza, comparing Gaza under Hamas rule with Nazi Germany: 'They are to blame for this situation,' Eiland wrote, 'just like Germany's residents were to blame for electing Hitler as their leader and paid a heavy price for that, and rightfully so.'[23] What may be significant is that Eiland was not reprimanded for expressing openly these extreme views, which are widely shared by the defence establishment and by the Israeli public at large.

One of the most vocal public figures in the dehumanisation of the Arabs as a group was the late Rabbi Ovadia Yosef, the spiritual leader of Israel's ultra-orthodox Shas Party, who called in 2001 in a sermon for the annihilation of Arabs: 'It is forbidden to be merciful to them. You must send missiles to them and annihilate them …'[24] When discussing peace-making with Arabs in 2009, he said: 'How can you make peace with a snake?'[25]

Moshe Ya'alon, then the Minister of Defence, underlined the dangers of terrorism by suggesting that children of three are trained to be terrorists: 'As long as three-year-old children are being educated to carry explosive belts at ceremonies and Israel does not appear on their maps, there is no chance for peace.'[26]

In a letter to his troops on the eve of Operation 'Protective Edge' Colonel Ofer Winter, commander of the Givati Brigade, wrote:

> History has chosen us to spearhead the fighting [against] the terrorist 'Gazan' enemy which abuses, blasphemes and curses the God of Israel's [defence] forces … God, the Lord of Israel, make our path successful as we go and stand to fight for the sake of your people of Israel against a foe which curses your name.[27]

Ayelet Shaked, a member of the Knesset for the Jewish Home Party, posted inflammatory messages on social media which were subsequently erased. On 1 July 2014 she posted on her Facebook page:

> This is a war. Not a war on terror, not a war against extremists, or even a war against the Palestinian Authority. All are forms of evading reality. This is a war between the two nations. Who is the enemy? The Palestinian people. Why? Ask them, they started. What is so shocking in understanding that the whole of the Palestinian people are the enemy. Every war is between two nations, and all of the people that opened the war, as a whole, is the enemy.[28]

In response to reports about the deaths in the 'boys on the beach' incident on 16 July, Minister Naftali Bennet stated on TV:

> I think it is terrible that Hamas is butchering its own children. I would never take my children and place them next to missile launchers. Here's what they are doing. Hamas is conducting massive self-genocide. They're taking women and children, placing them next to missile launchers, and shooting the missiles at Israel.[29]

The statements selected illustrate hostile attitudes towards the Arabs as a race, Muslims as a religious group and Palestinians as an ethnic group. The words uttered in public addresses by Israeli politicians, senior military and other influential figures could easily be qualified as 'hate speech'. The function of the 'hate speech' is to reinforce the projected division into two groups in a society – 'us' and 'them'. The 'them' group is invested with all evil and as a collective denied human characteristics in what is known in academic literature as a 'dehumanisation' process.

To say such things in a country so permanently in conflict with those dehumanised – to be permitted by that country to say such things without restraint by the law – is dangerous. Freedom to say such things will inevitably poison and degrade the humanity of the society itself. The freedom within Israel to say and hear such things makes it entirely likely that insincere reasons for attacking Gaza *might* be advanced by the government, knowing that a majority of the people will be untroubled about whether any reason given is strictly accurate or not. The misfortune of the dehumanised is that they cease to enjoy the normal regard of their fellow humans, making it possible/probable that the real intentions of the government will have them as the true object of the attacks under the pretence of the state acting in self-defence.

There are, of course, many strands of political opinion in Israel, including many that oppose the policies of Netanyahu. The reality for both sides of this conflict – just as the reality in Western lands presently thought peaceful that may yet experience extremist government to their great surprise – is that allowing dehumanising language that finds support in only part of a population can nevertheless drive political or military policies that can be criminal.[30]

THE HAMAS PERSPECTIVE

The questions about conduct asked of Israel are probably simpler to ask of Hamas and may be simpler to answer. Whether war crimes were committed by Hamas turns on why rockets that could *not* be accurately targeted were aimed at Israel with the risk of killing civilians, and whether tunnels would be used for incursions of Gazan fighters into Israel for combat purposes and with what likely effect.[31] As with Israel, things are said by Hamas officials, or those claiming affiliation, that read and sound similarly disregarding of the modern law on armed conflict. Indeed, the founding 1988 Covenant of Hamas[32] has regularly been quoted by supporters of Israel as showing criminal intent by Hamas. For example, Article 15 of the 1988 Covenant includes:

> The day that enemies usurp part of Muslim land, Jihad becomes the individual duty of every Muslim. In face of the Jews' usurpation of Palestine, it is compulsory that the banner of Jihad be raised … It is necessary to instil the spirit of Jihad in the heart of the nation so that they would confront the enemies and join the ranks of the fighters.

Further, dehumanising comments attributed to Hamas relating to the 2014 attack *can* be identified.[33]

However, it has proved much harder to find dehumanising language associated with Hamas for the 2014 conflict than to find – in quantity and character – such language emanating from supporters of Israel. It may also be of note that in November 2014 Hamas leader Ismail Haniya told me in an interview in Gaza that he would be willing for those he led to be investigated by the ICC.

TENTATIVE CONCLUSIONS

In well-constituted armed forces each level of command knows the laws of war and how to apply them.[34] Both sides in a standard two-party armed conflict should also be able to apply the law to the best of their abilities. Does that happen often, or is it more common to see one side acting within the law and the other acting as if the law is not for them? And international law generally will not be being followed by *either* party in this conflict if, although both parties' *fears* are genuine, they are not well-founded and their military responses not proportionate.

At any trial of both parties for war crimes would Hamas be able to argue that as an imprisoned state / entity it must be allowed to fire rockets that are not capable of being accurately targeted regardless of the letter of the law on armed conflict, because there is no other way to defend and advance its citizens' interests? Is Israel allowed to react beyond what that black and white letter of the law allows because the level of real risk (atomic weapon or similar from somewhere or other) allows breaches of rules that are applicable only to others?

If there has to be room for combatants to break unrealistic laws – or laws unrealistic in certain circumstances – then all surrounding factual circumstances become *the main*, not an associated, issue. The question whether Israel intends and is entitled through its own reasoning to destroy Gaza by pretending to obey the laws of war becomes not one pointer to possible criminality, but the critical circumstance that may answer the question whether the law should be applied at all. Were Hamas to be hiding an unwavering desire to push Israelis into the sea by reliance on the letter of the law in some way then the same issue arises. Does the rule of law really have any place in this conflict as presently structured and carried out?

Discussions with Zionists or supporters of Hamas bring arguments that often seem to the non-partisan to be extreme and beyond discussion – all contrary to the natural justice / Voltairean principle of listening to and actually attending to the other side.

Is what we are concerned with – in reality – whether the law should be applied at all or whether in this case (in some unappealing long-term utilitarian way) the parties should be allowed to battle it out to the extinction of one side or the other behind a closed wall of international inactivity? This completely unacceptable argument – logical though it may be and resonant of what happened in conflicts of centuries past – may drive us to ask whether either side should be trusted with anything. Must we wait for a two-state solution finally to emerge with boundaries marked by oppressive walls and fences separating peoples harbouring enmities? Should all walls – the notional Jabotinsky Wall, the physical wall in the West Bank, the wall of Palestinian intransigence to the existence of Israel at all, and the wall of international inactivity – be dismantled and the entire land of Palestine administered by outsiders until a single state of equal citizens can exist on the basis that there may yet be scope for true democracy of those peoples in a land they all claim to call home?

Chapter 14

Does the Citizen Have the Right to Protest on the High Seas?

The MV Mavi Marmara *was one of several vessels loaded with humanitarian aid that attempted to break the Israeli blockade of Gaza in 2010. A case has been started at the International Criminal Court, in which a fundamental issue (separate from the killings by the Israelis of ten people on board) is whether people should be allowed to protest on the high seas, as the passengers on the ships of the flotilla were doing, in part.*

Original lecture delivered on 4 November 2015.

In the last chapter I discussed how to approach the question of establishing whether war crimes were committed in the Israel–Gaza conflict, not whether they had been or not. In this chapter I look at an incident involving the MV *Mavi Marmara*, an event to be seen as within that overall conflict, when, in 2010, a flotilla of ships with humanitarian aid sought to break the blockade of Gaza.

The vessel was boarded on 31 May by members of the Israel Defense Forces some 73 nautical miles from the Gaza shore and nine passengers on the *Mavi Marmara* were shot dead by the IDF; one other was in a coma from gunshot wounds until he died in 2014. Hundreds of passengers were handcuffed and gravely abused. All were taken to the port of Ashdod under arrest but later released without charge of any kind. I have represented the states of Comoros (flag state of the *Mavi Marmara*), the ship's owners, bereaved and passengers at the International Criminal Court and elsewhere. Just as earlier I offered no conclusion about whether war crimes had been committed by either side – on the grounds of having insufficient access to material and witnesses – I will not do so on this occasion for similar and additional reasons arising from my representation of involved parties.

This is the last chapter here focused on the role of law in international armed or internal armed conflicts. In all chapters I may have revealed a concern, sometimes scepticism, about the application of law to war, but always, I hope, with a conclusion that there was a role for law. I have argued that there were reasons to press on with what could be seen as experimental judicial and quasi-judicial processes where states, state forces, paramilitaries and individuals have been, and are being, examined for criminality – whether done well or sometimes less well – by courts and tribunals. What else is there to consider on the topic?

THE CONCERNED CITIZEN

We live in a world where 'uninvolved' citizens are ever better informed of events by television, radio and social media. They form opinions and often enough recognise that their concerns and interests are not being reflected in what nations and international bodies do in their name. But experience shows that expressing opinions is of limited effect. Public demonstrations, 'letters to the editor' and even 'op eds' rarely achieve much. Yet the world citizen has a right to his/her opinion and, in a dangerous world, may have the right to express it and to seek to have it affect the way the world turns. But merely to say what your opinion is may achieve little or nothing.

For example, in the Israel–Gaza conflict generally there have been opinions by several international or otherwise apparently objective bodies adverse to the legality of some or many aspects of all sides of the conflict – Richard Goldstone's report, Mary Davis's report for the UN, the informal Russell Tribunal on Palestine's conclusions on the conflict, and so on. But these opinions count for little and often achieve nothing at all. Even the highly critical words of the UN Secretary-General or the UN High Commissioner of Human Rights about aspects of Operation 'Protective Edge' (subject of the previous chapter) had no apparent effect.

Yet the formal international institutions – including the UN itself – constructed to deal with such issues are inactive and silent. What can and what should the bystander do? Nothing? Something? They sometimes want to and try, as the hundreds of passengers on the *Mavi Marmara* did. But what is their standing when they do?

One of the four reasonably contemporaneous reports into the *Mavi Marmara* incident, the UNHRC Report chaired by retired ICC Judge Hudson-Phillips, QC, an inquiry that was not recognised by Israel,[1] dealt with this issue at its conclusion:

> A distinction must be made between activities taken to alleviate crises and action to address the causes creating the crisis. The latter action is characterized as political action and therefore inappropriate for groups that wish to be classified as humanitarian. This point is made because of the evidence that, while some of the passengers were solely interested in delivering supplies to the people in Gaza, for others the main purpose was raising awareness of the blockade with a view to its removal, as the only way to solve the crisis. An examination should be made to clearly define humanitarianism, as distinct from humanitarian action, *so that there can be an agreed form of intervention and jurisdiction when humanitarian crises occur* [my emphasis].[2]

This insightful and constructive proposition – revisited later – may not quite get to the issue of those who were 'demonstrating' on the high seas on board the *Mavi Marmara*.

Efforts to affect the course of world affairs by peaceful means other than the ballot box of their own nation will attract many categories of individuals: those whose anguish for the suffering they seek to remedy is high; those whose desire to engage in politics other than through being elected or appointed to office is high; those who simply enjoy meddling in the affairs of others; a last category may be of those travelling with the well-intentioned group but hiding political affiliations and subversive, or worse, intentions.

THE BLOCKADE

The Israeli blockade of Gaza was announced in 2007 and placed restrictions on the 'passage of goods, the supply of oil and electricity and the movement of persons' to and from Gaza, in response to a number of military-security concerns regarding Hamas, the newly elected leadership in the region. Sanctions tightened import of goods to only primary food, fodder and hygiene items. They prevented entry of items beyond basic humanitarian products, such as clothing and construction materials. The restrictions on Gaza's export industry caused its economy to become dramatically depressed and led to the continued impoverishment of its population. In 2015, more than half of the population suffered from food insecurity, 70 per cent continued to rely on humanitarian aid and exports of marketable goods remained at 6 per cent of what they were prior to the closure in 2007.[3]

The Israeli government remains firm in its justification of the blockade. The Turkel Commission, an 'independent' commission initiated by the Israeli government to examine the flotilla incident, reaffirmed Israel's compliance with obligations under international law and supported the proportionality of the blockade's military objective, even when considered in light of the suffering imposed on the civilian population.[4]

The legality of the blockade remains hotly debated. To cite from a few of its opponents, the International Committee of the Red Cross described the blockade as a 'collective punishment imposed in clear violation of Israel's obligations under international humanitarian law'[5] (and contrary to binding Geneva Conventions), and a report prepared as a joint enterprise by a number of NGOs and interested parties, including Christian Aid, Oxfam and Amnesty International, concluded that the imposition of the blockade was illegal under international law and a 'disproportionate response' to the threat posed by Hamas.[6]

Attempts by human rights organisations to breach this allegedly unlawful blockade soon began – over land and on sea – by delivering humanitarian aid to the Gazans whilst exposing their living conditions to the world. Amongst those organisations, the Free Gaza Movement ('FGM')[7] initiated a series of motor vessel trips to Gaza and was successful on five separate occasions. On each of these occasions, between August and December 2008, boats carrying humanitarian supplies and heterogeneous groups of passengers/delegates were able to reach the Gaza coast, tracked as they were by the Israeli military.[8]

In early 2010, a collective of FGM and a number of other NGOs known as the Freedom Flotilla announced its intention to form another humanitarian convoy of eight vessels that would attempt to break the siege on Gaza. The *Mavi Marmara*, largest and leading vessel of the flotilla, left Istanbul on 29 May.

Nearly everything that can be disputed by one interest or another has been disputed: whether the blockade was lawful; what were the real motives of the passengers or activists; were those on the vessels active or reactive in the violence shown to the IDF boarding party; was any firearm on board before the IDF boarded (there is no suggestion anywhere that one was actually used by passengers); whether the IDF fired on the vessel before boarding or when descending the ropes from helicopters; what was the level of abuse of passengers by the IDF; how long they were kept in handcuffs; how they were treated on the way to Ashdod, and so on. The inquiries established by the UN, UNHRC, Israel and Turkey have all been subject to allegations of bias of one kind or another. Nevertheless, some common features may be regarded as very broadly non-controversial.

The Freedom Flotilla was found to have carried an eclectic delegation in excess of 700 passengers[9] from more than 40 different nationalities, together with hundreds of tons of humanitarian aid, including medical supplies and construction equipment.[10]

At approximately 04.00 on 31 May 2010, in international waters 73 nautical miles from the coast of Gaza, the Israeli military launched Operation 'Winds of Heaven 7' by surrounding the six Freedom Flotilla vessels[11] and attempting to board by force. Non-lethal weapons, including stun and smoke grenades, tear gas and paintballs, were used on all of the vessels; the main passenger ship, the *Mavi Marmara*, was targeted with live ammunition fire and plastic bullets.[12]

The rights of protesters

Pausing in the narrative, to whom, if any, should those aboard be most likened? Fighters in the Spanish Civil War or those overseas volunteers who join the IDF under the Mahal scheme? Probably to neither – at their strongest the allegations against the *Mavi Marmara* passengers are that the 40 who were IHH (a Turkish NGO) activists were violent in their *response* to what happened to them when the IDF boarded, using 'cold' weapons including metal rods cut from the safety railings on the ship and kitchen knives; and none of the passengers was in a military or militarised force. Should they be likened to peaceful civil disobedience protesters in India, later led by Gandhi, who suffered violence from the British authorities, most seriously at the Amritsar massacre – for which David Cameron said 'we must never forget what happened here' and 'we must ensure that the United Kingdom stands up for the right of peaceful protest around the world'?[13] There is possibly some similarity, although the scale of death was very different and the protesters on the *Marmara* were for the most part international 'outsiders'. Or are they best compared to demonstrators around the world who attempted to move public opinion over the Vietnam War and who used some violence at demonstrations, for whom – as at Kent State University – some reaction by the authorities did bring death to the innocent? Possibly.

But whenever authorities use lethal force against protesters they expose themselves not just to criticism but often to forces of opinion sufficiently strong as to become part of the reason for long-term change of policy.

Or was the destruction of the Berlin Wall by people on both sides closer to what happened in 2010 on the high seas off Gaza? A boundary was being torn down and set aside but in Berlin people on all sides, after a time, were unopposed by the authorities on either side.

All of these examples may have something to say about how protesters *were* treated on land and how protesters *should* be treated.

What legal instruments, if any, give us guidance as to what the passengers on the flotilla could expect from a law-abiding state? The UN Universal Declaration on Human Rights, of universal application but itself without legal force, says that no one shall be subjected to arbitrary arrest or detention and that everyone has the right to freedom of opinion and expression and the right to freedom of peaceful assembly and association. The European Convention on Human Rights, that may have no binding application to this event but that may now be regarded as part of customary international law, includes more or less identical provisions regarding freedom of expression and freedom of peaceful assembly.

At first sight both instruments are irrelevant: they concern human rights law whereas armed conflicts are covered by international humanitarian law. Is the International Covenant on Civil and Political Rights (ICCPR),[14] which has been ratified by Israel, of any relevance? Two points are of interest.

First, in the ICJ case about the wall built by Israel dividing communities in the Occupied Territories,[15] the court found that the construction of such a wall constituted breaches by Israel of various of its obligations under applicable international humanitarian law *and* human rights instruments, including the ICCPR. It continued:

> As regards the relationship between international humanitarian law and human rights law, there are thus *three possible situations: some rights may be exclusively matters of international humanitarian law; others may be exclusively matters of human rights law; yet others may be matters of both these branches of international law* [my emphasis] …
>
> The Court would observe that, while the jurisdiction of States is primarily territorial, it may sometimes be exercised outside the national territory. Considering the object and purpose of the ICCPR, it would seem natural that, even when such is the case, States parties to the Covenant should be bound to comply with its provisions …

Powers to derogate from certain provisions of the covenant under Article 4 arise 'in time of public emergency which threatens the life of the nation and the existence of which is officially proclaimed'. Israel has neither claimed nor 'proclaimed' derogation from any part of the covenant in respect of the operation on the *Mavi Marmara* and it is thus arguable that Israel was exercising its jurisdiction on the high seas and that the covenant applied with full force to all that was happening.

Second, the terms of the ICCPR include:

> **Article 9**
> Everyone has the right to liberty and security of person. No one shall be subjected to arbitrary arrest or detention.
> **Article 10**
> All persons deprived of their liberty shall be treated with humanity and with respect.
> **Article 21**
> The right of peaceful assembly shall be recognised. No restrictions may be placed on the exercise of this right.

WHAT PROTESTING CAN BRING

Returning to broadly non-controversial facts, 'Winds of Heaven 7' resulted in the death of ten civilian passengers, the serious wounding of more than 50 passengers and injuries to many other passengers who were hit by plastic rounds or 'bean bag' charges.[16] Scores more were subjected to mistreatment, including overly tight handcuffing for extended periods, beating, denial of access to toilet facilities, denial of medication (such as for diabetes, asthma and heart conditions) and provision of only limited access to food and drink. Passengers were forced to remain kneeling on decks exposed to the sun (resulting in 13 passengers receiving first-degree burns), seawater spray and wind gusts from helicopters, and were subjected to various types of physical and verbal harassment such as pushing, shoving, kicking, and threats and intimidation (including through the use of dogs), and to being blindfolded or having hoods put over their heads.[17]

All vessels were rerouted to Ashdod where the fingerprints of passengers were taken and intimate body searches were conducted. The passengers experienced intimidating and coercive behaviour from Israeli officers and were denied access to legal representatives or consular representatives until their release some days later.[18]

There were several initiatives in response to questions about the legality of the flotilla incident, most notably those commissioned by the Israeli government and the United Nations. An Israeli military probe into the incident led by retired Israeli General Giora Eiland acknowledged 'mistakes in various decisions made, including at relatively senior ranks, that ended up in a result we [the Israeli military] didn't anticipate'.[19] This motivated the formation of the fact-finding Turkel Commission which concluded, on the information available to it, including witness testimonies from Israeli officials, that Israel's use of force was proportionate in all of the circumstances.[20]

The UNHRC Report (mentioned previously) found the blockade to be unlawful and that 'several violations and offences have been committed' with 'clear evidence to support prosecutions of crimes' under the Geneva Convention and concluded that the 'right to an effective remedy should be guaranteed to all victims'.[21]

A panel of inquiry established by the UN Secretary-General to investigate the flotilla incident (the 'Palmer report'), on the other hand, found the blockade to be lawful but also found that Israel's decision to board the vessel 'with such substantial force' was 'excessive and unreasonable', noting 'non-violent options should have been used in the first instance' and the 'operation should have reassessed its options when the resistance to the initial boarding attempt became apparent'.[22]

In May 2013, lawyers for the government of the Union of the Comoros ('GoCo'), the flag state for the *Mavi Marmara* and a signatory state to the Rome Statute, filed a State Referral with the International Criminal Court, requesting the prosecutor to initiate an investigation. Whilst the referral focused on the interception of the *Mavi Marmara*, the *Rachel Corrie* and *Eleftheri Mesogios* were later incorporated into a 'Situation' as within the temporal scope of the Court.[23] The prosecutor announced the opening of a preliminary examination and, later the same year, the Situation was assigned to Pre-Trial Chamber I (PTC I).

GoCo submitted Israel had committed a number of war crimes on board the vessels including wilful killing, wilfully causing great suffering and severe physical injury, torture and inhuman treatment and outrages upon personal dignity that were part of a wider policy or plan amounting to crimes against humanity (all contrary to the ICC's Rome Statute). The referral submitted witness evidence, autopsy reports and video evidence as part of the complaint.

The timing of events now needs thought. Hundreds of sincere civilians with mixed motives were subject to events on the high seas that gave rise to allegations of illegality/criminality of a very high order. They looked, through the reference of the Comoros to the ICC and by their own subsequent applications as victims, to the only court able to deal with the issue of criminality comprehensively for a decision about their suffering and whether it was the result of crime. They had to turn to that court knowing that it was thought to be vulnerable to US and Israeli pressure or interests. But they had hopes. The very first decision that the court had to make – simply whether to investigate at all – could have been made in days or weeks, if there had been will.

The only other route to criminal accountability – apart from in Israel, which has shown no appetite for investigating and prosecuting the IDF for these alleged offences – *might* have been via the Law of the Sea Convention; but neither Israel nor the Comoros has ratified the Convention. Alternatively, a national jurisdiction such as our own in the UK, where torture is a universal crime, could be a suitable forum if individuals responsible for any of the alleged crimes come into the jurisdiction; and the UK police are investigating with that possibility in mind.

Despite all efforts to have that simple issue of whether to investigate decided swiftly, 18 months passed before this was done. In the meantime, Operation 'Protective Edge' took place, in which 2,200 people were killed, mostly civilians and including 500 children. Suppose now that the court – probably seen by both sides until then as unlikely to dare to investigate the Israel–Palestinian–Gaza problem – had heard the prosecutor say she *would* investigate, and do so independently and quickly. Might participants on all sides have felt some reason to lower the temperature of the conflict? Might they not have done what they were to do? The prosecutor has said her function includes deterrence. How regrettable that with such an obvious chance to deter within her power nothing was done.

In November 2014 the prosecutor published her negative response to GoCo's request for an investigation on the basis that the evidence made available did not give rise to potential claims capable of surmounting the ICC's 'gravity' threshold. In her decision, the prosecutor recognised that there was reasonable basis to believe war crimes had been committed by the Israeli military, including wilful killing, wilfully causing serious bodily injury and the mistreatment of passengers, all within the scope of the ICC's temporal jurisdiction; however, she decided their nature, scale, manner of commission and overall impact were not serious enough to compel the court to investigate.[24] She further refused to make a finding on the legality of the blockade on Gaza.[25] The prosecutor stated she could not consider evidence beyond the court's jurisdiction, and with this in mind, found there was insufficient evidence of the incident contributing to a wider plan or policy.

GoCo responded with an application for review to PTC I, submitting that the prosecutor had failed in her duty to assess its referral according to the correct standard and in line with the spirit of the Rome Statute to prosecute perpetrators when there would otherwise be impunity for their crimes. It challenged her refusal to consider evidence that the wider context of the attack was relevant to crimes that were within the ICC's jurisdiction, dismissing the finding against the presence of a wider policy as 'surprisingly premature' when she had reserved her position on other important issues such as the lawfulness of the blockade.[26] The Review Application highlighted evidence available to the prosecutor that would reach the gravity requirement and demonstrate serious and aggravating factors in the commission of the crimes and criticised the prosecutor's attitude to 'unclear evidence' which, it was suggested, provided greater not less reason to invite a formal investigation.[27]

On 16 July 2015 PTC I decided by a majority that the prosecutor had deviated from her duty by her reasoning not to investigate, which was flawed, preferring GoCo's positions on unclear/conflicting evidence as a reason to initiate an investigation and not a basis to shy away from doing so, also affirming the position concerning the use of extra-jurisdictional information in reviewing crimes that were within the court's jurisdiction and concluding that she had ultimately erred in assessment of the gravity considerations.[28] PTC I requested that there be a prompt reconsideration of the prosecutor's decision, a request which is presently challenged by the prosecutor at the Appeal Chamber of the ICC but remains undecided.

If the prosecutor succeeds in her appeal, the hundreds of innocent civilians will be left with little or no prospect of remedy so far as bringing criminal proceedings is concerned and with no international recognition that their rights were disregarded. The appeal leads to time passing as the victims and Comoros wait for the chamber's decision. If she wins then the process will continue – more applications, more referrals to the court, more work by lawyers hoping to persuade the only person with appropriate authority to examine what happened, but no actual detailed analysis by that person of what did happen.

AT SEA OR ON LAND

Those engaged in seemingly unending conflicts around the world might consider the stance of the bystanders who may be appalled by what they see, may want to help and may feel increasingly alarmed and threatened by a world becoming daily more dangerous. Bystanders' interest in the *historic* rights and wrongs of any conflict wears thin measured against the growing anguish they may feel for the victimhood/suffering of others and is moderated by concerns they will have for themselves (as approaches to the recent refugee crises show). They may want, justifiably, to see authoritative answers to questions of the legality of actions in conflicts as a better way to a safer future if they can reduce or stop the killing of the innocent.

What rights do people have to demonstrate on the high seas? Probably as many or more than people who protest on dry land. Probably at least as many as those protesting in a secure capital city on some political issue, perhaps more given the danger to the protesters of the sea as opposed to dry land. It might seem a strange, or even illogical, thing to do but hundreds of well-intentioned, unarmed people from around the world risked the high seas with, as one reason for being on the vessels involved and exposed to IDF intervention, the purpose of drawing attention to the plight of Gaza and the Gazan people. Given that the *Mavi Marmara* was 73 nautical miles off the Gaza coast when attacked it might be appropriate to consider, as a very rough analogy, whether hundreds of demonstrators gathering on, say, Hampstead Heath for a protest they intended to make in Trafalgar Square could all be arrested, handcuffed and treated/abused in the way that happened on the high seas.

Those in my lecture audience who journeyed with me over my series of lectures, through consideration of many conflicts, have shown a continuing concern for the victims of atrocities and have demonstrated their willingness to consider with open minds how difficult it is to find ways to alleviate the suffering caused by states that go to war. For many, the specific Gaza question effectively asked by Hudson-Phillips may be of particular practical importance: should an independent agency, presumably the UN, arrange for aid voluntarily given in such large amounts to be transported to and distributed within Gaza in order to tap the manifest good will of the uninvolved but concerned citizens of the world? That *would* separate out one function – political protesting – from humanitarian relief. I am not aware of it being attempted.

The political function of the demonstrators would remain, and there is no reason to believe that people independent but anguished over suffering they believe to be unjustified might not again take to the seas in numbers to mark their desire for change. But for those who protest in such a manner, much stands in the way of their humanitarian aid getting through or of their having much political effect or of changing the thinking of those whose thinking may need to open up or change. What part can the law play?

The fact that everything about the attack on the flotilla is challenged, with the four major inquiries already conducted not being respected, shows a need for an independent court to investigate with full cooperation of all parties and to bring some definitive conclusions. And the very fact of a proper legal investigation happening may itself have a beneficial effect. Legal process, and even the beginning of activity towards a proper legal process, may have effects on parties in conflict, as has been revealed in other situations. The overall legal process may not cure any conflict, but may provide a blanket that dampens violence and allows other beneficial changes to come.

Legal process may be part of a bridge between parties that will ultimately have to be made politically but can be started or furthered once it is known that the supporting pillar of an accurate legal determination is being created. With such a legal process in place, and if physical aid can get through to those in need, then non-involved but concerned bystanders may not feel the need to put their legal rights to the test or to put innocent life at any risk on the high seas.

Chapter 15

Sex and the Law

Reputations tumble; men once popular and famous but too powerful are condemned and imprisoned. Others fear their reputations will not long survive their deaths. Others will 'get away with it' as presumably they always have. How will all this be viewed in decades to come? Witch-hunt or confirmation that Mary Whitehouse was right and the sexual revolution is to blame?[1] *If so, what should society have done that it didn't? What should it do now apart from lock up aged offenders? And what about juries? Will they, not judges, ultimately determine how the law can be fair on sexual behaviour – assuming juries can ever discuss these things candidly?*

Original lecture delivered on 2 March 2016.

This chapter is rooted in questions I found interesting at various stages of my professional practice as I dealt with several different kinds of sex-related crimes. Developments over recent years – in particular the investigation, prosecution and public condemnation of historic sex offenders – have possibly made the questions more likely to generate interest. However liberal as a society we think we have become, sex and the detail of sex is largely beyond public and even private discussion. Intolerance of ideas can lead to intolerance of permissible action, of what people should otherwise be free to do. So we must 'be bold' – as Kenneth Williams used to say in *Round the Horne*.[2]

SEX IS FUNNY BECAUSE WE CAN'T SPEAK ABOUT IT SERIOUSLY

We cannot talk about the mechanics of sex seriously and we have to laugh about them, however dull they may be. Go to any theatre and hear the audience laugh at any sexual term especially if also used effectively as a swear word. It can wreck many performances and all because the audience knows no other way to react. When depiction is on a film people will generally sit in silence and in the dark, *not* giggling, at detailed scenes of sex or at sex words or at bad language. Perhaps it is the dark of the cinema that makes it less the embarrassing *public* 'discussion' of a theatre where people must be seen to laugh at what they cannot cope with; or perhaps the dark is like the dark of private and secret imagination. Since I mentioned the radio programme *Round the Horne* we should also remember that that programme, and many other shows of different types, *used* humour in a positive way to break down taboos and to move society and its moral standards.

Fantasies

Sex has much to do with fantasy. Let me try to make the same point about our inability to talk seriously about sex by a fantasy I have had, one in which a parliamentarian acknowledges his own indulgence in violent sexual fantasy in a parliamentary debate about an imagined drug to be introduced into the drinking water that could restrict us from crossing from the line of permitted and enjoyable fantasy to impermissible realisation of fantasy. After all, research shows that fantasy by both men and women includes imagined violent or forceful sex.[3] No parliamentarian could *ever* make such an acknowledgement.

Talking about the realities of sex involves recognition of the risk, at a minimum, that fantasies stray beyond the boundary of what it is legally or culturally permissible to do and also that past actions of many men may have crossed that boundary – one that ebbs and flows over time.[4]

People cannot speak about sex because they may well harbour suspicions about their own pasts, about whether they have crossed lines that they have publicly to condemn in the strongest terms in others who do. They may also be inhibited because of what they know or strongly believe about the real behaviour of friends or work colleagues. And memory itself is degraded by the passage of time and the change in public mores. I recall a friend who worked on *Jim'll Fix It* observing how Jimmy Savile would look at under-age girls and refer to 'Mr Policeman', thus revealing his interest and that he knew his interest was, or would be, against the law. At its time it was probably irrelevant, although by today's standards it might be a most powerful piece of evidence in bringing a sex offender to justice.

I was surprised last year to turn up a letter written to me in 1965 by a schoolteacher I knew who ran a music / drama group for school leavers and people just in or out of university. He was, I guess, about 40. He wrote of returning to school to work, observing that, although the teaching was 'driving him mad', he was 'cultivating two gorgeous third formers – usual trick – let them do the seducing, then wham'. This letter reveals several surprising things. First, that a grammar school teacher had clearly been able – if his bragging was accurate – to seduce young girls and get away with it. Second, that he felt no fear in writing about intentions that would be the end of his career and possibly a route to the slamming of a prison door in today's climate, but, third and fourth, that I was apparently not shocked at receiving such a letter and was able to forget it completely, although I don't believe I saw the writer again. When I had calculated who it was from, I checked his name in case – 90 years old though he would be at least – he featured anywhere; he didn't. Time changes morality, public and private, and with it our sensitivity and even our memory.

ABUSE OF CHILDREN

My school seemed remarkably untroubled by the problems of some others. But once I went to university and got to know boys from boarding public schools I heard one or two accounts of what teachers assumed to be their rights that were beyond my understanding – that it should happen and that the boys did not object or tell their parents so that *they* could object because the parents probably wouldn't object. Some parents thought, so I was told, that regular thrashing of their sons was no bad thing.

And the sexual abuse at some of those schools was, I imagine, part of an arc of abuse that had regular physical abuse at one extreme, linked or not to the violent teacher's sexual fantasies. Only recently a thoroughly nice chap I know gave an account of the clear sadistic relish of his headmaster at a famous boarding school when administering beatings that were, apparently, to be endured without any hint that the boy's parents would be interested or that the long-term health or mental health of the boy concerned would be affected. I listened wide-eyed wondering whether I would have had anything like the *sangfroid* he had in dealing with what was taken for granted.

LIVING MEMORY

Our discussion might benefit from consideration of sexual behaviour in Greek, Roman, Elizabethan and Victorian times. But overall it may be sufficient to note that, in the last six decades since the start of the 1960s, simply *because* people cannot and will not say publicly much or anything about what happens in private, morality itself changes to a degree unobserved – and this can be risky for the unwary – the doers, or to those to whom bad things are done – and we have seen much of this in the last few years.

My professional career happened periodically to involve me in cases that gave me a view of how things were changing, as I can now understand.

First, in the 1970s I prosecuted a few prostitution cases. I learned about the warrens of rooms in Soho where prostitutes, with the security of a maid, would receive clients and periodically the scurrying figure of the rent collector who handed over the excessive rents the prostitutes paid to the true property owner. He remained as distant from the property as he could – except when he was in a cupboard peeping into a room through a hole in the door or, possibly, dispensing fatal injuries to a non-payer. There was some sense in the determination of the police to prosecute these men who profited so excessively from the risky and (to me) unappealing work of the women; but I could see more to prostitution than vice. Much later a relation left me some very honest and revealing tapes about the approach of respectable but not privileged men, such as my relation was, in the inter-war years who, coming from the blue-collar band of society, respectfully limited the scope of romantic liaisons until marriage and saw in prostitutes women who should not in any way be under-regarded. I recall how the Russian ex-princess teaching her language to South London boys at my school in the 1960s was happy to misquote Macmillan's 'You've never had it so good' as 'You've never had it so often' to make us laugh – the advance of liberty was well under way by then. This meant that if you wanted sex you were expected to be able to have it without pay; did this change the attitude to and downgrade prostitutes in the eyes of men and women?

I next found myself prosecuting dirty books. And how dirty they were. Unreadable. Often violent and, by way of one example, they frequently narrated so-called stories of the clenched fist going into places where it was never intended to go. I could barely understand how what I was reading could be of any appeal let alone how any such act could be of any pleasure to anyone.

The internet has enabled me to ask and answer a question that occurred to me back then in the 1980s. Was this 'fisting' a traditional practice of long standing? Not at all, says the Internet. This was entirely a 20th-century innovation rooted in San Francisco. If so – and assuming it would have been as alien to the caveman as would have been some of the other practices set out in these books – was writing about a physically damaging act of such excess corrupting? Did it show something about the vulnerability of humans by persuasion to enter the dark world of progressive degraded imaginations?

Trials of these books – for being 'likely to deprave and corrupt' – gave me the opportunity to be against the late John Mortimer, creator of *Rumpole of the Bailey*. He would never read the books, as he made clear by holding them upside down while giving the jury his freedom-of-speech address, that would always 'knock for six' my careful identification of pages here and there that must surely have demonstrated that they would deprave and corrupt. I always lost. Perhaps the jury were quite unable to discuss the realities of the terrible activities portrayed and accepted from Mr Mortimer that freedom of speech meant freedom to write almost anything. Perhaps they thought Mary Whitehouse a busybody and by voting for an acquittal were in some way rejecting the limited forces of conservatism battling sexual liberalisation of all kinds.

Dirty books that could be prosecuted were part of the much broader range of material known as pornography. Pornography – soft or hard – has its attackers and defenders. It cannot be said that it is necessarily nor overall likely to increase cases of sexual violence; some argue on the basis of statistics that it can have the opposite effect. Its burgeoning since World War II seems unstoppable and has effects one way and another. A very substantial majority of men and women have viewed it sometimes or often since the arrival of the Internet, all reflective of that changing morality that surfaces in spikes and at different places. Available statistics about the viewing of pornography and of its availability to children are – to those who fear it is capable of harming us – truly alarming. But it is now effectively a majority interest.

I got out of prosecuting dirty books as soon as I could, but was drawn back to prosecute and occasionally to defend cases of sexual abuse of children.

Dame Janet Smith's report into Jimmy Savile and the BBC contains an excellent chapter on general background. Dame Janet explains how, 'Since Victorian times, British society has recognised the need to protect children from sexual abuse, although it is only fairly recently that it has appreciated how much protection is needed.' She then quotes from *Child Abuse: Law and Policy Across Boundaries:*

> The single unifying term 'child abuse' encompassing all child maltreatment emerged in the late 1960s and early 1970s ... Even when the term 'child abuse' began commonly to be used in the 1970s, it was used primarily to refer to the physical assault of children. The term became all-encompassing in the late 1980s when the problem of child sexual abuse became more widely recognised. The, now common, use of the term 'child abuse' gives the impression of a universal consensus

> about what acts and omissions are abusive; however this is far from true.[5]

Dame Janet also sets out some of the relevant statutory provisions:

> The Criminal Law Amendment Act 1885 provided for offences of carnal knowledge of a girl under 13, and from 13 to 16. Later, a range of offences from rape to unlawful sexual intercourse, gross indecency and indecent assault, to name but a few, covered sexual acts against children. The Sexual Offences Act 1956, a consolidating statute, provided for offences in relation to children (girls) under 13 and children (girls) under 16, with heavier penalties for the former. There were separate offences of buggery and what was then termed 'gross indecency' between men. Further offences of indecent conduct were provided for in the Indecency with Children Act 1960, which used an age limit of 14 years. There was (and still is), however, no legal definition of 'paedophile' in English law …[6]

I prosecuted a couple of large child sex abuse cases in 1990 and 1991 and they included what had already become standard suggestions of 'paedophile rings'. Many technicalities still affected proof of crimes, but what was most obvious to me was that these crimes were committed by people of very limited chances in life, limited education (possibly actually limited intelligence), who lived in pretty unsatisfactory accommodation and were unlikely to have a great deal to do with their lives outside work, if they had any. In most or all cases there was indication – or even hard evidence – that the abusers had themselves been abused. At what stage does a person of limited ability have to be punished for things done that maybe he can't resist? And what a terrible waste of life – any life, the life of the abuser, and, more importantly, of the abused.

HISTORIC SEX CRIMES

All of which brings us to Jimmy Savile. Was he excited by what he achieved or was his a horrible body to inhabit and was it one that may itself have been constructed by abuse perpetrated on him? One thing is now clear – he had or developed an appetite that society's structures did little or nothing to restrain. Dame Janet said this in her opening statement:

> Most important of all, in the 1970s, 80s and 90s, child protection was very low on the BBC's radar. In this, the BBC was far from alone. At that time, our society did not recognise the prevalence of sexual abuse of children; complaints were disbelieved and therefore rarely made. We were not sufficiently shocked by the signs of older men being sexually involved with teenage girls and we were unaware of the damage which such unequal relations could cause. Sexual harassment was not taken seriously.[7]

And these things were all happening, it now seems to me, just when the strongest undercurrent in society was working *against* any control in an environment where even to criticise relaxation of sexual controls might attract a reputation for being old-fashioned, repressive or worse. And there was, of course, good reason for much liberation: the long process of an individual's sexuality being publicly acceptable and something that would no longer prejudice her or him was in train and clearly – at least according to nearly all European standards – needed encouraging. It was likely to be difficult to be permissive and encouraging of acts recently regarded as criminal by the law and many in society on the one hand, and yet to be trying to tie down permissive acts on the other.

And so things were done in lax environments where there was probably misplaced admiration for the liberties some men took by their more timid friends and colleagues. The doers thought they would 'get away' with what they did. They probably often thought it was not even something that needed getting away with. They thought they could be as immune as rock stars (for the most part) appear still to be, but they overlooked that the liberal public morality they thought would protect them was never publicly stated (it could not be) and could be denied when the reality of harm done by them to the objects of their interest became known. And once that started to happen, the line dividing fantasy from acceptable reality was moving against them. They should have left as fantasy what they put into effect.

Dame Janet's report provides snapshots by particular witnesses of reality:

> A journalist told me that, while working at the BBC in the 1980s, he had seen a crowd of young girls standing in the corridor waiting to get into the *Top of the Pops* studio. He said that it was hard to tell their ages as they were '*made up to the nines*' but from the conversations he overheard, he had the impression they were there in the hope of '*bedding the presenter*'.
>
> Tina Ritchie, who, in the early 1990s, worked as a newsreader on BBC Radio 1, described hearing of '*a lot of sort of bottom slapping of women in the office*' at Egton House, which contrasted with her experience in current affairs at Broadcasting House. She attributed the contrast to: '*these incredibly famous men surrounded by people who did exactly what they wanted because they were incredibly famous. It is sort of one feeding the other, and everybody surviving slightly on a culture of fear, because one word from a presenter and you would be in trouble, which is why I didn't say anything.*'
>
> One witness, who worked in BBC Radio 1, said there were lots of '*wandering hands, comments about your body, chaps just felt it was perfectly fine to put their hand on your bum and other places*'. Another who also worked in BBC Radio 1 described how a colleague would put his hands up the front of her jumper while she was working. When she complained to her manager, the reaction was to ask her if she was a lesbian. In the witness's view, '*if it didn't come from the top,* [this culture] *was supported and endorsed and allowed to continue from the top*'.

These very general considerations may set the scene sufficiently for me to ask the questions that arise from the title of this lecture. But there is something else we might want to have in mind. The culture – and the legal cases that have brought the culture into consideration – is largely one of, and for part only, of our present society. In our multi-ethnic, multi-national society there are many other groupings, some of which have cultures that *seem* to treat women with much greater distance and possibly much greater respect. But do they? We can certainly read of men in societies abroad deprived of the company of women altogether until a dowry is raised and paid, and of the effect that that will have on the sexual conduct of men with men – and we can know that these alien societies may soon be parts of our own society. But we may know nothing of what happens in private – locked away from us by double doors of privacy and secrecy. It is hard enough for us to deal with our present problems derived from changing national private and public morality and immorality in which crimes against children have only recently been properly understood, and where in the 19th century Oscar Wilde could be pilloried in public for what was – apparently – largely acceptable in private among the ruling class. Other societies – other sections of our rainbow society – will have as many conundrums to unravel if universal standards are to be applied, as all our present public thinking would appear to demand.

CRIMINALITY, WICKEDNESS AND SUFFERING

I have no difficulty in thinking the men (occasionally women) who do these things to be wicked, even if they are only repeating in adult life what they experienced as children. But, as one of a number of really unappealing questions to be asked in this modern age, is it possible that in particular environments victims – like my friend from a famous public school – are NOT affected, as he claims is the case for him, by physical violent abuse? Is it possible that another friend was not affected after he was sexually assaulted on his very last day at school, by the headmaster of the famous public school he attended? In fact I was never sure he was right when he maintained that he was unaffected, but his family certainly made no complaint.

Should we hope both these men when young were unaffected (because it means they will not have suffered or been changed) or should we today seek extraction and articulation of their suffering so that we can be more condemning and seek more punishment for the people who abused such children, however long ago?

This brings me to the almost unaskable question that arises from many exchanges with mature women friends as they hear or read about the abuse of young women by famous, usually much older, men. Often I hear exasperation from my friends at the fact that such a 'to do' is made over something they would have dealt with, or did deal with, by a slap round the face or similar, and that they would not conceivably have been as changed by the experience as victims say they have been. Are my friends actually suppressing the reality of what happened to them in such incidents? Were they in fact damaged but unable to acknowledge as much?

CAN WE PROGRESS?

Throughout the time I have had occasionally to think about these things I have been quite unaware of active steps by government to change our private or public morality save to the extent the law and criminal cases may deter – all too late, for so many victims, it must be thought.

Access to pornography barely regulated, limitations on what can be shown on TV and the screen all but abandoned – and with the enthusiastic support of all liberally minded people like me. Scornful contempt for people like the wretched Mary Whitehouse, for those who remember her. Or was she so wretched after all? Her nemesis at the Bar was Jeremy Hutchinson, QC, 100 years old last year. His professional life covered the very period of our present concern – and he was always on the liberal wing of society into which he had been born personally privileged. He successfully defended Penguin Books on charges of obscenity when they published *Lady Chatterley's Lover* in 1960, and did similar work for the film *Last Tango in Paris* and the play *The Romans in Britain*. Charles Moore wrote a congratulatory piece about Lord Hutchinson that showed how sometimes great age can take someone into a world they might never have expected. Moore explained: 'Mrs Whitehouse's warnings about the exploitation of women in the brave new liberated world were seen as fuddy-duddy at the time. They now seem almost fashionably feminist …'[8]

CONCLUSIONS

I am not sure that even now if Mary Whitehouse were around I would support her. But I can be sure that those caught up and punished heavily for what they did decades ago might wish she had had more sway and been of more effect. The Stuart Halls and Rolf Harrises of this world are unlikely to think the short-term pleasure all those years ago was worth the long-term suffering and disgrace in which their lives will end. They would probably say it would have been better for there to have been a moral compass set that encouraged them to keep what should be fantasy at best – or worst – as fantasy, so that they could have succeeded in public life with all its trappings without abusing their positions. Instead there were no restraints effective on them.

But there is nothing we can put in the drinking water to control us. Ultimately it is our society that must do what it can to bring under control behaviour derived from the animal need to reproduce. But the impulse that serves that need should not be extended for commercial reasons – or by reason of fashion – incrementally to behaviour that has no place on the streets, in the studios and the work places of powerful men, in the unhappy homes of people subject to limitations or even in the bedrooms of the otherwise fortunate and well educated. Expressed at its simplest – and perhaps most unrealistic – we should find better things to do.

Chapter 16

Human Rights: Whether in Europe or Out?

The campaign over Brexit has covered many different subjects, but what will the result mean for human rights? Has the debate been framed to bring a better understanding of the issues and processes involved?

Original lecture delivered on 6 April 2016.

The lecture on which this chapter was based was delivered before the European referendum and obviously before its result was known. I have decided to rely mainly on that original text for the content of this chapter, writing it on the basis that the vote is yet to come as I think this is helpful in considering the issues I wish to discuss.

This referendum raises issues about open democracy, including whether many important issues should be dealt with by referendums and, if so, of what type. Should there, perhaps, be specialist voter panels for highly sophisticated referendum issues?[1] Or will the opposite happen, and matters great and small be thrown to an electorate under-informed and insufficiently educated on the subject to form any valid view? Or, alternatively, may referendums be avoided in recognition of many political problems being too complicated for the ordinary voter and best left to politicians?

Being honest about how many of the highly technical political, economic, cultural and legal issues that fall for consideration in this referendum are beyond most of us to deal with competently raises another question. How are those voters who are less interested in detail, or even simply less educated, being addressed? It is easy to say that they are subjected to simple-minded xenophobic excess by the tabloid and other Brexit-inclined press. But many of them, along with many who would claim better education and knowledge of public affairs, have had their minds opened a bit in the public debate. As an example, until a year or so ago the easy-going public house – *or* Pall Mall club – conversation would have had the UK subjected to 'human rights' imposed from Europe. But the debate in the media has slowly acquainted some readers and viewers with the fact that the Council of Europe is not the EU, that the Council of Europe established the ECtHR, and that the European Convention on Human Rights was drafted substantially by UK politicians, and right-wing Conservative politicians at that. Even if this detail is not registered by *all* sectors of society, the Brexit campaigners know that they cannot allow the 'own goal' of overlooking this historical reality in a diatribe against Europe.

CONSEQUENCES

The consequences of the referendum are not, I fear, just limited to being in or out of Europe. And they are to be contrasted with the

1975 decision to be in a new Europe that came in the first of only two UK-wide referendums held to date (the second was the Alternative Vote Referendum of 2011). That 1975 referendum under a Labour government followed entry into the EEC, precursor of the European Union, a decision made by the Conservative government of Prime Minister Edward Heath without direct reference to the electorate. The result was strongly in favour of staying in: 67 per cent on a 65 per cent turnout. Changes that followed – backed by a significant majority – were inevitably gradual, and heated divisions at the time of the referendum could cool to manageable differences of opinion.

Denis MacShane, former Labour Minister of State for Europe, itemises a number of significant points of difference between the 2016 and 1975 referendums. For instance, in 1975, Britain had been in the EEC for just two years, and few voters were aware of any change being in had brought; the press was overwhelmingly in favour; the majority of business leaders supported the 'In' campaign; the referendum took place at the beginning of a Labour government, at the time popular amongst the electorate, particularly as the premiership of Edward Heath from 1970 to 1974 had been so unpopular; the Tory leadership, including Margaret Thatcher, was strongly supportive, and there was cross-party support; the only minister with status who spoke against Europe was Tony Benn; and the In camp outspent the Out camp by 12 to 1.[2]

But even this sobering analysis fails to deal with the consequences – beyond the economic and political – for voters. If the result of the referendum is to stay in, the grumbling and division will continue until and unless the UK takes a lead in Europe and makes its workings more acceptable to all, or unless the economic benefits of continued membership become obvious so that sceptical opinions can be swamped by consumer contentment. Or perhaps unless a horrible armed conflict reveals the security advantage of having a leading role in such a large political entity.

If, however, there is a vote to leave, followed by immediate problems that persist: currency collapse; housing market collapse; reduced employment; Scottish separation and its joining Europe; reduced UK power in Europe and in the Northern Hemisphere; loss of Security Council seat at the UN – what then? None of these outcomes is certain, but all are possible. What will voters who went one way say of those who went the other? Will we, the nation, be able to pull together? And if one part of the effect of voting out – and getting out – is to reinforce xenophobic aversion to foreigners, then what may happen to internal integration of races in this country, always a sensitive issue, never one so very far from being problematic?

SHOULD WE, THE PUBLIC, EVER HAVE BEEN ASKED?

The reality is that this is a problem for the nation that the electorate cannot properly solve by referendum because there is no consensus. Without consensus it is *change itself* that should have been avoided,[3] and for the same reason countries with written constitutions often require substantial majorities in their parliaments for significant constitutional change.

Party politics led to a promise that should not have been made if the interests of the people were to be paramount. Unnecessary fear of UKIP and an overwhelming desire to win a general election played their parts in calling for a decision by the electorate insufficiently equipped to handle the confusing material laid before them, so that *chance* may decide what cannot properly be achieved by argument. Why are our politicians incapable of presenting clear facts for us to decide on? It is into this exciting discussion that the topic of human rights is casually thrown.

This is not a democracy functioning in a way to impress others.

HOW THIS IS VIEWED BY OTHERS

Unsurprisingly, a sometime French-favoured description of Britain, 'Perfidious Albion' ('Treacherous England'), is back in use. If our voters want our country to be regarded as different from those of mainland Europe, will it be for this epithet to stick? The description is not something of which we should be proud. It reflects how we voluntarily joined an organisation – call it a club, as people often do – knowing there would be duties and benefits and that there would be rules. It seems clear that we have a potential leadership role in the club and that many other club members want us to remain and probably to take a lead in the club's affairs. We could stay in, determined to improve the club.

Instead we look for all ways in which the club is not to our liking and invite our own islanders to decide on pulling out and giving up club membership altogether.

SOURCES OF EUROPEAN LAW THAT AFFECT THE UK

In addition to the UK's own Human Rights Act of 1998, that by incorporating equivalent European human rights laws has made many references to Europe unnecessary and that has been regarded as setting the way for other countries, there are two principal 'foreign' sources of law. The 1950 European Convention of Human Rights (ECHR) dealt with at the European Court of Human Rights (ECtHR) established in 1959, sitting in Strasbourg; and the 2000 EU Charter of Fundamental Rights (CFREU) having legal effect from 2000 at the European Court of Justice (ECJ) that had been established in 1952 in Luxembourg.

Thus when we joined the EEC we had already had experience and some understanding, through our participation in the Council of Europe that drafted the ECHR and established the ECtHR , of the value of pooling knowledge and experience in the law. The Council of Europe, it has to be emphasised, is not the EEC or the EU and never has been. The ECtHR preserves for our citizens and for others in Europe what had been identified in the ECHR as (universal) human rights, rights that cross national borders and demand recognition and respect in all lands. By joining the EEC and then the EU we, as a country, extended this experience by involvement in a more formal system in which the even broader human rights of the CFREU could from 2000 be given statutory force by the ECJ.

It might be unsurprising if the product of shared expertise is, on occasion, disturbing *at first* to some. 'Pooling' experience of different nations may expose one nation's law's shortcomings as measured against the laws of another nation or the law emerging from the pooling exercise. That exercise will not, in any case, necessarily get things right first time and emerging law may need future refinement. Each of these possibilities can cause disquiet and even resentment in the citizens of nations formerly used to having only one legislature and one court system to understand and to challenge, if at all, and then on 'home turf'. In proof of this, reactions by several countries, not just the UK, to the best efforts of the Strasbourg court (ECtHR implementing the ECHR) have been surprisingly extreme. In a newspaper article in 2011 Sir Nicolas Bratza, President of the Court in 2011–12, said ,'The vitriolic – and I am afraid to say, xenophobic – fury directed against the judges of my Court is unprecedented in my experience, as someone who has been involved with the Convention system for over 40 years.'[4]

Despite this, there is no present proposal, even with Brexit, that we should depart from the Council of Europe, so that withdrawing from the European Convention on Human Rights may not be realistically possible.

The margin of appreciation

Decisions of the ECtHR are binding on member states, but the court has no enforcement powers. States generally comply, but not always, and not always quickly – as shown by the UK government's long-term impasse with the court over prisoner voting rights. But such impasses are rare not least because, little known by the public, within the Council of Europe's human rights decision-making processes there is a 'margin of appreciation'. The French term, *marge d'appréciation,* is more accurately translated as 'margin of assessment/appraisal/estimation'. This refers to the Strasbourg institutions' recognition of cultural and other differences in Council of Europe members that justify differences in how they may be expected to meet obligations under the European Convention on Human Rights.[5]

Here are a few examples to show how this has worked out.

The October 1981 ECtHR judgment in *Dudgeon v. the United Kingdom* found a violation of ECHR Article 8's right to private and family life in Northern Ireland law criminalising homosexual activity. Respect for Northern Ireland's margin of appreciation – based on the country's moral conservatism – was outweighed by the detrimental effects the relevant law could have upon the private lives of gay adult males in Northern Ireland.

The 1993 ECtHR judgment in *Brannigan and McBride v. the United Kingdom,* however, respected the UK's wide 'margin of appreciation', accepted that the UK government had direct responsibility for striking the proper balance between taking effective action and respecting individual rights, and upheld the UK law on detention and questioning of the applicants for periods of 6 days 14 hours and 4 days 6 hours respectively under anti-terrorist legislation. The United Kingdom government relied successfully on a (23 December

1988) right to derogation of their obligation under Article 5's right to liberty and security to be brought promptly before a judicial authority *in time of war or other public emergency.*[6] The applicants failed; the UK's powers to detain and question were upheld.

In the 2013 case of *Vinter and others*, 'whole life' sentences for grave crimes were held contrary to Article 3, which prohibits torture and inhuman or degrading treatment and which the court held *required* there to be some 'reducibility' of any sentence when changes in the life-sentence prisoner are so significant, including by progress to rehabilitation, that continued detention could no longer be justified penologically. Regard to the margin of appreciation meant the court would not prescribe when and by what process that review should take place, although from comparative international practices a review 25 years after imposition of a life sentence, at the latest, was required. Absent such a review, a whole life sentence would breach Article 3 of the Convention.

Further, a whole-life prisoner is *entitled* to know, when sentenced, what he must do to be considered for release so that 'incompatibility with Article 3 … already arises at the moment of the imposition of the whole-life sentence and not at a later stage of incarceration'.[7]

Do these cases represent an imposition of wholly unacceptable law from outside on our funny little island? Or may they seem a reasonably satisfactory result of careful consideration by intelligent men and women of the problems that will come from applying high-level principles of human rights to the particular problems of individually different states?

Leaving the EU would not make a difference to the UK's duty of compliance with the ECHR. What it would mean is that the UK would not be covered by EU human rights laws that are contained in the CFREU that came into force after ratification of the Treaty of Lisbon in 2009. These rights have not had as much of an impact as Convention rights, but are in some ways more wide-ranging.

In the negotiations leading up to the signing of the Lisbon Treaty, Poland and the United Kingdom secured a protocol to the CFREU rights in their respective countries.

The protocol, in Article 1(1) states:

> The Charter does not extend the ability of the Court of Justice of the European Union, or any court or tribunal of Poland or of the United Kingdom, to find that the

> laws, regulations or administrative provisions, practices or actions of Poland or of the United Kingdom are inconsistent with the fundamental rights, freedoms and principles that it reaffirms.

Article 1(2) then says that Title IV of the Charter, which contains economic and social rights, does not create justiciable rights, unless Poland and the UK have provided for such rights in national law. Academic views have been expressed that the protocol has no legal binding force, instead having a 'chilling' effect, being 'declaratory' in nature and intended to restrict the 'judicial creativity' of the EU courts.[8] Judges here have said that it is 'far from clear' what it does achieve, and it certainly has not prevented them from ruling that UK law has to be 'disapplied' because of a conflict with the Charter in several recent cases.[9]

BREXIT AND HUMAN RIGHTS

Threats by the Conservative Party and government to abolish the UK Human Rights Act that sets in UK law the provisions of the ECHR obscure the reality that the big 'threat' to parliamentary sovereignty remains EU membership, *not* the operation of the HRA.

A Brexit vote would leave the ECHR intact, as it would the ECtHR's watch over these rights. However, withdrawal *not* from the ECHR and ECtHR but from the EU, EU Charter and ECJ, could eliminate or reduce some particular EU labour rights. For example, paid holiday, maternity leave and other employment rights could be significantly affected, not least because transfer of undertakings rules protect workers whose jobs are transferred or outsourced.

HOW BAD HAVE HUMAN RIGHTS LAWS BEEN FOR US?

There are many organisations enthusiastic about the development of human rights law in Europe and elsewhere. I turned to one[10] to select three of the most important human rights cases – not necessarily European-driven but reflecting law that is consistent across Europe – that have affected the UK.

The right to freedom

In 2001, after 9/11, Parliament declared a state of emergency, giving the Home Secretary powers to detain foreign terror suspects indefinitely. In 2004, three men arrested in 2001 challenged their continuing imprisonment without charge. The judges of the House of Lords, then the country's top court, decided that with a 'near permanent' state of emergency the UK could excuse itself from some human rights obligations in order to deal with the terror threat. But indefinite imprisonment without trial, that 'wholly negated' the right to liberty, was disproportionate. Also, as the new powers applied only to foreign people even though part of the terror threat came from British citizens, they were unreasonably discriminatory. The law was declared incompatible with the Human Rights Act, and although this did not invalidate the law Parliament subsequently repealed it. Lord Hope said that an independent judiciary holding the government to account is 'a cardinal feature of the modern democratic state'. Even in an emergency, the law cannot be ignored. And everyone's right to freedom must be protected.[11]

The right to freedom of journalistic expression

On 2 November 1989 Mr Goodwin, a journalist, received information from a company called Tetra of its confidential corporate plan. A UK court that ordered the papers not to publish the confidential information also ordered Goodwin to reveal his source. Goodwin refused and was fined £5,000.

The ECtHR, highlighting the importance of a free press in a democratic society, held that the order and fine violated Goodwin's Article 10 right to free journalistic expression, one of the essential building blocks of a democratic society in which the press inform the public on matters of public importance.[12]

The right to life (and death?)

In 1999 Diane Pretty was diagnosed with motor neurone disease from which she would suffer a protracted and painful death. Diane wanted someone to help her end her life. The government refused to guarantee that her husband would not be prosecuted if he helped her to die, so Diane took her case to the ECtHR saying that the Article 2 right to life included the right to choose whether to go on living. The court decided that none of her human rights had been unfairly restricted and that the right to life was not determined by the *quality* of the life in question and was not a right to die.

Although Diane's right to choose how to end her life was within the scope of her right to respect for her private life, the UK's decision to make assisted suicide illegal had a legitimate objective in trying to protect vulnerable people. Diane died a month after the ruling. A number of cases have followed Diane's, and on each occasion the courts seem to have inched a little closer to the result which Diane wanted. Ultimately the right-to-die debate may have to be resolved by our Parliament.[13]

THE BENEFIT OF DIALOGUE

Sir Nicolas Bratza has demonstrated how the majority of references to the court against the UK are rejected immediately, how the UK Human Rights Act has led the way for other countries and is much respected, and what would be lost should the UK withdraw from the convention system. He says:

> The Human Rights Act, and the manner of its implementation by judges of the United Kingdom, have set a shining example to other states of how Convention rights can be brought home. The withdrawal of the United Kingdom from the Convention ... [would] do immeasurable harm to the standing of the United Kingdom within the wider community of Europe in which it plays such an important part.[14]

He further explains how Strasbourg has, on occasions, drawn upon English law to determine issues of wider interest for contracting parties; in one case, the thorough analysis of the Immigration Appeal Tribunal in England helped the ECtHR decide a case that could affect national practice in a number of European jurisdictions, including those of Denmark, Finland, France, Germany and the Netherlands.

Joshua Rozenberg, the UK's leading legal journalist, summarised the seminal case of *Horncastle* in which the UK did not follow ECtHR law over when hearsay evidence could be used to secure a conviction, the UK court distinguishing between the European approach and the UK approach that *did* have enough safeguards to ensure the use of hearsay does not violate Article 6 of the ECHR.

The UK was thereafter able, effectively, to challenge the earlier ECtHR decision of *Al-Khawaja* that had set the ECtHR hearsay law with which it disagreed on the basis that the ECtHR had misunderstood UK law and practice on hearsay. The ECtHR then accepted that a conviction based wholly on hearsay does *not* inevitably constitute an Article 6 breach, thus modifying its earlier *Al-Khawaja* ruling. Rozenberg summarised the more general arguments that flow from the case about the interaction of national and European courts and the wisdom of withdrawal of the UK from the ECHR, something discussed as possible by many politicians, as follows:

> The Horncastle dialogue has a deeper lesson … Sure, there is no 'democratic override' – no parliament can overturn the decisions of the court's grand chamber – but the European court, like any other institution, is capable of getting things wrong. And, when it is persuaded that it has made a mistake, it is not too grand to think again. Crucially, it was persuaded to do so in this case by the careful reasoning of the court of appeal and the supreme court. That's what the court would lose if the UK pulled out of the human rights convention.[15]

Given the intention forged in 1948 to share decision-making with others through the Council of Europe, an exercise that has identified and reinforced rights through a court accessible to individuals as well as to other entities, given the margin of appreciation of ECtHR matters and given the overlap of the Convention and the EU Charter, that has NOT to date brought many judgments hostile to the UK, why are we now being invited to revert to nation-state law on the basis we always know best, cannot learn from foreigners and no longer wish to colonise others with our ideas as we often enough trumpet we did when colonisation was in full swing?

May it be that those wanting to break ties with the rest of Europe need to frighten voters into their camp, and there is nothing better to create fear than a good enemy – preferably a distant, anonymised one – a 'they' of the familiar '*they* stop us doing this', '*they* make us do that' kind, without the '*they*' ever being fairly assessed for what they actually do? It was always inherently unlikely that judges from European countries with many common features of culture and background, working together to find solutions to immensely difficult problems about life, death, freedom and human rights in all their forms, would be hostile to the interests of any state in the EU. Why would they? Job satisfaction for judges is in getting the right solution. Judges normally want the best for all those they serve. And there is no evidence – none – that any decisions of judges in the ECtHR or the ECJ have revealed *any* animosity towards the UK. They are given by judges from *all* countries approaching, say, the problems of assisted suicide, abortion and so on – on *all* our behalves. Politicians, however, have fewer scruples when they want to get their own way. Attacking as enemies individuals who are doing what we as a country asked them to do when we joined the Council of Europe or the EU – *any* individuals – who can be anonymised and even dehumanised into a group of 'theys' can be an easy route to getting something through a combination of fear and little more, sometimes, than common abuse.[16]

This is why, although I express no view on the referendum itself, I do doubt whether consideration of human rights law should play *any* part in what might better be decided on security and economic grounds.

Chapter 17

Law and Lawyers: Not All Bad?

Law should not be of that much concern, most of the time, to non-lawyers if it delivers what the citizen needs. Identifying what may interest and inform a Gresham audience is never easy for Gresham law professors. Confronting that difficulty, having to understand better what citizens, not lawyers, need from law – made me understand better that a critical issue for our modern world is how to make law the servant and not the master or mistress of the men and women it serves.

Original lecture delivered on 4 May 2016.

There are, I think, different types of lawyers. Throughout my four years of lectures and their revision in this book, you may have detected in me the odd sign of scepticism from time to time about the law in this country and about the law around the world. But remember, in our country, there are many lawyers, particularly in the criminal field, who day in day out take society as it is. They are not worried, as I am, about *why* people commit crimes; they deal with the business of crimes being committed in a society regulated by law, and they can do it not only well but absolutely brilliantly, without having any of the angst that I have. And then there is another cadre of lawyers, absolutely brilliant, intellectual, informed, who go on to become the senior judges. And again, they may not have the scepticism that has peppered my lectures. They do an extraordinarily demanding and difficult job conserving, but also developing, the laws by which the ways we spend our lives are constrained. So, be careful about how I have approached things, because I may simply have been completely wrong – from time to time or often.

In this country, we tend to see the law, and lawyers, as for the good. I'll come back to that proposition in a quotation from someone else much later, for it contains a hidden risk. But if you look back on our statute law, whether it is against slavery, or on the enlargement of the electorate, on divorce, on abortion (although that is always going to remain controversial), on abolition of the death penalty, and indeed on human rights, the law of this country has progressed in a way that society has found ultimately comfortable and positive. And it is not just the statute law, it's the judge-made law. Many of you will know of Lord Denning. Although he may diminish in stature if you read about how he dealt with the Profumo affair, the rest of the time his judgments from the Court of Appeal and for a short time in the House of Lords were sometimes provocative, but advancing of the law. And, in our country, the judges have opportunities to make the law, something worth bearing in mind at a time when others are saying that we shouldn't share law-making with others in Europe. Sharing law-making at home between the legislature and the judiciary has worked well; why would sharing – legislature to legislature via the pooled wisdom of ECtHR and ECJ courts – be less beneficial?

An example of judge-made law at home is a case called *R. v R.*, when, as recently as 1992, it was made clear for the first time that a man could be guilty of rape if he had sex with his wife against her will. The Law Lords made this law. Several other European countries made similar changes between 1980 and 2005.[1] The common law approach to 'making' law in this particular case is well explained by Lord Keith:

> The common law is, however, capable of evolving in the light of changing social, economic and cultural developments … Hale's proposition involves that by marriage a wife gives her irrevocable consent to sexual intercourse with her husband under all circumstances … In modern times any reasonable person must regard that conception as quite unacceptable.

This is an example of the flexibility of our law, that can be changed not just by statute but by the judges.

This change in the law – like many other significant changes – reflects substantial changes in our society and in how, as a society, we wish to behave or have our fellow citizens behave. Looking back critically at changes in the law requires us to be careful about looking with today's standards at yesterday's behaviour, as I must do with the following two bits of retrospection.

The first is Hillsborough. It took 27 years for one narrative to change completely to the other. How many parts of the overall system bear responsibility? Just the police? Need we worry – as former Labour minister Andy Burnham recently suggested – about the adversarial system itself that allowed unacceptable accounts to be peddled and pushed? Is a *system* of law that allowed this to happen to be trusted simply because it makes a correction in the end? Lord Taylor got most of the way in his first inquiry to the correct answer. But we know that there were lawyers, civil servants and all sorts of people of great skill involved in the justice process, and it took 27 years to put it right.

The *Jogee* case, decided by the Supreme Court in February 2016, involved the criminal law of joint enterprise liability for murder. The courts had held for a very long time that if someone is involved in a general, concerted criminal act *not* having the intention to do a very serious crime but foreseeing that another member of the enterprise *did* have that intention, then a jury could conclude that the person with the 'lesser' intention did intend serious harm and could therefore convict him of murder, making him liable to life in prison.[2] The Supreme Court overturned this law. One lawyer appearing in the case explained the history of joint enterprise, tracing it back to 1984 and to the case of *Chan Wing-Siu v The Queen*:

> Here the law made its wrong turn ... although foresight may be evidence of intention, it had never previously been treated as a substitute for intention, and should not be confused with it ... When a judge calls an argument 'bold' or 'novel', they really mean it's barking mad. So when the Supreme Court bluntly says Chan Wing-Siu was an 'error' ... the gloves are off.[3]

Why bring these cases to your attention? How do you, the citizen, value your overall legal system? Are you content that the law changes in the end, and *ultimately* gets things right? Or are you concerned that it was in disrepair for so long?

We British regularly boast of our legal system as the greatest in the world. If this boasting leaves you feeling protected from any bad governments that might yet come, turn to the Provost of Gresham's *The Third Reich in Power*,[4] and read all the indexed references to law and lawyers, and see what can happen in civilised countries when extremes take hold and lawyers do nothing to resist. It will disturb your sleep. And one thing we should consider – as some people say 'chuck the European Convention on Human Rights and write our own laws' – is that however safe we may *seem*, having another level of supervision, and another level of court to which we can turn, may, in uncertain times, be something of very great value.

Lord Neuberger, Presiding Justice of the Supreme Court, reflected:

> ... due to our fortunate history [in the UK], we tend to take the rule of law for granted, and we blithely ignore threats of the break-down of the rule of law ... In other words, the complacency engendered by decades of internal peace and democratic government, endangers the rule of law.[5]

So should we be more vigilant in checking whether our legal system needs to be more carefully checked, calibrated, 'stress-tested'?

COURAGE, ADVOCACY ... AND MONEY

A few words now about advocacy. But first, let me mention a third category of lawyers, to set alongside the professionals and the high intellectuals. This third category of lawyers, little thought of these days, are the radical lawyers. They first became apparent in the 1970s. They drifted away from mainstream sets of chambers and did astonishing things, like *only defend*. Or *bring cases against the police*. Or *represent the IRA*. The rest of us, embraced warmly by the establishment system to which we'd all succumbed from whichever social background we came, perhaps looked down on them. Judges would barely be able to speak *to* some of them, or *of* some of them. But they carried on. Some of them acquired a bit of fame. For example, many of you will know the name Michael Mansfield. Fewer of you will know (but should know) the name of Ed Fitzgerald. These are people who have done a great deal – and there are many others – by being prepared to be 'radical' in advancing difficult arguments, sometimes for unappealing clients. I am sure they will be seen to have been of great value to our society, despite Britain, in its usual, subtle way moving towards them and making them less visible.

You need courage in many jobs, in many professions. When you go into the law, you don't know whether you're going to have the courage within yourself to represent your client, or to cope with a difficult judge or to face a 'hostile' court. As with all professions, there are heavy, sometimes very heavy, psychological demands made on lawyers, to which they sometimes, all too tragically, succumb.

But let me say one other thing about advocacy. If you read Cicero, sometimes thought to be the greatest of advocates, who put so much of himself into his arguments to draw so much out of 'jurors' he thus engaged, you realise that advocacy can be an exercise by the advocate of power or even of leadership. Lord Neuberger may have acknowledged as much when he said:

> It is not entirely clear to me quite why oral argument is of such benefit, given that we so often have first class written arguments, but it clearly must be something to do with the way the mind works – the human mind, not just judicial mind.[6]

Perhaps it is the power that advocacy gives to lawyers that makes them so expensive, at least in the UK.[7] I, however, confess to finding it impossible to regard the huge sums of money some lawyers earn as justifiable, even in societies where levels of wealth are diverging ever faster. For commercial cases the level of earnings by the merchants encourages – or even invites – very substantial payment to lawyers. I remain unreconstructed in several ways, one of them in finding talking about, or even thinking about money slightly demeaning, and remain suspicious of any well-intentioned task being over-rewarded. I am probably wrong in that.

For most of my professional life I earned modestly; and in the last few years when hourly rates have risen I have, I hope, moderated the total bill by application of a multiplier to the rate to achieve a substantial understatement and never the reverse. I know many other lawyers do the same thing. And, of course, much of the work I do – like very many lawyers around the world – is by choice entirely without pay.[8]

JUSTICE SERVED?

Two decisions of the ICTY in 2016 tell us something about those courts, and offer something of an update and a contrast to our own legal system. The first decision was the case of Radovan Karadžić, the leader of the Bosnian Serbs, on trial for seven years overall, convicted of some of the most egregious of crimes in international criminal law, including extermination as a crime against humanity and genocide. He was sentenced to 40 years in prison. In mitigation, Karadžić presented evidence about an agreement he claimed to have made with the American envoy Richard Holbrooke in July 1996 whereby Karadžić resigned from public and party office and withdrew from public life on the understanding that he would not be prosecuted at the tribunal. The chamber took this into account as a mitigating factor. This is a man who was involved in the genocide of 5,000 people, and many other crimes. After his meeting with Holbrooke he went into hiding for ten years, never said sorry, didn't plead guilty, and fought the trial. What mitigation is that? The judges got it completely wrong – why? Perhaps there was a lot of 'horse-trading' between the judges about the sentence (as it is understood there was at Nuremberg). The victims were of course looking for a life sentence – 40 years did not work for them. They left The Hague disappointed and even distressed. Karadžić, it was easy to calculate, could be free again if he lives to 90, able to walk the same streets as those whose family members were brutally exterminated for political objectives in a genocidal mass crime. Yet again we come to the point I've tried to make time and again in these lectures: victims' interests seem often to count for little. Those interests obviously required the court to do the maximum it could to help the victims make progress in lives that are almost impossible to live with the knowledge of what happened to their loved ones.

Another extraordinary case is that of Vojislav Šešelj, a propagandist who said the most terrible things in public about non-Serbs, and was charged with committing crimes against humanity and war crimes personally ('directly'), as well as by inciting commission of those crimes by Serbian forces through his participation in a joint criminal enterprise. His trial lasted nine years. At the end of it, a majority decision acquitted Šešelj of all charges.[9] The dissenting minority judge Lattanzi, however, wrote that the court had

> the requisite evidence to conclude that he incited the crimes charged in the Indictment … he denigrated and dehumanized the Croats comparing them to 'primates' and 'vampires' … he called the Bosnian Muslims 'balija' or 'pogani' which he himself translated as 'excrements'. I hold that [by] the use of these terms, together with his constant references to 'genocide' … Vojislav Šešelj also took the risk that murder, torture, cruel treatment and destruction would be committed.

Finally, Lattanzi said – and this is something that I have never heard said in any other court:

> … the majority sets aside all the rules of international humanitarian law that existed before the creation of the Tribunal and all the applicable law established since the inception of the Tribunal in order to acquit Vojislav Šešelj.
>
> On reading the majority's judgment, I felt I was thrown back in time to a period in human history, centuries ago, when one said – and it was the Romans who used to say

> this to justify their bloody conquests and murders of their political opponents in civil wars: '*silent enim leges inter arma*' [In time of war the laws fall silent].[10]

How much are the interests of victims honoured by a court that was publicly this much in internal conflict? What will victims think of a court that, after ten years of trial, reaches no conclusion of any coherence? The ICTY is still a new(ish) court entitled to understanding of the difficulties new enterprises always face. But if justice processes can be regarded as systems, are there similarities between uncertainty of the kind shown in the Šešelj case and the uncertainty 27 years of Hillsborough judicial processes visited on the victims of that tragedy? Must we be for ever alert to the shortcomings of legal systems, as Neuberger warned?

A SUMMING UP

In digging out material for these lectures I found this passage in Charles Darwin's *The Descent of Man*:

> As man advances in civilisation, and small tribes are united into larger communities, the simplest reason would tell each individual that he ought to extend his social instincts and sympathies to all members of the same nation, though personally unknown to him. This point once reached, there is only an artificial barrier to prevent his sympathies extending to men of all nations and races.[11]

Given my interest in why people behave badly, does this provide, in the first sentence, a non-religious reason for behaving well in self-interest? Does the second sentence allow us to go a little further and justify a continuing approach to territorial neighbours, even across the English Channel? It certainly would be in contrast to Nigel Farage saying: 'Perhaps our own opposition to even the level of European integration we have now, let alone any more, is well known.'[12]

The village of Downe in Kent has provided homes to both Charles Darwin and Nigel Farage; the words of one of them will be remembered for a very long time.

As an inexcusable act of vanity I had the College of Heralds construct a coat of arms – of single generational use, I fear, as I have three daughters and coats of arms pass for use only through sons – with heraldry a last bastion of sexism in an old-fashioned land.

When it came to a required motto I was perplexed. By looking back on where I had come from and on all the good fortune and luck I have enjoyed in life, I decided on this aspiration, and it is aspiration only:

Ut Alienas Meis Anteponam Causs
'That I may place others' causes before my own'

Sir Thomas Gresham looked to God for guidance in his life, and the Gresham family motto was

Fiat Voluntas Tua
'Thy will be done'

Is it pressing my connection to Gresham College too hard to find some connection between the two, secular though our age is, but because much of holy scripture points to the duty to help others?

One of the things barristers are supposed to do (or not) is to persuade an audience that black can be white – or the other way round. So let me persuade you that maybe the two mottos are not so very far apart.

Thomas Gresham, by his will,[13] provided public education free of charge. Not quite the same as the lawyer serving the interests of a client at a moment of distress – but certainly putting other interests and a form of public service ahead of his own or his family's. Lawyers are not by any means all bad – notwithstanding the scepticism I occasionally express and the criticisms I make – and at their best do provide a form of public service and do put that service ahead of self-interest. May they continue to do that; just as Gresham College puts the will of Thomas Gresham, presumably written as the will of his God, in the selfless service of others through the agency of those lucky enough to be professors of his college.

Postscript

June 2017

4 MAY 2016
My last Gresham lecture

23 JUNE 2016
UK votes at a referendum to leave the European Union; Prime Minister David Cameron resigns, and Theresa May is appointed Prime Minister

8 NOVEMBER 2016
Donald Trump is elected President of the US

15 MARCH 2017
The Netherlands rejects far-right candidate Geert Wilders, whose party nevertheless made gains and attracted considerable public support

16 APRIL 2017
President Recep Tayyip Erdoğan of Turkey obtains 51 per cent of the popular vote, granting him extreme autocratic (right-wing) powers

7 MAY 2017
France rejects far-right candidate Marine le Pen as President; she gained 34 per cent of the vote

8 JUNE 2017
UK snap election results in a hung Parliament; Theresa May's Conservative Party forms a minority government based on a 'confidence and supply' agreement with the Democratic Unionist Party of Northern Ireland.

None of us is here as a volunteer. From the first scream of birth and until the graves we are born to seek,[1] we will be in conflict or competition with other non-volunteers. Conflict and competition have led to the human genius of mechanical invention, of arts and of societal organisation as well as to the worst wickedness of inter-societal or intra-societal conflict. Little surprise, then, that understanding how to limit wars – a core subject of the lectures and of this book – will intrigue humans until the end of their time on earth, however that collective death comes.

In the very years of the lectures, and as contemplated in the lecture on Europe, parts of the world have been in the process of quite unprecedented changes in the way their populations were thinking. Those changes can be sensed and may now highlight or explain various things that I have raised in this book but that otherwise could have passed as fit only for armchair discussion.[2]

These changes – if they continue – in allowing or welcoming more extreme and more authoritarian governments are significant and potentially dangerous. Policy differences between generally beneficent states and states that are content to commit gross human rights abuses may not actually be so very great. Once a population as a whole makes even a small shift towards endorsement of extremism, the gap between 'good' and 'bad' states becomes smaller. The smaller the gap, the easier for the 'good' state to tolerate the 'bad', and that may be something we should fear.

What is true of states is equally or more true of the leaders of states as they size each other up, wondering how far they have to go to appease a public conscience when they would prefer to get on with the nuts and bolts of ruling. Trivial examples of how individuals acted, and how these actions were perceived, can be revealing. The infamous moment when UK Prime Minister Mrs May held hands with US President Trump, who had happily bragged of sexually assaulting women (whether he did so or not), said nothing about the UK having values different from his – assuming that it does. It spoke of surrender at any price to the power of a country from whose core philosophies (for example, the one on guns) we should in many ways maintain immense distance. But by then, coming after the referendum on whether the UK should leave the European Union, the UK's own philosophy of living had changed and it was as unsurprising as it was demeaning to see the UK's leader running after such a person.

Before that referendum, even to discuss sending immigrants back to countries from whence they came was not acceptable in most parts of UK society. 'Native' citizens understood that to discuss sending 'home' those who came to our territory with our consent would negate essential, universal human rights. Not so post-Brexit.

In the post-Brexit debate the concept of *essential* and *universal* human rights – identified in 1948 and then again in 1952 – may be passing from citizens' understanding as they are led to think only of the UK granting rights as it chooses, without regard to higher-level rights that have to be respected, come what may.

These anecdotal examples of life in the UK are mirrored in other European countries that have toyed with extreme nationalist policies – the Netherlands and France, for example, and in Turkey and elsewhere.

In the US President Trump felt able to speak casually of torture that 'absolutely' could 'work', whereas many people around the world – grapple with the famous conundrum about torture[3] as they might – would generally regard its use as barred by a universal human right. Trump's many observations about Muslims would appear to show complete disregard for the seminal work Eleanor Roosevelt and others did drafting the 1948 Universal Declaration on Human Rights that identified what is entailed in being human and asserted to what rights a human being is entitled.

The UK referendum on leaving the EU and the following demands by 52 per cent of those who voted to quit (i.e. 37.5 per cent of the registered electorate) gave 'Brexiters' an expectation, publicly expressed, that no other argument could be heard apart from theirs, and that it could then be developed and articulated entirely as their leaders chose.

'Remainers' felt silenced – and were. Incoherent arguments and comprehensive dishonesty by both sides of the debate (but probably more on the Brexit side than the other) could count for nothing. Even if an opinion poll were now to show a majority of the population to think the referendum result was a clear error, nothing might happen. The jackboot decision of the referendum had stamped on the mouths of any who might dare to say it was a blunder; and that is where it will stay until the deed is finished.

On 26 May 2016 I spoke at a public debate with Dominic Grieve, QC,[4] in favour of remaining in Europe; we were against Matthew Elliott, CEO of 'Vote Leave', and Daniel Hodson. Dominic spoke extremely well; I, less convincingly as a debater, focused on the good neighbour values we would lose by Brexit. My arguments, I dare say, were responsible for the two-vote shift towards Brexit in the before–after audience poll! I touched on the language of the political debate and, very gently, on the risk of violence it created. The moderator, Gresham Provost Sir Richard Evans – historian and author of authoritative books on Hitler, who knows a thing or two about hate speech – ticked me off in his summary at the end of the debate for scaremongering. Three weeks later, on 16 June, MP Jo Cox was murdered by an extremist in circumstances where it could be said the language of the politicians' debate may have allowed the killer to act as he did. I relate this not so much to show my prescience but for what followed. In a mournful House of Commons debate no one, I think, beat their breast wailing of what we as a country had done to ourselves by language that abused reason, created and fuelled enmities and that may have allowed such a thing to happen.[5] No one, neither Boris Johnson, nor the extravagant Remainers, even attempted to express a collective sadness for what we – *we as a nation* – had done and were doing to the fabric of our society. And within a day or so David Cameron was back to jesting from the green benches. The country had already moved on: this death was a consequence for which no one would accept responsibility. Jo Cox is, it is true, regularly remembered publicly with sadness, but not with any agony of farewell to the better public culture we lost and might not recover. And, of course, few remember the 40-year-old migrant worker Arkadiusz Jóźwik, killed on 28 August 2016 in not dissimilar circumstances in Harlow Essex. What might this say about the ease with which societies move under the sway of strong ideologies – in this case, to leave Europe, come what may – from hitherto beneficial ethical norms?

But if, as argued, the cause of these woes – around the world, not just in the UK – is in part the failure of the 'liberal elite' to understand the lives of others, we must ask *not* what we should do *now* to atone for our guilt, and then yield by silence to the referendum-dominant voice as the easy way out. We need to be honest about what went wrong and yet stick to liberal values. Being honest brings this difficulty. The blue-collar worker – if his vote was in part the cause of the mess – may fear losing his job, or the hand of his daughter, to a man of a different colour or to a man who speaks a different language. His fear is genuine; it is not a fear he *thinks* he has but should not hold according to liberal condescension – or even to any Voltairean fight for his right to be heard[6] before his argument is crushed as baseless. The fear is real, just as a child's fear of the dark is real, even if on one view unfounded. Telling the child or the blue-collar worker that there is nothing to fear respects neither and will not work.

Members of the now notorious 'elite', believers in a 'liberal consensus', often enjoy positions of comfort and privilege from which to judge others. Such vantage points are not ideal for seeing what went wrong or for planning how to map a way ahead if liberal values are to survive being trampled on by Trump in the US, Brexiters in the UK and nationalists rising in other places. But knowing what happened when political theories prompted war (Vietnam), or religious leaders drove wickedness (Iran), or the desire to hold office at any cost prolonged conflict (African cases at the International Criminal Court), or ethnic separateness could be prayed in aid by political leaders seeking hegemony in the Balkans (Milošević) – and other topics discussed from the armchair – can tell us something of what we should do if we are to enjoy some prospect of a peaceable life.

So, what now? What next?

As an 11- or 12-year-old I learnt a few bits of poetry at home, including a couple of verses from Edward FitzGerald's paraphrase of *The Rubáiyát of Omar Khayyám*. They set as in wax and stuck as in marble.[7] One advised against reaching to the sky – an 'inverted bowl' – for help. I always understood that as meaning religion is unlikely to answer anything much, a view I continue to hold. The other read:

> *Myself when young did eagerly frequent*
> *Doctor and Saint, and heard great argument*
> *About it and about: but evermore*
> *Came out by the same door where in I went.*[8]

Is that where I am now, leaving the discussion of the lectures and of this book by the same door as in I went?

I started this book focused on how states – and indeed international organisations – will never confess to doing wrong, on justice and on how to calibrate individual goodness.

LYING TO THE CITIZEN

The way states lie to their citizens – consider Japan on the Comfort Women, Serbia on Srebrenica, the UK on torturing the Mau Mau or the legality of the war against Iraq – is unlikely to change. Should we face reality and speak more of the citizen's right to know and less of a state's right to keep its secrets? It was one thing for medieval peasants to be slaughtered at the whim of victorious warlords or kings and to know little or nothing of why they or their loved ones had to die. It is entirely another for civilians in the modern internet age to suffer – as millions do – in addition to the injury or bereavement resulting from armed conflict, because it is deemed necessary to hide the truth, often on spurious 'national interest' grounds. The citizen should proclaim his right to know. Whistle-blowers, even if they merit condemnation in some instances, are providing momentum. But a major change in the centres of power – the UN, the 'permanent five' of the Security Council, and other leading nations – would be essential for this new right to equal or overrule others, and that would require an Eleanor Roosevelt to draft an addition to the 1948 Universal Declaration. It may never happen.

JUSTICE

The suffering of hundreds of thousands, indeed millions of people killed, displaced and persecuted through innumerable acts of injustice around the world is beyond ready categorisation, and for that very reason easier for political and societal leaders to accept as unavoidable because no common thread can be found. But there is an entirely unsurprising common thread for much, or perhaps most of what people suffer at the hands of their fellow humans, even if I only worked my way towards it by a roundabout route.

My school's ultimately austere headmaster, William Hecker, employed teachers who were outstanding or brilliant at what they did but not at all of Hecker's mould. For example, one teacher – important for me – was Welsh poet Tom Earley,[9] who had been a Marxist, communist, pacifist, member of the CND[10] and an anti-Vietnam protester. Hecker, who could summon for two successive Annual Speech Days guests of honour Field Marshal Montgomery of Alamein and Field Marshal Auchinleck, saw the wisdom of engaging such a man as teacher of English and prep school headmaster. Hecker clearly had the personal confidence to fill the staff common room with men such as Tom Earley, despite maintaining distance, it seemed, from those he appointed and almost absolute distance from pupils and parents. Was he just a clever manager? Or did it say something about diversity, not a term then used, something that was not just accepted but encouraged and embraced? In a valedictory to Hecker in 1967, the schools' second master noted that Hecker had 'the facility of being able to pick out from the applicants for teaching posts … those men who could best …. [develop] a variety of methods in dealing with boys rather than a single rigid system which forced all into the same mould.'[11] So we fortunate boys were educated in a system that took diversity for granted in the values education instilled. It did not even need to be articulated, and wasn't: it was simply part of our experience. And I am reasonably confident it will have fed in many others an instinctive recognition that diversity is good and being against diversity is incomprehensible.

A boys' school for the fortunate in the 1950s was no organ of world government, and who knows how the headmaster or the masters might have responded to having black teachers or Muslim women teachers in burkas. For me the unspoken essence of diversity was invaluable, endorsed by a similar attitude at my home and, even, in the book-lined flat Tom Earley, his wife and two daughters – one of whom became my first significant girlfriend – lived in on the north side of Bloomsbury Square. It was there on 22 November 1963 that Tom climbed the stairs, opened the door, and told us all that Kennedy had been assassinated. Our facial expressions were blank, from puzzlement more than shock; but our minds – even Tom's, despite Vietnam – sensed an end to whatever optimism Kennedy inspired. Tom's language was not of hostility to the president, as I recall, despite his profound objection to Kennedy's approach to the conflict in Vietnam. He acknowledged differences of view that did not eliminate other qualities, the central demand on anyone seeking to be a true exponent of diversity.

Can I expand from this very narrow example of simply one 'domestic' inbuilt diversity?[12] Can I ask – really, honestly – why there is no broader instilling of the love of diversity in places where armed conflicts break out, in particular those armed conflicts that seek resolution by moving populations or killing them? An immense leap, but one I am prepared to attempt, and perhaps readers with other examples of instilled acceptance of diversity will understand.

Diversity is to be honoured wherever it appears; it is not something to fear. We all emerged – black – from Africa, and became brown, yellow, white and all sorts. We 'interbreed' to add more diversity. Seeking to undo diversity – recreating silos of some homogeneity – often means creating glass jars of white people, armed and prepared to guard their glass jars against all-comers, mindless of the fact that glass jars can and will shatter. Once a remembered homogeneity of population – often enough falsely remembered – is gone it can not be recovered, and attempts to recreate it are likely to be wickedly dangerous. But mendacious political leaders of all eras have known how easy it is to tempt their supporters, and even democratic voters, to indulge in memory of near-forgotten golden ages and to reject diversity as an enemy in itself.

Now think of the millions of deaths of innocents 'clocked up' by the massacres of the Jews in World War II, of communists in Indonesia, of Hutus in Rwanda, of non-Serbs in the Balkans. All these deaths were rooted in feelings of hostility to diversity or were generated by leaders who saw they could exercise power through driving people to feel hostility to diversity.

Diversity cannot, as often thought, be eliminated by moving populations – whether by criminal ethnic cleansing or by peace-negotiation 'repatriation'. Separated populations may live behind neighbourhood fences but only for a time until a demand for Lebensraum or some other cause brings on another war.

Post-conflict trials of all parties in two- or multiparty conflicts do little or nothing to quell policies premised on anti-diversity that may easily outlive the trials: the fellow-nationals of someone convicted at an international criminal trial feel enhanced dislike of the victim group 'winners', who themselves feel reinforced in their determination to have nothing to do with the fellow-nationals of the person convicted. Further, as I have publicly argued on many occasions, one of the great ironies of the Balkan conflicts was that all peace plans – even before a shot was fired – favoured ethnic separation, something specifically but ironically 'respectful' of anti-diversity emotions.

Once diversity is with you, standing in its way – by any two-state solution, by sending immigrants back, by barring families of existing immigrants family rights, by shifting populations around – may do nothing except store up for tomorrow more of what happened yesterday. And that way, no one wins.

PERSONAL GOODNESS

Calibrating personal goodness in the course of ageing is to add one task to an already difficult battle. Growing old is, probably, the greatest battle many will face, not least because the outcome is certain and victory or defeat will be assessed only by how defeat is handled. Many – perhaps most – of us who have spent some of life wondering how we have contributed, approach the end of a conveyor belt that is going to tip us over a cliff into an unknown emptiness, unable properly to assess what we have achieved but already beyond use to the society of which we were a part. The last two verses of Tom Earley's poem 'Rebel's Progress',[13] about his life from Marxist to anti-Vietnam War demonstrator, sets out how his activist's political journey would end:

So now I'll leave the politics to others
And not be an outsider any more.
I'll go back to the valley, to my mother's,
And never set my foot outside the door.

Except to go to chapel on Bryn Sion
And maybe join the Cwmbach male voice choir,
I'll sit at home and watch the television
And talk about the rugby by the fire.

No Welsh valley or talking about the rugby for me, as it happens. But surrender of a lifetime of thinking constructively about world affairs to little more than reminiscing about cosy times past – is this what ageing lemming gangs of skilled surgeons, school crossing keepers, scientists, judges, street cleaners and astronauts all face, knowing the cliff is near? Leaving some record, little better than a message in a bottle thrown into the sea before this particular lemming falls, may be a better thing to do.

Acknowledgements

Sir Thomas Gresham – a businessman of great acumen and success – who for four centuries has made it possible for those who thought they had things to say to do so to audiences interested to listen to them.

To the audiences who came to my lectures and kept me on my toes.

To the two Provosts of Gresham College: Sir Roderick Floud, for appointing me; and Sir Richard Evans, who on one occasion with Valerie Shrimplin defended my right to freedom of speech against fierce opposition.

To all Gresham College staff under Academic Registrar Valerie Shrimplin: James Franklin, Dawn Fulks, Alex Mee, Richard Taverner, Tinko Georgiev and Georgina Calver, who dealt efficiently and imaginatively with the unreasonable demands I made without complaint.

To those who took part in or assisted with the preparation of individual lectures:

Dr Nevenka (Nena) Tromp
Shokoufeh Sakhi
General Sir Nick Parker, KCB, CBE
Professor Avi Shlaim
Sarah Clarke, QC
Rodney Dixon, QC
Dr Dimitrios Giannoulopoulos
Hamid Sabi
Haydee Dijkstal
Rukshana Pervin Hoque

To those who supported me, and the project generally:

Caitriona Fogarty
Tim Dutton, QC, CBE
Sappho Dias
Paul Spencer

Tom Earley (1911–1998), schoolmaster and poet

A great debt of thanks is due to:

Neil Titman, for bringing this project to Scala, and acting as consigliere throughout; and

Hannah Bowen, my editor, whose diligence, unflagging attention to detail and (not least of all) good humour and unflappable calm have been priceless assets throughout the development of this book. Much of what you see here is the result of her efforts.

With Thanks To

The publisher would like to thank the following people and organisations for their assistance:

Shokoufeh Sakhi, for permission to include her testimony in Chapter 7: Japanese 'Comfort Women' and the Iran Tribunal.

Professor Vernon Bogdanor, for permission to reference his Gresham College lectures in Chapter 8: The Law as a New Religion.

The UN Permissions Team, for permission to reproduce an extract from the 'Report of the detailed findings of the commission of inquiry on human rights in the Democratic People's Republic of Korea', A/HRC/25/CRP.1, by the Human Rights Council, © 2014 United Nations, in Chapter 10: Burma and North Korea: Avoid the Law Unless Convenient.

General Sir Nick Parker, for permission to reproduce his text in Chapter 13: Gaza–Israel: The Legal and the Military View.

Dame Janet Smith and the BBC Trust, for permission to reproduce extracts from the Dame Janet Smith Review in Chapter 15: Sex and the Law.

Jean Earley, for permission to reproduce two verses from the poem 'Rebel's Progress' by her father, Tom Earley, in the Postscript.

Michael Christoffersen, for permission to use film stills from his award-winning documentary, *Milosevic on Trial* (2007). Thanks also to film editor Niels Ostenfeld for extracting the film stills for print publication.

The Press Office at the ICTY, for supplying video footage and photographic evidence used in the trial of Slobodan Milošević and for permission to reproduce this material.

Nena Tromp, for permission to use the ethnic majority maps of Bosnia–Herzegovina, 1991 and 1997.

Iain Reid, for digging in the ICTY archives.

Linda Lundin, for book design; Laura Fox, for clearing image permissions; Neil Burkey, for proofreading; and Marie-Pierre Evans, for the index.

Introduction to Appendices

These two appendices cover in a little more detail things already touched on in the lectures. They are in part autobiographical and demonstrate how my experience as a lawyer shaped my personality as I grew to understand the need to react immediately in particular circumstances, private or professional, and however difficult.

In Appendix 1 I explain, by examples, how professional standards that I had applied without trouble for nearly three decades in England and Wales came into conflict at the UN Tribunal with decisions of an over-powerful manager who was responding to other, possibly political, objectives. The problematic consequences of these decisions – for the case I prosecuted, for the setting-out of the conflict's history more generally, and eventually for me – were very serious. Over time I discovered how immediate my response *had* to be to problems of this kind, previously outside my experience. Lawyers in well-functioning legal systems can sometimes seem to be little more than skilled technicians operating a well-made machine; but when laws, or even mere rules of procedure, are about to be broken by any manager the lawyer has to be ready to react immediately, even with ferocity and at whatever personal risk, if the 'rule of law' is to be followed and injustices of many kinds to be avoided. Then, being a mere technician is not enough.

Appendix 2 covers my return to what I thought was, indeed, a well-functioning machine comprising the courts of England and Wales that included the Privy Council, final appeal court for many jurisdictions including the Channel Islands. In all the British Isles, I may have thought, there would be no need for immediate reaction to risk of injustice. Surely the gentle countryside of the island of Jersey and the civilised court buildings of its capital, St Helier, would be home to no wilful disregard of the rights of any individual – the defendants I was to try there, or even me? And, with equal confidence, there could be no interference with my human rights by the Privy Council, sitting in the Supreme Court opposite Westminster Abbey and Westminster Hall, just down the river Thames from the Inner Temple where I had practised for 30 years and where, in the 13th century, King John started negotiations for Magna Carta, Article 39 of which is a root of the right to trial by peers and the law:

> No free man shall be seized or imprisoned, or stripped of his rights or possessions, or outlawed or exiled, or deprived of his standing in any way, nor will we

> proceed with force against him, or send others to do so, except by the lawful judgment of his equals or by the law of the land.

But I was to learn, after a couple of years, how things were not so very different in St Helier and London from how they were in The Hague. My conscientious efforts in Jersey to apply the law fairly were crossed by other currents which in due course swept me towards personal destruction at the hands of an overmighty court that, true to the nature of all overmighty institutions, declined to confess or even to discuss its own shortcomings, pressed into limited acknowledgement of error though it was.

The appendices touch on developing ill health, included for necessary context. Overall ill health served my work well. Perhaps because having a serious medical problem to cope with meant other problems seemed less significant and were more easily managed. Or, perhaps, because my body showed me how bodies react when attacked – more or less immediately and to a purpose[1] – and taught me that I should act in the same way when interests that should be preserved by law were imperilled.

But was a developing appreciation of the advantage, for my job, of decisiveness over indecision any more than recognition of the wisdom in 'he who hesitates is lost'? I think there is a bit more.

Decisiveness is natural to some but alien to others who, like me, are inclined to prevarication. For the indecisive, training or education or some particular activities can help, although by never having played team sports and never having been in the armed services I missed two experiences that *might* have instilled some rapid-reaction. I had reserves of resilience, supplemented by the experience of ill health; but I needed something more.

Practice at the Bar had provided some limited training in public decisiveness. The rules of the game of an adversarial trial always favour the advocate who has prepared properly so that he should never be seen to falter or to be embarrassed, although seeming to act instinctively. Thus the advocate who attacks a witness or even an advocate opponent – combatively, aggressively – caught out saying something provably untrue does himself no harm. Similarly the barrister who strikes on the spot the bullying judge, staying the judge in his tracks by a protestation of right against might, is also usually the 'winner'. But the action is always somewhat stylised.

There will be many barrister advocates, like me, whose essential indecisiveness in private or in the office can enjoy a happy coexistence with the public display in the courtroom of certainty, or even of bravery.

My apprenticeship in the imperative of immediate response *out of court* came late in life. It was often an uncomfortable experience. Eventually it provided some certainties, including that the imperative to react immediately when in the right should be matched by the imperative to confess immediately to error when in the wrong – a more difficult rule to follow.[2]

These Appendices, that supplement material touched on in chapters 1 and 6, explain something about that apprenticeship.

Appendix 1

Inside the International Criminal Tribunal for the Former Yugoslavia

I joined the International Criminal Tribunal for the former Yugoslavia (ICTY) in 1998. Justice Louise Arbour, the Prosecutor and head of the Office of the Prosecutor (OTP), was a former Canadian Court of Appeal Justice.[1] She wanted to add a UK Queen's Counsel (QC) to her team. She had never practised as an advocate, going straight from academia to become a Canadian judge; but she, and her Australian Deputy Chief Prosecutor Graham Blewitt, understood the adversarial system and the way counsel in the UK and in other similar jurisdictions worked.

Louise approached her leadership role in such a way that those in her team would take problems to her by choice, feed the problems in and get rapid, reliable and usable responses. All in the OTP turned to her, and indeed to Graham, for advice and her staff operated in a happy, healthy, professional environment.

I was recruited to prosecute the case of Dario Kordić and Mario Čerkez, two Bosnian Croats charged with crimes committed against Bosnian Muslims. But I also finished the case against Goran Jelisić, a Serb charged with genocide and crimes against humanity for his killings of Bosnian Muslims. I took this case over from an American prosecutor who had to leave The Hague for family reasons. Jelisić had murdered very many Muslims and had been photographed doing it on one occasion. He pleaded guilty to the killings as 'crimes against humanity' but not as 'genocide'. The presiding judge of the trial chamber – French Judge Jorda – urged Louise privately to drop the genocide charges because Jelisić was a 'low level' killer and to let him be sentenced on the basis of his pleas of guilty to crimes against humanity. Louise resisted and the trial on genocide charges went ahead but did not finish before Louise had resigned and left The Hague – before the end of her term, and too early for the good of the institution.

Louise's replacement, Carla Del Ponte, was very different. She had been a controversial attorney general of a Swiss canton. She operated the office in a way that suggested she was happy for her staff to dislike and to be fearful of her while always allowing junior lawyers to go behind their team leaders' backs in reporting to her. Before long, lawyers running particular cases focused on keeping their cases sealed from her involvement and a very different environment developed.

When Del Ponte arrived the Kordić–Čerkez trial was coming towards its end. Although it had been the ICTY's largest trial, and a trial of a politician at that, it was of no great interest to Del Ponte or the wider world. It was narrower in scope and lower in gravity than other cases being prepared. As a result, I was left pretty much to get on with it.

But one event showed how changed things were going to be under Del Ponte. The judges got their way in the Jelisić case by acquitting of genocide without allowing the prosecution the right to argue the issue. In court, Judge Jorda refused me the right to say a word and insisted on my sitting down before reading out a judgment many found hard to understand. Judge Jorda's and my relationship in the sentencing proceedings that filled many subsequent court days was, inevitably, somewhat strained.[2]

This acquittal decision, as all senior OTP lawyers agreed, had to be appealed. But Del Ponte had a private meeting with Judge Jorda, declining my offer to accompany her. I was never to be told what was said at the meeting but was concerned that a provisional 'deal' may have been struck where the appeal by the prosecution seeking a trial on genocide would be withdrawn. My response to the meeting was swift but I did not have to confront Del Ponte directly. I ensured that other lawyers endorsed my opinion on the need for an appeal. Any agreement by Del Ponte – if in fact contemplated or made – had to yield. The appeal was heard and the prosecution won on every point, although no retrial was ordered. The issue of Jelisić's culpability for genocide was never resolved.

Del Ponte's willingness to negotiate behind closed doors with other parts of the ICTY from which she might have maintained independence signalled what was to come.

I left the ICTY in January 2001 never expecting to return – although I had left a clear message that I would come back if Milošević was surrendered and if I was asked to lead his prosecution. I returned in

November 2001 to do just that, but the OTP had become a very different place by then, and here is why.

The *way* in which any country's lawyers work can determine the fairness of a trial quite as much as the law itself does. The UK legal system historically depended for its integrity substantially on the *independence* of its barrister advocates – usually genuinely and completely independent practitioners – who earned fees on a case-by-case basis and whose only saleable assets were their reputations.[3] They knew that one obvious professional blunder or a breach of ethical standards could be terminal for reputation and career. Whatever their internal inclinations they were normally pushed by powerful vectors to behave honestly, honourably, openly and in compliance with professional standards. They had too much to lose if they didn't.

Institutional law offices – such as the OTP of the ICTY, itself part of the hugely bureaucratic UN – are necessarily different. There will be a 'line manager' – in my case, first Louise Arbour and then Del Ponte – whose instructions have to be obeyed as a matter of employer–employee contract. Non-obedience to a management instruction can have far more personal consequences for a lawyer than breach of some professional guideline that will probably never come to light if the management wants to hide it: loss of job, being overlooked for promotion, being ostracised by management, and so on.[4]

In the UK, teams, even big teams, of properly led, strong-willed lawyers holding divergent views on a particular topic can usually come to a consensus around the single objective of winning the case according to applicable legal, procedural and ethical norms. The trouble with Del Ponte was that she had objectives other than success of the individual cases. Some of her objectives, such as having Mladić and Karadžić handed over by Serbia for trial, were clearly worthy. Others, such as obtaining publicity for her office, looked less worthy. But to allow these objectives – worthy or not – to affect decisions that should have been made in the interests of particular cases was always likely to cause unforeseen and unpredictable damage. Del Ponte came from a working life in institutional legal offices and understandably expected complete compliance with her orders. Ethical scruples troubling individual lawyers on her team coming from other jurisdictions might not trouble her as much as they would the lawyers concerned, all part of a somewhat isolationist approach to the immense issues involved in any war crimes trial.[5]

Early on I knew that my independence – on which the integrity of the trial might depend – was to be challenged: first by an approach to management within the office that allowed subordinates to undermine me, and second by Del Ponte seeking to overturn policy decisions – sometimes ethically driven – that I made.

I, like any other lawyer in her office, had to confront her formidable personality. Unlike many colleagues who had moved families to the Netherlands and for whom loss of a job would be immensely disruptive, my children were grown up and in England and I could return across the English Channel and pick up on work at home without any real risk of being unemployed. But if I lost my UN job then I would lose the best and most interesting work I had ever had; and losing it would have other consequences for how I would be regarded elsewhere. I was, whether I liked it or not, in many ways as vulnerable as others to the pressures Del Ponte could apply and that she thought should win complete obedience.[6] In early meetings with her I felt the anxiety of uncertainty and I had got nowhere close to the immediacy of reaction that I had to find, and that it was my duty to deliver, if integrity of outcome was to be achieved.

Del Ponte's management style was not just a result of her coming from a different legal system. It was the extraordinary power of her office – allowing her to decide whom to indict or not, how to deal with requests for evidence, etc. – that made it difficult to reason with her. Her office was subject to no auditing system and to no real oversight of whatever decisions she made. She was, and *anyone* elected to the job was likely to be, pretty much as those who made her – the Security Council – would have wanted her to be: someone who reported to a political arena twice a year and who might remain subject to political influence. If things did go wrong it was by no means all her fault: she was probably doing what her masters wanted of her.

I had not been in employment (as opposed to self-employment) since a couple of short jobs after university and was not immediately responsive at speed to the difficulties coming my way. Circumstances, reflecting an office culture different from Louise Arbour's and far removed from the way barristers in England and Wales worked, compelled me to change. Here are some of them in sequence, reduced to a few explanatory sentences.

2003: The Supreme Defence Council (SDC) records were the best possible documents the prosecution knew of in 2003 (see also chapters 2 and 3). They recorded the precise, stenographically recorded words of Milošević, President of Serbia, and the Presidents of Montenegro and of the federal body of those two republics (the Federal Republic of Yugoslavia, or 'FRY') at meetings throughout the period where Serbia's support for the Serbs at war in Croatia and Bosnia was discussed. Del Ponte struck an arguably unnecessary deal where she would not oppose the best – i.e. the most interesting or damning – parts of these records being blacked out from public view. The trial chamber respected the deal although the ground relied on for protection was not one known to the law of the ICTY. The heavily redacted records available publicly at the ICTY were then, surprisingly, what the International Court of Justice (ICJ), the world's top court, relied on in the Genocide Convention case started by Bosnia against Serbia in 1993. The decision in that case delivered in 2007 determined, in part, that the state of Serbia itself was *not* responsible for genocide in Bosnia, an immensely important and controversial conclusion. Both courts obscuring from the public what these documents actually showed created anger in Bosnia but led – by parallel approaches of Del Ponte and the Belgrade authorities – to other similarly valuable documents being hidden from public view on later occasions.

I heard of Del Ponte's plan to agree to Serbia's request – possibly by chance – and wrote her a memorandum saying there was absolutely no need for the concession and that it should not be made. But, I knew, the decision, however unwise, was technically within her powers. I could not force the issue further if she disregarded my advice. Indeed, to fulfil my duties as a subordinate I had to help with any drafting required for the 'deal' she made.

February 2004: It became clear that presiding Judge (Sir Richard) May was ill when there were only seven days of hearings left for the prosecution to finish its case. The case adjourned and, within days, the nature of his medical condition became known to a few of us; he was never going to return to work. The rules of the tribunal allowed trial chambers to sit with two judges for up to five days *only* if the third judge was to be absent for a period of 'short duration'. In light of what was known of Judge May's medical condition the hearings had to stop *immediately*. Del Ponte conceived of a plan to condense the seven hearing days of the prosecution case into five, and to have the chamber sit as a two-judge court. No one – in particular Milošević – was to be told of the real state of the judge's health. This was clearly wrong and not a trivial matter as she, and the rest of the court, including its president, seemed to think. Milošević was entitled to three judges, although he would probably have said he could not care how many there were and whether they were judges or baboons. And if a court breaks rules for public relation objectives, Del Ponte's apparent reasoning for her decision, then the court loses all integrity. I pressed Del Ponte to allow Milošević to be told enough to challenge the lawfulness of the hearings. She refused. My professional ethics body – the Bar Council of England and Wales – confirmed my view that unless this was put right I had to leave the case. I contacted the Foreign Office's chief lawyer and asked for help to get the court to conduct itself lawfully; he told me I was on my own. Other lawyers were asked for their opinions by Del Ponte, who may have assumed they would be too fearful of their futures to cross her. Some were, but mostly their written opinions were as they should have been: after all, the answer was completely obvious. At a meeting of many lawyers Del Ponte declined to consider telling Milošević, and said I had 'blackmailed' her by checking my position with the Bar Council. I told her that she had no choice but to make the proceedings lawful by letting Milošević know enough and she could either withdraw the suggestion of blackmail or I would – there and then – provide my memorandum that set out the history to all the court's judges to force the issue. Which is what I did.

Del Ponte could not sack me for this. She ordered me not to go to court; I disregarded this edict and she and I met in court on a day when I would have corrected any statement anyone might have made misrepresenting the true position. She asked why I was there in light of her order not to attend. I told her I had been instructed to run the case and would carry on doing so. No further demonstration of disobedience was required because the judge now presiding announced that Judge May was 'indisposed', and the hearing was immediately adjourned.

At about this time I was summoned to the room of the president of the court – the judge who led the entire institution and presided over the Appeals Chamber to which any challenge to the procedural propriety of these days of two-judge hearings would have to be made. To my surprise Del Ponte was with him as was a note-taker. I was challenged, without warning, for having breached Judge May's privacy by *any* discussion of his health with anybody in the office, an elementary disregard of where priorities lie where lawfulness of court hearings demand discussion by professionals of how a trial should proceed. The purpose of the encounter – with UN note-taker in the corner – I assumed was to keep me quiet. I wrote to the president and Del Ponte immediately afterwards explaining precisely the unlawfulness of what they were doing. They did not reply.

In the following days and weeks, a compromise was hammered out in which prosecution evidence was concluded with Milošević just about adequately informed of the realities. I tried to get for Del Ponte publicity I assumed she might enjoy: there were two French-speaking defence witnesses to come; would she like to cross-examine them? We would help in preparation, as we did. The cross-examinations were, however, not a success. I remained in charge of the case and pressed ahead.

Ethical or near-ethical considerations, not always a top priority, on this occasion won, but only just. And yet, although Del Ponte would never have understood this, I could only go so far to achieve what had to be done; namely to confront her and to compel her to agree to do what was right. I could not stroll across the court to fellow barrister Stephen Kay, QC, who was effectively amicus curiae to the court, and alert him privately to the rule that he may have overlooked and that made the proposed five hearing days unlawful. Had I done that, he could have done my 'dirty work' for me. But that would have been in direct disobedience to my employer. I could not and did not do it.

From this moment on any disagreements I had with my line manager were likely to prove even harder to resolve.

2005: It was known that intercepts of phone calls existed between Milošević and Mladić, the commander of the forces at the time genocide was committed in Srebrenica.[7] Efforts to obtain those intercepts from a third-party state were well advanced when Del Ponte was instructed by an external entity to withdraw the prosecution's application to obtain them; she complied. The instruction was never explained to me but fits with the theory that the more the 'West' may have known of what was happening at Srebrenica – as it would have done by having listened at the time to these intercepts – the greater its responsibility for the mass killings that happened there. Making the transcripts into publicly available exhibits could have revealed this to the world. For the trial, however, transcripts of these intercepts could have been absolutely critical to the issue of Milošević's knowledge and thus his potentially criminal state of mind – *mens rea* – at the time of Srebrenica: did he encourage Mladić to genocidal killing? Or did he instruct him to act in accordance with the laws of war? The transcripts were denied to us then and to the world ever since.[8] But again, Del Ponte's decision to do as she was instructed was well within her authority. Apart from resigning – which would achieve nothing – I could not claim there was an ethical imperative by which I could force her to refuse to bow to the pressure to withdraw the application. If Milošević ever raised in his defence a suggestion that the West influenced the production of evidence in the trial to obscure its own complicity in what had happened we would have had to reveal the OTP's vulnerability to external pressure as 'exculpatory material' – i.e. something favourable to a defence argument. But by the time of his death Milošević had made no such suggestion.

2004/2005: Ramush Haradinaj was prime minister of the tiny state of Kosovo that had recently declared independence. He was an appealing target for Del Ponte's office. But a couple of teams of in-house *courtroom* lawyers told Del Ponte that there was insufficient evidence to bring a prosecution. She rejected that advice and ordered three *management* lawyers, who never appeared in court as advocates, to draft an indictment. They did as bidden although two of them seemed to age quickly in the process, perhaps fearful of the consequences of the indictment becoming public. In fact Haradinaj was well advised – including by MI6 – to call on his supporters to remain peaceful and to surrender when publicly indicted. Which he did, and no street violence followed his transfer to The Hague for trial.

Another senior lawyer and I wrote a memorandum to Del Ponte saying that peer review was really necessary for such important decisions as whom to indict. She responded to our advice with scarcely contained fury and no acknowledgement of the possible value of what we said. Haradinaj was detained in custody for several years, tried and acquitted; tried again and acquitted again. However, my colleague and I both accepted, I think, that her decision – however professionally wrong *we* judged it to be, however damaging for the institution, for Kosovo and for the region – was within her power. Another possible (purposeless) resigning matter but not one for forcing an issue on ethical grounds.

2005: General Božidar Delić was a defence witness called by Milošević. He gave evidence for a number of days relying on maps specially created by a unit of the Serbian army *after* the conflict, inexplicably substituted for original war diaries and battle maps that showed what Delić and his troops were *actually* doing. His account – as a sceptical observer might caricature it – was almost of tanks driving around handing out sweets to children rather than killing Kosovars in the wanton ways evidenced. He had written an appalling so-called PhD thesis full of racist condemnation of Kosovar Albanian fecundity and was a treat in store for cross-examination. Unknown to me, Del Ponte and her Chief of Prosecutions Patrick Lopez-Terres had been negotiating with Serbia to secure favourable pension terms for Delić. She wanted him as a prosecution witness in the case against former Kosovo Prime Minister Ramush Haradinaj that Lopez-Terres and the two other management lawyers had indicted, and other more junior lawyers were about to conduct. Just before I was to start cross-examining, Del Ponte summoned me to her room where – with Lopez-Terres present – she said I would *not* be cross-examining at all! She explained she needed Delić as a prosecution witness against Haradinaj.

My reaction was immediate and emphatic. Did she not understand that NOT to cross-examine Delić on his nonsensical evidence would mean that the judge would be obliged to take his evidence at his word and to act as if it were the truth – more or less the unavoidable consequence in an adversarial trial process if a significant witness is not cross-examined? Did she not understand that Delić covered so much of the Kosovo case that to lose all the allegations to which *his* evidence was connected in detail would mean the end of the entire Kosovo case? Her extraordinary first reaction was that she would drop the Kosovo case completely. My vigorous persuasion turned via shock to explosion. There was, after all, nothing left but force. And yet an *order* to me not to cross-examine would have been within her powers as manager, as would a decision to drop the part of the case that had taken over two years of court time and cost the UN's tax-paying funders around the globe very many millions of dollars. These, again, were not in themselves ethical issues that I could elevate into irresistible arguments. Of course, had she pressed ahead with her initial intention to drop the entire Kosovo case I would have walked away – but with probably limited effect. In the event Del Ponte yielded quickly and I did walk away, but only from her room, in a state of unbelieving. Shortly after that Lopez-Terres slid round my door to show me the letter by which Del Ponte had been trying to help this defence witness to a better pension from Serbia, the very country that, in our general case theory, was behind the mass killings committed in three former Yugoslav states. This, indeed, was the first I ever heard of this part of the background and I assumed that I was only given the letter then for fear that Delić might mention it during my questioning and embarrass Del Ponte's office by my knowing nothing about it. Delić kept quiet on the subject, as it happened.[9]

2005: Playing in court an extract from a video showing the Skorpions paramilitary unit killing six very young men from Srebrenica was, in some ways, the single action in the case of greatest benefit to the region (see chapter 10, pp. 178–82). By this stage there was a pattern of management decisions that I thought were damaging for the case and that seemed to favour Serbia (SDC records; intercepts; Haradinaj). So I kept all preparations from Del Ponte and her senior management non-courtroom lawyers expecting that she would have done something – one way or another – that could wreck my plans. Was I justified in doing this as a contracted member of her staff who would normally owe some duty of good-faith disclosure to her? Quite probably not. The extract was played in court; as a result the whole tape was played in Serbia the same day. Serb public opinion was transformed overnight into acceptance that the Srebrenica massacre had actually happened and was not mere Bosnian propaganda. Three things of interest followed: I was immediately subject to an inquiry from Del Ponte aimed at finding fault: 'had I checked in advance with the parents of the six young and identifiable men who were killed so that the parents could be prepared for what would be shown?' Of course I had. What little trust; or perhaps what hope of an opportunity for payback; and certainly no word of praise for one of the tribunal's most successful achievements. Second, Nena Tromp,[10] investigators and I went immediately to the scene of the killing in Bosnia to investigate, something we could not have done before for various security reasons. That investigation – on an inevitably cool trail – was aimed at identifying responsibility of Serbia proper for these particular killings which were part of the 8,000-plus Srebrenica killings. Del Ponte stopped the investigation, an action that favoured Serbia, without giving a reason. Third, Del Ponte and Serb human rights activist Nataša Kandić, who asserted inaccurately that she had provided us with the Skorpions video, got themselves nominated for a Nobel Peace Prize relying on the broadcasting of this video.

Assume, for the purposes of argument, that these decisions by Del Ponte were bad for the case and might have harmed other formal or informal processes under way, including the ICJ Genocide Convention case, the development of public knowledge, and some resolution of the suffering of victim survivors and bereaved by their knowing the how and why of what happened. What does this history show?

First, that any over-powerful prosecutor elected by politicians, with the expectation of the appointee being willing to act politically, is a real risk for what is so often vaunted as the 'rule of law' – a rule that can *only* be effective if *all laws and all lawful procedures and ethical principles and essential professional practices* are followed. Although a fantasy, I often wondered how the OTP would have been if it had been led by one of the personally *modest* gods of the legal system, such as the late Lord Bingham from the UK, or the many similar others from elsewhere.[11]

Second, by such appointments, unless the power of the post holder is diluted by enforced peer review of critical decisions, and controlled by the existence of strong *internal* professional bodies (the UN had none) to which lawyers could turn for help when under pressure, then the individual lawyer will be conflicted between loyalty to a business structure that must be obeyed, certainties about what is best for the case that can only be reflected by useless resignation from a job, and ethical rules that must also be obeyed but that will only very rarely enforce proper decisions.

There is little reason to believe that the UN – or other bodies, such as the Assembly of States Parties of the International Criminal Court, which controls that particular court – would really understand these conflicts, or care about them. We are still a long way away from true consensus that the rule of law in the resolution of war crimes trials should never be subject to hidden political interference.

HEALTH

My work at the ICTY was all against a background of ill health, first discovered at the medical required by the UN in 1998. Louise Arbour and Graham Blewitt were happy to continue with employment of the medically imperfect and for my first period until 2000/2001 I had to do nothing but be tested every three months. My body coped well enough with that even if I was feeble every time a test result was due. Back in England from January 2001 my consultant suddenly required me to act, which I did by undergoing fancy surgery, all to be fitted together with getting new UK work, being appointed head of the chambers I had been invited to join and many other things. Then, to everyone's surprise, Milošević was handed over to the ICTY and I got the job of prosecuting him. I left for Holland the day after extended post-operative treatment ended.

In fact the operation did not work, although it brought a few more years of nothing more difficult than three-monthly tests. Until the beginning of 2006, that is. Again my consultant demanded immediate action. Another different 'cure operation' by a different consultant; seen immediately. The operation required a week off work. Judge Bonomy, the UK replacement judge for Judge May, now deceased, knew enough to arrange a week free of hearings without giving anything away.

But while I was enjoying a patch of some optimism, a new problem. A staff member had made a complaint against me. Initially I asked only its date, assuming, accurately, that it would connect to the day I had notified Del Ponte that I had had to write to New York about her conduct. The complaint was drafted the day after. I assumed, also accurately, that Del Ponte or her office may have had a part in drafting the complaint. There was nothing in the complaint meriting investigation but Del Ponte, instead of dealing with it as a manager, had it processed through New York, with maximum and extended effect on me. Inquisitors were appointed to see if an inquiry was justified.

The week I was operated on in London, thus, had anxiety for me of one kind, hope of another and, then, two extraordinary pieces of news. Immediately after the operation I heard that the witness Milan Babić, the Croatian Serb who had served our case so well in giving evidence against Milošević, had hanged himself in his cell. During my first day or so of post-operative recovery, having got the inquisitors to tell me (over the phone I think) the summary of the complaint, I wrote a full account of any and everything that could be relevant before reading the complaint and not one word of anything I wrote was ever challenged as incorrect. At the end of the week, back home for one night in the English countryside, David Tolbert, Del Ponte's deputy, telephoned to tell me Milošević was dead – found in his cell; natural causes; no foul play suspected. I drove back at once (unwise, I dare say) and dealt with the immediate aftermath. The inquisition was postponed – by just one day. Nena Tromp collected me by car from outside the Peace Palace where the inquisitors were at work, appalled beyond belief at the sight of someone dragging himself – and one or two obscured post-operative devices – from a quite unnecessary ordeal forced on me by a completely ungrateful institution.

Del Ponte and her press spokesperson had to answer the questions I raised with the inquisitors about the baseless complaint; sadly, not in my presence, as the UN had no idea of due process at the time. She and her press spokesperson fell out dramatically in the course of the inquisition; perhaps because the attack on me had been handled so badly that Del Ponte had been implicated.

She had the nameplate ripped from my door and twice overnight from my personal in-tray in the corridor and then, without notice, had the locks changed on my door. No advance notice; no explanation of why; and of course no remonstration of any kind from her senior team of lawyers David Tolbert and Gavin Ruxton. Just as when no lawyers came to support me over the institution as a whole trying to hide Judge May's state of health from Milošević.

Del Ponte may have thought killing me off – figuratively – could allow her to present the closing stages of the case herself. She had no idea how impossible it would have been for any other lawyer even *with* knowledge of the case to close it for the prosecution. Resources had become limited and teams reduced. I had been telling management and my team in encouraging confident terms that the case could be closed on time but barely believed what I said because there had been simply too much evidence to deal with by the team then at my disposal. Why, if concerned about the outcome of the case, as she should have been, would Del Ponte *not* have dealt with the complaint herself, to find that there was nothing in it?

Senior colleagues shunned me for being the subject of some complaint that they must have known about, although I was apparently not to discuss it if I was to honour my terms of employment. They felt obliged to give me a farewell dinner – that I felt obliged to attend – at the usual farewell-party restaurant, where

I sat alone on one side of the square table because no other would dare associate with someone Del Ponte now so publicly opposed. Eventually one colleague self-consciously moved to my side.

What an unimaginably unpleasant experience and what an extraordinary 'to-do' generally.

And what *was* I to do? Disease, the power of the body, the support of my family and Nena had confirmed me in the certainty of the need to respond immediately, to be prepared to attack but then to press ahead.

Anne Fosty, an inspiring member of the UN's pro bono 'Panel of Counsel', formerly a very senior UN lawyer in New York, compelled the UN on my behalf to face up to what it had done, something that cost the UN a couple of years of earnings in damages; but that came with no apology from Del Ponte or anyone else. In the world of lawyers, confession is only for others.

I gave a lecture at Columbia University. I spoke at other events in New York. Nena gave a terrific farewell champagne party in The Hague for my team, judges, shorthand writers, the British Ambassador and others. I planned ahead. I applied to become an English High Court Judge and passed the test, but not enough vacancies came up for me to be appointed; good thing probably. I went with my wife to give a lecture at Flinders University in Adelaide, Australia, for a senior lawyer in Louise Arbour's team who left the ICTY once Del Ponte arrived. From there I went to New Zealand where, a few weeks after leaving the UK, I was woken in the middle of the night by a telephone call asking whether I had received the letter offering a knighthood. That cheered me. And the year drew to its close.

But not before a friend on his deathbed got me offered the position of Commissioner – ad hoc judge – in Jersey to try a large, complicated and urgent case in their Royal Court. I was sworn in before Christmas and returned in January – now knighted – to get on with what looked like interesting and enjoyable work, and perhaps a move to something different.

Appendix 2

Immediate Action in Defence of Self

In November 2009 the Privy Council judgment about the case I presided over in Jersey in 2007 – *R. v Peter Michel and Simone Gallichan* – might well have destroyed me (see also chapter 6). Indeed it is easy to think that reading the judgment drafted by Lord Brown could have raised such an expectation. It was said that in a reasonably long and complicated trial I had asked too many questions, and in a particularly unpleasant and inappropriate way; such terms as 'snide' were used of me by Brown. I was, it was effectively said, against the defendant Michel. A conclusion wholly incorrect in every detail as evidence later showed.

This is a more detailed account of what happened and of the lessons to be learned from the conduct of the lawyers involved, but most significantly from the conduct of Lords Brown, Phillips and Neuberger and Baroness Hale. The fifth judge, Lord Rodger from Scotland, died some time ago.

JERSEY: THE ISLAND, THE CASE AND TWO TRIALS

To start at the beginning: how was Jersey for me – someone who can, perhaps, be too easily charmed by new experiences?

Michel was an accountant. Gallichan was his loyal, long-time non-qualified office manager. The case against them that I had been appointed to try was what was left after a previous Commissioner had dealt with only one count of a many-count indictment, declining to try the balance.

The case reflected a 1999 change in Jersey law. Until then 'Exempt Companies' in Jersey could receive funds and pay them out in cash, or other ways, with no questions asked provided the source of the funds was neither weapons nor drugs. Those entitled to the funds – receiving them in cash in England and elsewhere – could avoid paying tax. Many lawyers and accountants on Jersey had got very rich by operating these companies for 'offshore' clients. Many – perhaps most, or all – of the firms of those lawyers I was to encounter in Jersey had, until recently, operated such companies. But the law had changed. Michel, unwisely, had not; he appeared to have been continuing a practice after it had become illegal. This brought him, represented by counsel, to trial in Jersey's Royal Court.

It had been necessary, I learnt, to apply some pressure to encourage *any* Jersey counsel to accept the Michel brief. Was this because what was being investigated was a bit too close to home for *all* lawyers on the island, in a case where Michel may have been something of a scapegoat? Was this to be a trial where a 'successful' conviction of one man who had failed to follow the new law might blur the longer view of a legal system that had allowed piles of £50 notes to be passed from Jersey banks via Jersey accountants and lawyers to those who would then defraud their own tax regimes? All the banks – including Barclays and HSBC – had allowed accountants like Michel to have their office juniors make any number of cash withdrawals per day in sums up to £9,950 without raising any query. So strong was the need for £50 notes, even for some time *after* the change in the law, that special provisions had to be made for Jersey's ATM machines to be adequately stocked from the UK with crisp '50s'. Michel's account in his evidence of planes to London being populated by accountants with metal briefcases bursting their hinges with cash was not at all unlikely – and not even challenged by the prosecution.

As Commissioner – ad hoc judge – in Jersey, I would work with different law, different procedures and two of a limited pool of 'Jurats' – almost professional jurors – who decided all issues of fact and verdicts.

At the previous trial of one count in the indictment, the then Commissioner's two Jurat colleagues had determined that both Michel and Gallichan were guilty of the single charge facing them. In due course it was easy to be surprised that Gallichan had ever been pursued by the Jersey police given the number of other office staff who undertook exactly the same tasks as she did. Indeed, qualified accountants who had joined Michel's firm when the previous 'lax' law was effective, and who had no doubt hoped to be part of Michel's thriving business, had been called as *prosecution* witnesses despite never having remonstrated with Michel in any way over his firm's practices. None of them, I recall, had an adverse word to say about Gallichan. I might have acquitted her myself at the end of the prosecution case if there was insufficient evidence *in law* for a conviction, but felt there was just enough circumstantial evidence for the case to proceed. After a full trial the two different Jurats sitting with me acquitted her of everything in no time at all.

One other thing I feel I can say about the previous trial: Jersey counsel for Michel had had no trouble in having stand-up rows with this previous Commissioner over procedural issues so noisy as to be reported in the Jersey press.

UNDERCURRENTS AND REACTION

Jersey legal life was genteel. There were Norman French prayers to start the day and a Humber Super Snipe motorcar from the 1960s to drive me to and from airport, hotel or court. Jersey's top lawyers, the Bailiff chair of Jersey's parliament, the Deputy Bailiff and the Attorney General, who traditionally enjoyed an almost dynastic elevation from one post to the next – welcomed me at various social functions. All agreeable and, in many ways, beguiling. Life with a civilised 1950s feel, but in the early years of the 21st century.

At one of those events, however, another judge told me that although the Jurats were to decide facts and pronounce verdicts, the Commissioner retired with them and could, by what he said to them in retirement, affect their verdicts.

I found this less agreeable, less civilised and realised I had to be *en garde* against operating a judicial pattern of work – generally long-gone in England – where judges used to 'push' juries for particular verdicts. That would not happen in my court.

So in due course I required counsel on all sides, in addition to providing standard closing oral and written arguments, to submit detailed documents that would remind the Jurats of counsel's most important arguments on all separate components of each alleged crime – normally two or three component parts for each. This was to help deliberations in the event of the Jurats getting 'stuck'. I had no intention of becoming a judge who 'nudged' Jurats in difficulty to a particular factual conclusion: facts were for them and law – nothing more – for me. This system worked well. What it showed of my true nature and of my personal disinterest in verdicts seems to have been completely missed by the Privy Council. As were several other critical things that would not have been missed by an intelligent non-lawyer citizen sitting with the Privy Council to fill the gaps in their experience or common sense, as I later explained to Lord Neuberger by letter.[2]

Before the trial began the two Jurats due to sit with me, unlike jurors in the UK, pre-read the 12 lever arch files of exhibits in the case and understood the detail of the case as well as, or better, than I did. The case started on 26 January 2007.

TWO CONSIDERATIONS, AND WHAT MAY HAVE HAPPENED IN THE APPEALS

There are a couple of things the reader may wish to know before reaching a roughly chronological account of events and then my correspondence with the Privy Council.

First, given the Privy Council suggestion that I had been in some way adverse or hostile to Michel, something that may emerge from my Gresham lecture series as a whole. I have no pleasure in seeing individuals convicted and none in sentencing them. I tend to see offending as a failing of society, rather than the reflection of essential wickedness in any human. My only real interest in any court is to get at the truth – not the actual objective of the adversarial trial system, that has winning by proof or blocking of proof as the parties' aims – and to operate the trial system according to its rules. The Privy Council judges, none of whom knew me at all before they pronounced their judgment, may have assumed that someone who had worked in criminal courts would hold entirely different views from those I actually hold and always have. Such a superficial view of theirs, if held, could have been consistent with some UK appellate judges' views of criminal case work as intellectually less demanding than the areas of work in which they mostly practised before passing (often as quickly as possible) through the junior judicial ranks to reach high office. Not only had none of the Privy Council judges ever seen me as an adversary or as counsel in court, none of them had ever practised, so far as I know, in criminal courts.

If they harboured thoughts that I was an intellectually limited, unimaginative criminal practitioner, then they were in serious error. Indeed, it would have been reckless of them for *any* prejudgment to enter their thinking – even subliminally – merely on the basis of a transcript and concessions made by counsel who had never been in my court in Jersey.

And I was not then or since going to accept the assault on me in the way public schoolboys may have been expected to tolerate and forget abuse at the hands of masters or prefects, whom they should have thanked for a flogging.[3] I was certainly not going to tolerate the errors of others in the interests of preservation of the reputations of legal systems, in the UK or Jersey.

Second, there remains in the legal professions operating in England and places like Jersey the remnants of a 'boys' club' culture that should long ago have disappeared, but where judges and lawyers sometimes do things that suggest they believe they are the masters of the law and of legal processes, not the other way round. In England, just by way of example, I recall a couple of attempts made by domineering counsel in multi-defendant trials where I was appearing for one defendant to force all other counsel to get their clients to plead guilty to selected counts in the indictment. The domineering counsel hoped thereafter to bargain with the prosecution and the judge that pleas of guilty by all defendants to the selected counts should be accepted in order to achieve early conclusions to the trials, regardless of the real justice of the outcome. Counsel forcing the issue may have had other cases to go to, other self-interests to serve. I never fell in line; but these things used to happen. Once collateral objectives are set the law can be made accommodating.

Once such things start they can develop a momentum that is hard to control. Did that happen in this case, where counsel for Michel, on one occasion only in the many hearing days, asked in a deferential, muted tone if the number of questions coming from the bench could lead a defendant to question the independence of the court? Nothing was said then, or ever in the trial, about improper tone; nor could it be. I was unfailingly polite throughout as all counsel knew. Did that one muted question, from the same counsel who had had stand-up shouting rows with the previous Commissioner, lead to a mischievous Jersey Court of Appeal hearing where the same counsel misrepresented the way I had asked questions? Having said nothing by way of criticism during the trial, he saved any complaint – injected with incorrect representation of how I spoke – for the Jersey Court of Appeal. He discovered there was no one there to correct him and no tape recording that the court would listen to.

Gallichan's acquittal meant that her counsel, Caitriona Fogarty, an extremely experienced, very senior trial lawyer with a background in academia, who showed meticulous attention to detail in her client's case, had no further part to play in the appeal proceedings. She had been the only woman counsel in the case and would emerge later as a person of both courage and integrity. But having left the battleground following her client's acquittal, there was no one else in court to say how things really were.

Thus, at all subsequent stages of Michel's appeal in the Jersey Court of Appeal and the Privy Council, only male counsel and their male solicitors (I understand) were present, many having personal interests in the Jersey legal system. English counsel – not allowed rights of audience in Jersey – would 'sit by' local counsel to advise and feed questions. These 'sit-by' counsel often came from the same chambers as the non-island ad hoc judges – unlike me, a newcomer to this legal scene.

Having gone that far, when the case reached the Privy Council, where neither counsel who addressed the court had seen or heard one word of what actually happened in my court, had a pact been formed – silently maybe – between prosecution and defence to let the judge (me) go? Jersey counsel now, by a form of ventriloquism through the English sit-by counsel, knew there was no one who would challenge the version advanced providing the prosecution gave up on me, as I have been informed they did.

Mixed objectives may have coincided: give Michel a chance of appeal; never again have to put up with a judge who would question the way Jersey was actually run – something until then given minimum publicity?[4]

It is now clear that the single muted intervention by Michel's counsel had grown – Caitriona Fogarty was later to use the term 'snowballed' – beyond any connection to the truth. It served in an arguably devious way as just enough to preserve a position for appeal that required the record to be recast from what it actually was. Not impossible, once Caitriona Fogarty was gone.

And if it did happen like this, did the Privy Council judges – perhaps unaware of what they were doing – inadvertently join the club when they heard from counsel they probably knew personally a common line about a judge they knew not at all? They would accept what they were told – Lord Phillips more or less said as much in his first reply to me – despite having nothing evidential but a transcript. They overlooked a judgment of their own court cautioning against depending on transcripts that can all too easily mislead. But they missed much else besides. Other counsel who have read the transcript for other reasons – but who knew me – found absolutely nothing out of order in what they read. They knew how words in the transcript would sound when coming from my mouth. The Privy Council had no idea.

Two wholly independent records of events – what Caitriona Fogarty could say, and the tape recordings – were not turned to by the Jersey Court of Appeal or by the Jersey Attorney General who chose, without reason, to abandon me in the Privy Council, knowing that to lose the case might lead to Michel being acquitted and cost the Island a very great deal of money. Caitriona Fogarty was able – I was not – to listen to the tape recording of the Jersey Court of Appeal hearing and was absolutely shocked to hear how counsel for Michel characterised – to the amusement of two of the judges – how the written word had sounded. All 'fair game', it might be said, in the combat of the adversarial trial process. Had the tape been called for and were the contrast between reality and counsel's performance revealed, not only might the appeal have been forthwith dismissed but defence counsel would have had embarrassment of his own to face. Before the Privy Council hearing the Attorney General had not bothered to check with Caitriona Fogarty or to listen to the tapes; yet neither he nor counsel appearing for the defence had been in my court at all during the trial. They were to rely on sit-by counsel from Jersey or England. Was this all the end point of a 'boys' club' event, casually started and never stopped, that would happen to see the end of a troublesome judge who asked questions the island would not want answered? Perhaps; I will never know for sure. My reasons for thinking these things is now for others to assess.

BACK TO THE TRIAL

On the second day of the trial I had to get to a Jersey doctor, rapidly. He in no time at all identified the problem my insides were suffering. A hole had been blown in an unfortunate place. I phoned the London consultant who had performed the March 2006 operation. He acknowledged immediately that his operation was to blame, hardly surprising as several other chaps – collectively a 'cohort', despite cohorts being groups of the strong not the disabled – had already suffered the same problem. Yes, he said, the damage *might* be repaired to a degree, although this could not be guaranteed. The process would take up to two years and he listed the operations – in the end something like 11 general anaesthetic procedures over 18 months in my case, I think. The procedures listed were absolutely dreadful to contemplate.

The Bailiff was all understanding and, of course, I could have quit and spent months in England waiting for operations. But the trial was urgent; its timetable was, in any event, not of continuous days and it was possible to get a few of the preparatory operations done within that timetable. The Bailiff and Deputy Bailiff, and their all-seeing PA, knew enough of the detail of my condition and of my own anxiety about its affecting my performance to keep a sensible eye on me. The courtroom and court's offices were intimately close together, making observation of what was going on very easy. Most days I reported informally to the Deputy Bailiff, whom I knew from early days at the Bar in England where he then practised, on what was happening in court, including about issues that were concerning the Jurats and even about questions asked by me for all three of us. I pressed ahead despite truly ghastly medical problems, often in immense pain of the kind dealt with by banging my head on the wall out of everyone's sight or a double Scotch back at the hotel.[5] My sole task was to get the trial completed properly: which I did. Had I behaved in any way inappropriately I would have been spotted and corrected – and if that was thought to be due to my medical condition, it could have been decided to stop the case. Listening to the tapes shows why that was not necessary. Nothing remotely inappropriate emerges in what I asked – or how – and nothing of my suffering shows. The body drives and keeps the person on track.[6]

We – the Jurats and I – did not find the prosecutor or counsel for Michel to be raising all the issues we felt should have been raised. I was advised by the Deputy Bailiff that the Jurats' questions *had* to be asked by me (I would have preferred the Jurats to ask their own questions), and with a sequence of detailed charges and the 12 or more lever arch files full of documents to read it was inevitable that we would raise issues count by count as the case proceeded. And that was what – much later – was suggested as excessive in number as well as improper in tone by counsel addressing the Privy Council.

I had no possible interest in getting Michel unfairly pushed into jail. Indeed I dared to ponder whether there might be some unargued defence that was not being articulated based on the nature of Jersey society of which he was a part. None occurred to me *in detail* although I think I raised the issue with his counsel. My summing up was entirely neutral but I may be thought to have gone quite a long way to make it *logical* for Michel to be *acquitted* of the major count in the indictment if his co-defendant was acquitted, as she was.[7] In the event the Jurats exercised their complete and unaffected independence to convict him of this count despite acquitting her. They convicted him of all other counts as well.[8]

After the case was concluded (before sentencing, I think) I gave all involved dinner at a local restaurant, with the Bailiff's approval. I had noted a lack of collegiality among all counsel appearing – Jersey and English – and wondered whether replicating habits of the mainland UK Bar might be a happy experience for Jersey counsel. It was, I thought, reasonably successful. Jersey counsel for Michel, notwithstanding how he was later to characterise my words in the Court of Appeal, thanked me fulsomely, noting *himself* the lack of collegiality in Jersey. Caitriona Fogarty was similarly grateful in writing and I recall the greffiers who had served us so well were similarly appreciative. The English 'sit-by' counsel seemed palpably underwhelmed and possibly unhappy at my initiative. The stranger in their midst?

LIFE WENT ON

By now I was able to function reasonably normally courtesy of all sorts of mechanical cleverness, but professional appearances were tricky. Nena made sure I never gave up on a thing. Life went on: lectures abroad, sitting as a part-time judge at the Old Bailey, with various risks of embarrassing collapse to guard against and obscure from all, combined with regular general anaesthetic procedures and events in the Balkans. Once – facing a full hall of Serbs in Belgrade on a complex subject – I sensed disaster coming in the middle of my keynote speech, the last five minutes of which were a fine balancing act: speed up delivery a bit and look casual, then saunter (while actually almost running) out for a short break before returning to listen to keynote speaker two, with the internal grin of having got away with a problem. In the middle of a panel discussion another problem that might not have been overlooked and yet again after rejoining the panel listening to a very distinguished fellow panellist, who I either confused or offended by hasty retreat. And really difficult pain day and night; but the body moves on; the human within as passenger travels, copes and sometimes enjoys. Afterwards, later that day, peaceful encounters in the local market with Serbs, who seemed to recognise me, and were keen to tell their personal stories – memories from the time of wars – despite my having prosecuted their one-time hero. Ill health really does add piquancy to the flavours of an ordinary life.[9]

THE TRIAL IS OVER – BUT THE ORDEAL WAS TO COME

The case was finally finished sometime in 2008 and by 2009 all operations were over; by mid-2009 I was returning to maximum function with limited remaining restraints on working life. On 4 November I gave a 50th dinner party for a former pupil and on the following day someone rang me – I think one of the Privy Council judges' clerks, but otherwise unidentified – to say the Privy Council judgment was in the newspapers.

A quick read was enough. I had to act. Face the insult and respond – immediately and without let-up. My family and Nena, as ever, were completely supportive, but friends less so. There is a strong desire in any community to be on the side of the strong, and that was not me for the time being. I wrote to all I knew – immediately – to explain that the judgment was wholly in error; itself an unusual act by someone in my position. The victim in these circumstances is supposed to put up with the authority of a superior court, even when the court is wholly wrong. Not a form of respect I had any intention of showing. And then confrontations with the Privy Council judges who had taken something of a risk with my life, for it would be easy to imagine the subject of such a judgment preferring the front end of a tube train to continuing treatment as a pariah. Some to whom I wrote were sympathetic but for the most part I must be damned.

I guessed that there might be one person prepared to tell the truth – Caitriona Fogarty, whom I knew only as the well-prepared, concise and articulate counsel who had appeared before me, and who had been one of the many entertained to dinner. Her client had enjoyed no favours at my hand – the Jurats, not I, had acquitted her – and there was no reason for her to help me unless her honest opinion might favour me. But I felt I could not raise another account of the trial, should she provide one, for provision to the Privy Council until Michel's case (then due for retrial) was completely concluded. I could not even contact her until then; my response to the rule of law not entirely different from the way I nearly always respected the contractual rules binding me to the UN hierarchy, whatever I thought of a decision by my boss.

I wrote to the Privy Council explaining – without Caitriona Fogarty's contribution at that stage – the many errors of their ways. All I got were refusals to engage largely based on procedural justification for what they did; they also tried, to begin with, to justify their judgment, although those efforts were to dissipate over time as they slowly confronted reality.

Substantial extracts from the correspondence follow and they may enable the reader to reach conclusions about the conduct of the Privy Council in this case that will be reasonably free of the effect of my personal recollection.

Once the Michel case was definitely finished I wrote to Caitriona Fogarty. Her reply explains all that a reader might like to know. Fearless of consequences for herself she explained to the Privy Council judges all that they needed to know to do justice. Her letter constitutes a detailed lesson in basic aspects of legal process that should be followed by all – high or low – who operate legal systems. The judges seemed unable, or perhaps unwilling, to learn.

True friends did emerge from the mass of those who had rejected me. Above all Paul Spencer, barrister of Serjeants' Inn, showed himself one with a genuine but tough sense of justice. Tim Dutton, QC, and Sappho Dias who added immense generosity of time to their appreciation that I had been wronged. Others, including Desmond Browne, QC, and Rodney Dixon, QC, showed real loyalty while Baroness Ruth Deech joined in, following Paul Spencer's determined persuasion, with the reluctance of someone in the House of Lords having to be prepared to criticise her friends. Never easy, certainly not for her.

Much later, when Tim Dutton and Desmond Browne had written an article in *The Times*, I received many more written and oral expressions of support, a number having a common thread in the opinions they gave of the author of the judgment, as well as of others on the court. I had just about known Brown to say 'hallo' to, no more. I had no idea what his reputation was among those who appeared in front of him. I do now, including from all levels of the judiciary up to the Court of Appeal.

A letter by many senior lawyers to Phillips drew a reply to Baroness Deech worth reading – extract below (see p. 340). Peer to peer acknowledgment of error?

Later, and only days before his death, Graeme Williams, QC, who knew me but not very well, concluded writing *A Short Book of Bad Judges*.[10] He included a reference to the Jersey case but it was the Privy Council, not I, who were to be counted as bad, if only by inference in his generous, elegant Introduction.

One interesting aside. Shortly after the judgment was delivered I appeared in front of Neuberger in a case called Perinpanathan.[11] After it was over my opponent, Hugo Keith, QC, told me that Neuberger had contacted him asking him to apologise to me for having failed to use my title when addressing me, something I had not noticed and could not care about. He also asked Hugo to say something about 'these things [the Michel judgment] passing', clearly intended as a sympathetic message. Now why did he do that?[12] It is true most people speak well of Neuberger as being a kindly enough fellow. But why bother to send this message after being party to an utterly destructive judgment?

If Neuberger ever reads this he will, I hope, excuse my guessing: seeing someone for the first time – appreciating that he is human, polite, decent, honourable or however he saw me in his court – made him understand that in the Privy Council I had been dehumanised in a way that allowed the merciless attack. Because of this he felt he had to treat me as human, something the Privy Council had signally failed to do.

He will also excuse my observing that there is a ladder of acts of dehumanisation and nearly all of us stand on one rung or another from time to time, most obviously as we pass wrapped piles of despair in sleeping bags on our streets without stopping, suppressing internal shame at our failure even to try to see the pile as a person. Recognition of the dehumanisation process by those on the worst rungs of the ladder, those engaged in terrible killings in wars, are sometimes arrested in what they are doing: 'That thing I was about to kill is not a thing, it is a person. I must not pull the trigger'.

Unhappily Neuberger, along with Phillips and Brown, refused all suggestions of meeting to discuss what they had done. Procedurally unprecedented and therefore not possible; or lack of courage to face the person?

The Privy Council judges could have done one of several things:

- Provided me with a transcript of the hearing before them – none was available;
- Spoken to me – over time I offered to meet three of them, but they always declined;
- Listened to the tapes that showed the truth; so far as I know they never even sought to do so;
- Heard an account from Caitriona Fogarty – they clearly never thought of doing so, although she is a woman of about their age with a background in academia, and someone you might think they could trust;
- Offered a complete and public apology, rather than the staggeringly muted sentence from Phillips to Baroness Deech;
- Written a corrective to be put on the internet to neutralise the effect of the entries there that may have caused me immense damage but that show nothing of the Privy Council's grudging acceptance of error.

There is, I should observe, no reason to read the correspondence with sympathy for me. The risk taken by the judges and the immense damage done to me are now in the past. I have, to my surprise, found benefit in the experience forced on me by what they did. I now know, with absolute certainty, that no organ of state will own up to anything where its own interests may be affected. And this reinforces how calibrating personal value, as I said in the Preface, is the responsibility of the individual, no one else.

In my lectures I tried to stimulate my audience to ask fundamental questions and not simply to stick with shock or surprise at some particular event. Here the reader may want to ask questions about how much trust we should repose in our legal system – brag about it to the world as we do – and about the reaction of powerful organs of state to criticism.

Sir Geoffrey Nice, QC, to Baron Brown of Eaton-under-Heywood

16 November 2009

Peter Michel v The Queen (2009) UKPC 41

I was the trial judge in the above case. I was given no advance notice of any of the complaints raised in the case or indeed that the case was being heard.

Had I been sent the skeleton arguments prepared by counsel who appeared in the Privy Council and been asked to comment by the court – which could have been done – there were several matters, some fundamental, that could have been raised with the Privy Council but were not raised.

I consider I should have been sent the skeletons and asked if I wished to comment.

Procedural unfairness – failing to hear the other side – can lead to fundamental error making the resulting decision simply wrong, and it can lead to completely unwarranted collateral damage.

I have, I believe, an unblemished record at the Bar for 38 years and as a Recorder for 25 years. I have also worked extensively for students and the profession throughout my professional life at the Bar in the UK and for developing international criminal law.

In my view it would have been appropriate and fair to have allowed me to respond to criticism targeted towards me in my judicial capacity ahead of judgment.

On 20 November 2009, Lord Brown, Justice of the Supreme Court, replied, stating that it was not usual in a case of this kind to send skeleton arguments to the trial judge for comment; that nobody present at the hearing felt able to defend my conduct; and that the transcripts '[spoke] for themselves'. Further, that this did not amount to procedural unfairness or a failure to hear the other side, as '[t]he two sides before the Board were the appellant and the Crown.'

Sir Geoffrey Nice, QC, to
Baron Brown of Eaton-under-Heywood
9 December 2009

Thank you for your letter of 20 November.

Your reference to my not being defended rather reveals who was the true object of judgment in this case. Yet I was without voice or representation. Such a person may well be the person whose defence most needs exploring.

The judgment of the Privy Council does not expressly deal with the following:

The degree to which I acted on an understanding – or misunderstanding – about how engaged the court could be with witnesses when the court was composed of a Commissioner and Jurats….

The fact that I was asking questions throughout the case – including in the defence case – not only on my own behalf but also on behalf of the Jurats (who, I was told, had to ask questions through me).

The fact that questions critical of aspects of the prosecution case – in particular where the probity of some Jersey banks was asserted – showed the even-handed approach of the court.

The fact that three senior members of the Jersey Bar and David Farrar, QC, sat through the many days of this trial without once suggesting – formally or informally – that the engagement of the court in the trial process was more than would normally be expected. One interpretation of this could be that the trial felt fair to those present. The single objection by counsel for Mr Michel was not endorsed by the prosecution. Despite every opportunity – morning, afternoon, mid-morning or mid-afternoon breaks, before or after court, formally or informally, with or without Jurats present – no hint of concern was raised by the prosecution or the defence.

Your characterisation of the questions asked by me of the defendant, if accurate, would likewise have drawn more than the single comment by defence counsel. Other interpretations of the style of the questions different from what might seem to emerge from the cold transcript could include that a light-hearted approach was required to get the defendant to face the difficulties of what he was saying. It could be – and may have been realised – from the questions I was raising that there was concern that the defendant's answers had to be seen in the setting of a society that may have been treating him as a form of scapegoat but that the court wanted him to confront the real difficulties not simply to say things that did not confront reality.

Someone coming to the end of his working life – or even towards the end of life – may find himself sustained by his reputation and his certainty of personal worth and goodness.... For an individual to have this support removed without warning and without the chance to defend his worth is a very serious matter. To find himself in the situation where people who he has known for decades turn aside in embarrassment is to cause contemplation of more than just damage to reputation....

I seek nothing for myself. I do, however, ask that if you find yourself minded in future to deliver a similar judgment on a judge without giving him or her a right to explain then you give thought to this letter and to what it contains.

On 17 December 2009 Lord Brown replied, saying that none of the judges involved in the proceedings felt any further comment was required.

On 28 February 2010 I was informed by Sir Anthony May, President of the Queen's Bench Division, that my application to sit as a Deputy Judge of the High Court had been unsuccessful.

On 30 April 2010 May wrote again to acknowledge that the Privy Council decision in Michel had had a bearing on his decision not to nominate me for an appointment as a section 9(1) deputy High Court judge. This consequence for my career was effected without Lord Justice May – or the Lord Chief Justice, Lord Judge, who had to deal with such applications – asking me for my view, and without either of them listening to the tapes that might have eliminated their concerns.

Sir Geoffrey Nice, QC, to:
The Right Hon. the Lord Phillips of Worth Matravers, Justice of the Supreme Court
The Right Hon. the Lord Rodger of Earlsferry, Justice of the Supreme Court
The Right Hon. the Baroness Hale of Richmond, Justice of the Supreme Court
The Right Hon. the Lord Brown of Eaton-under-Heywood, Justice of the Supreme Court
The Right Hon. Lord Neuberger of Abbotsbury, Master of the Rolls
CC The Right Hon. Lord Justice Anthony May; The Right Hon. Lord Justice Goldring
7 February 2011

R v Peter Michel

… I forecast – accurately as I now know – that the damage done to me by this judgment would be irreparable.

I realised, absent any formal route to complaint, that I would have to take the matter further with the Privy Council direct – as I now do – but that I could not do so, or take other necessary steps, until any retrial of Mr Michel was concluded lest his case should come again to the Council.

I had known with certainty from first reading of the Court of Appeal decision that counsel in the appeal were allowing, or even encouraging, a completely incorrect account of the trial to be drawn from the transcript. That certainty was confirmed on reading the Privy Council judgment. I knew that the questions I had asked during the trial were appropriate and necessary and that I had been polite and courteous to counsel, witnesses, defendants and staff from first to last and that the descriptions of the trial in both appeal court judgments were plainly and completely wrong. I would have been writing to the Privy Council now about this case regardless of whether further evidence were to be available. As it happens there is such evidence and I include it with this letter. This evidence concerns the conduct of the trial and makes it absolutely clear that both the Court of Appeal and the Privy Council were let down by counsel appearing before them and thus allowed to err….

Normally, failure to correct a judge – if he is said to have erred – is explored vigorously on appeal with counsel for what inference may properly be drawn about *counsel* and about the *real strength* of their complaint on appeal. No such exercise appears to have happened either in the Court of Appeal or in the Privy Council and yet there had to be reason for counsel's conduct.

NEW EVIDENCE

Ms Cathy Fogarty, the person to whom I wrote, was Jersey Counsel for Mr Michel's co-accused Simone Gallichan. Following her reply we spoke by telephone. I discovered a number of things about the Jersey jurisdiction generally and about the Michel case in particular of which I had been unaware at the trial....

I write this letter, and provide Ms Fogarty's, to enable the Privy Council to review its decision, assuming that any court that may have committed a serious injustice would prefer to know about it than to be kept in ignorance....

REVIEW

Number of questions asked: I clearly believed that a Commissioner in Jersey was allowed, or expected, to be more active and inquiring than is a judge in England, not least because he is the mouthpiece of the Jurats who are the sole judges of fact in cases where they sit. And no one at any stage disabused me of this understanding or misunderstanding – there is simply no single comment or criticism about the number of questions asked from the bench....

Tone of questions: The judgment listed epithets that have, no doubt, been the principle cause of the enormous damage that I have suffered, but did so without identifying the questions to which each epithet may have referred. Without particulars it is impossible to defend. Some of the very few counsel and judges who have spoken to me about the case have remarked on this as an obvious failure of basic due process. Clearly it is.... If, even at this late stage, the Privy Council identifies the passages for each epithet then I can review the transcript and listen to them on the tape recording, assuming it still exists....

While waiting for resolution of the retrial of Mr Michel I was approached months ago by an English criminal QC who had had to read the *whole* transcript of Mr Michel's evidence for other reasons.

He failed entirely to see what all the fuss was about.... But he had the advantage, as he explained, of knowing me to be unfailingly polite and that may have informed his reading of the transcript....

Content of questions: As a result of the way the case was presented I, on my own and on the Jurats' behalf, asked questions aimed at discovering more about the real culture of the financial community at the time and about Mr Michel's business.... Prevailing culture could clearly be relevant.... Questioning was driven by the court's knowledge of the papers and its desire to have answers to obvious questions that were not being asked by counsel....

... It may be that counsel were loath to have a non-Jersey Commissioner explore these issues that would otherwise be kept from public scrutiny.

The Jurats (through me) and I being straightforward about the financial culture may have hit raw nerves.... To be so blunt in enquiring about the nature of Jersey's financial culture may not have been appealing to the island or its advocates but it was essential for the court trying two people for alleged serious crime. The suggestion that it was inappropriate to ask these questions when neither prosecution counsel nor counsel for Mr Michel was prepared to expose the reality baffles me now, as then. How could a proper verdict be returned by the Jurats if this was *not* explored?....

In one of the closing written documents ... Mr le Quesne for Mr Michel wrote:

> Without the benefit of colour, context and perspective there is real danger of injustice. What the prosecution paint as a badge of criminality was often merely an industry standard.

This is irreconcilable with the agreement by counsel as to [the] inappropriateness of my questioning....

In the letter of 9 December 2009 I commented on Mr Michel being a scapegoat, a possibility rather reinforced by what I have since learned generally and by the attitude of counsel and the Court of Appeal to this line of questioning when the very obvious justification for the questions had never been challenged at trial....

GENERAL

… One member of our own Court of Appeal observed to me how this case may demonstrate the need for judges to have rights of involvement in these circumstances. Another member of the Court of Appeal observed how, in the absence of such rights, Court of Appeal judgments are tempered generally, and certainly as to tone, by recognition that a judge subject to complaint has *not* been heard….

SUMMARY

The Privy Council has, of course, to be seen as an infallible court. When such a court lays waste to the future career, however short, of someone who has worked courteously and fairly to all for some 40 years it also lays waste his past. He has neither opportunity to challenge the decision nor life ahead enough to rebuild his lost reputation. He will ask how it could be that judges at the top of his chosen profession, who did not know him, could do such damage without sufficient information about the realities of the case at first instance and, seemingly, without regard to the very rules by which he has worked. He may be left wishing he had applied his skills in some entirely different career.

Caitriona Fogarty to Sir Geoffrey Nice, QC

7 February 2011

Michel & Gallichan v H.M. Attorney General

... The propositions that your questions were excessive in quantity or inappropriate in tone are simply wrong. Questions asked by you on behalf of one or more members of the bench were relevant, necessary, and required to be answered if the interests of justice were to be served. All questions were asked with civility and brevity....

I can say that although Counsel were much thrown together over the course of this trial – in court, in the robing-room, in our respective offices, in coffee shops and restaurants – I heard not a word of informal criticism or dissatisfaction with your conduct of the trial during the whole of that time. This has never before been my experience and I am only too well aware that Counsel generally have a tendency to gripe, in particular when they perceive evidence or rulings going against them.

As you know, I acted for the defendant Mrs Gallichan during both the first and second trials heard in Jersey between 2006 and 2007. I was present throughout the entirety of each trial. I accordingly record my astonishment, on reading firstly the judgment of the Court of Appeal [2007] JCA239 and, later, the judgment of the Privy Council [2009] UKPC 41 upon which this letter is principally focused. It is not, of course, for Counsel to opine upon the outcome of those appeals and I do not do so. However, the trial I read about in both these judgments is unrecognizable as the trial which I attended. Had it not been for the inclusion of names, I would have assumed that those judgments referred to another case entirely....

Nobody, and certainly no experienced advocate, who sat through that trial and both saw and heard the proceedings could possibly have stated these conclusions in those terms about the character of your interventions on behalf of one or more members of the bench, or the atmosphere of the trial. In particular, nobody could have concluded – and most importantly nobody did conclude, or else they would have made submissions on the point, that you were demonstrating on behalf of the bench as a whole or on your own behalf, either bias, incredulity or profound disbelief.

This in my view is why evidence of manner, which is of course not apparent from either the transcript or any extract from it, and which was entirely absent from the Board's consideration of the case, is so crucial....

... At no point did any counsel, whether English or Jersey, indicate to me in the course of the trial that he considered that you were intervening too much or in a 'hostile', 'sceptical', 'incredulous', 'sarcastic', 'snide', 'mocking' or 'patronising' manner. No counsel could have done so firstly because the questions were asked quietly and with respect for all those involved in the trial process, and secondly because none of us could know (save for ... some questions where you made it plain that the Jurats were their source) which questions were asked at the instance of the Jurats....

All in all, I find it profoundly disturbing that personal and professional character assassination of such a serious type could be accomplished on a mere selection of excerpts from the written record alone by any court, even the Privy Council....

It could be said therefore that as this case progressed through the courts, a mere grain of concern which was not considered to be an issue by experienced counsel in the court of first instance, gathered a momentum of its own during each appellate hearing to the extent that findings were made by the Privy Council on, it seems, excerpts from the written record as to your conduct of the trial which bore no resemblance at all to what in fact took place; hence my astonishment and dismay that an appeal was mounted on a basis which could not have been considered sustainable had full knowledge of your conduct of the trial been known to counsel or the Board.

I had little doubt on reading the judgment that it must have been very hurtful from a personal point of view, and professionally very damaging. Although we do not know each other socially, you have informed me subsequently that this was indeed so. I have told you that for my part, and insofar as one can say this of a long trial, I have very happy memories of it and would have been certain that my client had had a fair trial even had she been convicted. It would give me great pleasure to appear again in your court, although I doubt in the circumstances that you could be persuaded to return to the jurisdiction.

On 30 March 2011, Lord Phillips of Worth Matravers, President of the Supreme Court, replied, confirming that the Michel transcript had made an adverse impression on the judges. He said that this 'perhaps' raised the question of whether the adversarial process in such cases – 'in which the judge whose conduct is under attack has no role to play and is not represented' – was satisfactory, but concluded that the Board had followed established procedure in this instance, so nothing more could be done. Was this putting procedure above fairness?

Sir Geoffrey Nice, QC, to The Right Hon. the Lord Phillips of Worth Matravers
CC The Right Hon. the Baroness Hale of Richmond;
The Right Hon. the Lord Brown of Eaton-under-Heywood;
The Right Hon. Lord Neuberger of Abbotsbury
20 July 2011

… You will recall that, in summary, there were criticisms of the number, tone and content of questions I asked on behalf of the court. There are two issues with which you might assist me.

First, who was the individual who used the term 'snide' in the hearing before the Board and to which question or questions of mine, asked on behalf of the trial court, was it applied? The hearing was a public one and anyone could have been there. Indeed I, or someone on my behalf, might have been there had I had notice of it and been alerted in advance to allegations that were made. In these circumstances, it is entirely appropriate that I, as the object of the epithets applied to me, and the victim of the damage done by them, should know how it was that they arose.

Second, it is clear that the prosecution … asserted before the Court of Appeal that the trial was fair, and that the Court of Appeal concurred….

In these circumstances it is clearly appropriate that I should know how it came about that the prosecution 'abandoned' me before the Board. The transcript or audio recording of the hearing before you might have revealed what happened and how it was that counsel on both sides … the Attorney General for Jersey and Peter Knox, QC – seemed to act together to abandon defences available to the judge as to the number and content of questions whilst introducing, or reviving, baseless allegations about tone….

I may not have been alone reading the judgment in Shoesmith[13] to have contemplated the relevance to my position of the passage cited (in part) from the judgment of Megarry V-C in *John v Rees*:

> It may be that there are some who would decry the importance which the courts attach to the observance of the rules of natural justice. 'When something is obvious,' they may say, 'why force everybody to go through the tiresome waste of time involved in framing charges and giving an opportunity to be heard? The

> result is obvious from the start.' Those who take this view do not, I think, do themselves justice. As everybody who has anything to do with the law well knows, the path of the law is strewn with examples of open and shut cases which, somehow, were not; of unanswerable charges which, in the event, were completely answered; of inexplicable conduct which was fully explained; of fixed and unalterable determinations that, by discussion, suffered a change. Nor are those with any knowledge of human nature who pause to think for a moment likely to underestimate the feelings of resentment of those who find that a decision against them has been made without their being afforded any opportunity to influence the course of events.[14]

There has been no attempt by any judge of the Privy Council to meet me. Indeed I experienced the destruction by people as unknown to me as I was to them (I had, at the time, appeared before none of the Privy Council judges) in a public setting, without any notice. This extraordinary experience was, and continues to be, as shocking as an assault. I, of course, am entirely content to meet you, or any of your fellow judges, to discuss this case. What I am *not* prepared to do is to leave for public consumption ... an uncorrected record that does so much completely unwarranted damage to me, to my reputation, to my family and, even, to my income.

On 25 July 2011 Lord Phillips acknowledged my letter of 20 July, stating that he was unable to answer either of the two questions raised. It is unclear whether a recording of the hearing existed, but was denied me. If so, it was rather like the Court of Appeal hearing that was unavailable to me, although Caitriona Fogarty found a way of accessing it.

On 28 June 2012 The Times *ran an article by Desmond Browne and Tim Dutton.[15] This next letter was written following an exchange of letters between Baroness Deech, Desmond Browne and others and Lord Phillips.*

Sir Geoffrey Nice, QC, to The Right Hon. the Lord Phillips of Worth Matravers, Justice of the Supreme Court
CC The Right Hon. the Baroness Hale of Richmond, Justice of the Supreme Court; The Right Hon. Lord Neuberger of Abbotsbury, Master of the Rolls
3 August 2012

Dear Lord Phillips,

I received your letter of 25 July 2011 but did not reply at the time, in part because I already knew that others were intending, on their own initiative, to take action on my behalf. Baroness Deech, Desmond Browne and others wrote to you on 29 March 2012, and you replied to Baroness Deech on 17 May 2012. After your reply had been received, I was provided with copies of both letters.

In your reply to Baroness Deech you said:

> If Ms Fogarty's assessment was justified then the Board's assessment was not and the criticisms made by the Board of Sir Geoffrey's interventions were not justified.

… Wholly unexplained is why you made to Baroness Deech a concession that you did not make to me in a letter where you urged me put the matter behind me. In whose interests, I am bound to ask, did you suggest that? Not mine.

On 28 June 2012 *The Times* ran an article by Desmond Browne and Tim Dutton.

That article has done a considerable amount to make public the 'counter-narrative' to the completely incorrect account given in the Privy Council judgment. It has elicited much support for me from colleagues and friends at the Bar and on the Bench….

Surprise has been shown among those who have approached me that audio recordings of the trial were not requested by the Board. The failure of the Privy Council to take note of its own warnings to the Court of Appeal of Jersey in the case of Edmond O'Brien about reliance on written records of trials has also been noted.

Many people have asked whether – and several have expressed an expectation that – the Privy Council will apologise publicly to me.

I have no such expectation….

Sir Geoffrey Nice, QC, to Lord Phillips of Worth Matravers and Lord Brown of Eaton-under-Heywood
22 July 2016

... It may, I think, be very difficult for you and others of the Council to live with the reality of how you took such risks with the livelihood, and even the life, of someone of whom you knew nothing but who you were prepared to destroy without giving him the opportunity publicly to correct the gross errors the Council made.

The Times article by Desmond Brown and Tim Dutton did much to correct the damage done by the judgment and the Introduction by Graeme Williams to his book *Bad Judges* – finished very shortly before his death – points independently to the errors made....

Should you be willing we can meet privately to discuss what went wrong – I seek nothing from you publicly or otherwise. The meeting need not be confrontational. There may yet be lessons to learn....

I appreciate Lord Phillips and, later, Lord Neuberger, declined to discuss the case on paper or in person. But that was all some years ago.

On 19 August and 3 September 2016, respectively, Lord Phillips and Lord Justice Brown each definitively declined to discuss the matter further or to meet with me in person.

Endnotes

Chapter 1

1. In 2014 a powerful UN Human Rights Council report led to the UN General Assembly urging the Security Council to refer North Korea to the International Criminal Court. At the time of writing there has been no referral.
2. The continued involvement of African states in the ICC remains uncertain in light of individual states having made moves to withdraw and the African Union having proposed mass withdrawal, all linked to pressures for reform of a court regarded by African states as anti-African. Whether African states will actually withdraw is at present uncertain.
3. Quoted by Judge Radhabinod Pal at the Tokyo Tribunal of 1948 and cited in Noam Chomsky, *American Power and the New Mandarins* (New York: New Press, 2000), p. 198.
4. 'Judgment of The International Peoples' Tribunal On the Dropping of Atomic Bombs On Hiroshima and Nagasaki', 16 July 2007: www.k3.dion.ne.jp/~a-bomb/Judgment-07-7-16.pdf.
5. See, for example, https://www.hrw.org/news/2008/12/12/rwanda-tribunal-should-pursue-justice-rpf-crimes.
6. Letter dated 26 July 2002 from the Permanent Representative of Rwanda to the United Nations addressed to the President of the Security Council, 1.5 Alleged Failure to Cooperate in Investigations of Human Rights Violations by the RPA in 1994.
7. Kingsley Chiedu Moghalu, *Global Justice: The Politics of War Crimes Trials* (Palo Alto: Stanford University Press, 2006), p. 113.
8. C. Jalloh, 'Immunity from Prosecution for International Crimes: The Case of Charles Taylor at the Special Court for Sierra Leone', American Society of International Law, October 2004.
9. C. Jalloh, 'Immunity from Prosecution for International Crimes'.
10. Aroun Rashid Deen, 'Libya: Indict Muammar Gaddafi Now for War Crimes in Sierra Leone', 12 March 2011: www.shout-africa.com/top-story/libya-indict-muammar-gaddafi-now-for-war-crimes-in-sierra-leone; Moghalu, *Global Justice*, p. 110.
11. Editorial, 'Cambodia: Burying the past', *The Guardian*, 25 June 2011.
12. William Schabas, *Unimaginable Atrocities* (New York: OUP, 2012), p. 106 *et seq*.
13. Nuremberg Charter Article VI, (c) Crimes Against Humanity. Emphasis added.
14. From the judgment: 'The Tribunal therefore cannot make a general declaration that the acts before 1939 were crimes against humanity within the meaning of the Charter, but from the beginning of the war in 1939 war crimes were committed on a vast scale, which were also crimes against humanity; and insofar as the inhumane acts charged in the Indictment, and committed after the beginning of the war, did not constitute war crimes, they were all committed in execution of, or in connection with, the aggressive war, and therefore constituted crimes against humanity.'
15. Forty-first SDC Session held on 14 August 1995,ICTY Exh. 667.41, ERN 0345-8372-0345-8405/ ET 0345-8372-0345-8405: 21.
16. Dr Cees Wiebes, 'Srebrenica: a "safe" area. Appendix II – Intelligence and the war in Bosnia 1992–1995: The role of the intelligence and security services', Nederlands Instituut voor Oorlogsdocumentatie (NIOD), p. 221. http://www.niod.knaw.nl.

17. At the time of writing, no protocol granting the court criminal jurisdiction has been adopted. Dynamics for progress may change if, as threatened, African countries withdraw from the ICC, making the need for an effective international criminal court for Africa that much greater.
18. Lara Nettlefield, *Courting Democracy in Bosnia and Herzegovina: The Hague Tribunal's Impact in a Post-war State*, Cambridge Studies in Law and Society (Cambridge: CUP, 2010).

Chapter 2

1. Milošević case: '16 June 2004 decision on motion for acquittal': www.icty.org/x/cases/slobodan_milosevic/tdec/en/040616.htm.
2. One slightly surprising feature of Serb history has been a recurring pattern of important political ideas being written down and then kept as secret documents – although said to be effective or instrumental – over decades. These include the 'Načertanije' of the mid-19th century, Čubrilović's 'Iseljavanje Arnauta' of 1937, Moljević's 'Homogeneous Serbia' of 1941 (not itself kept secret) and the SANU Memorandum of the 1990s, all of which embraced Greater Serbia in one form or another.
3. Go to the ICTY website (www.icty.org) and listen to the accounts of those few accused who, like Babić, confessed; not in truth to the judges and lawyers who have never experienced war, but to some inner standard they realised – few actually do – that they should have followed.
4. See 'Decision on Strategic Objectives of the Serbian People in Bosnia and Herzegovina', ICTY Exh. 451, tab. 12, ERN 0114-6063-0114-6063/0190-2431-0190-2431.
5. Intercept and SDC records and research, Nevenka Tromp, 'The unfinished trial of Slobodan Milošević: Justice Lost, History Told', PhD thesis, University of Amsterdam, 18 September 2015: http://hdl.handle.net/11245/1.485852.
6. ICTY Exh. P 613. 25 (31 July 1991), ERN 0212-8559-0212-8568/ET 0212-8559-0212-8568.
7. ICTY Exh. P 613. 60 (10 September 1991), ERN 0206-6177-0206-6180/ET 0206-6177-0206-6180.
8. Nevenka Tromp, 'The unfinished trial of Slobodan Milošević'.
9. 'Record from a meeting of highest political and military leadership of the Federal Republic of Yugoslavia and Republic of Serbia' ('The First Dobanovci Meeting') held on 25 August 1995, ICTY Exh. 469, tab. 20: 8.
10. Decision on Motion for Judgment of Acquittal, 16 June 2004: www.icty.org/x/cases/slobodan_milosevic/tdec/en/040616.htm.
11. 2 June 2005: www.icty.org/x/cases/slobodan_milosevic/trans/en/050602IT.htm.
12. Tromp, 'The unfinished trial of Slobodan Milošević'.

Chapter 3

1. Hannah Arendt, *Eichmann in Jerusalem* (New York: Viking, 1963), p. 243.
2. James Gow, *War and War Crimes* (London: Hurst, 2013).

3. Gregory Gordon, 'The Trial of Peter Von Hagenbach: Reconciling History, Historiography, and International Criminal Law', 16 February 2012: https: // papers.ssrn.com / sol3 / papers2.cfm?abstract_id=2006370.
4. Michael Kirby, 'The Trial of King Charles I – Defining Moment for our Constitutional Liberties', 22 January 1999: www.hcourt.gov.au / assets / publications / speeches / former-justices / kirbyj / kirbyj_charle88.htm.
5. Laura Lunger Knoppers, '*Paradise Regained* and the Politics of Martyrdom', *Modern Philology*, Vol. 90, No. 2 (November 1992), pp. 201–02.
6. Show trials are, by definition, for an audience apart from those directly involved. In normal trials the audience – the public – is admitted for them to see that justice in their name is being properly administered; trials are not public in order to send political or other messages.
7. And was the trial of Saddam Hussein – for which I had indeed pressed when a member of an NGO gathering evidence against him – really much different from theatrical summary judgment with something purporting to be a trial between capture and execution?
8. 'Oral Summary of Judgment, Kupreškić et al.' (IT-95-16-T), 14 January 2000, p. 2972: www.icty.org / x / cases / kupreskic / trans / en / 000114it.htm.
9. Patricia Wald, 'The International Criminal Tribunal for the Former Yugoslavia Comes of Age: Some Observations on Day-To-Day Dilemmas of an International Court', *Washington University Journal of Law & Policy*, Vol. 5, No. 87 (2001), pp. 116–17.
10. Tromp, 'The unfinished trial of Slobodan Milošević'.
11. See 54 bis Motion Litigation (3 June 2003). T 21661:16-21661:23: www.icty.org / x / cases / slobodan_milosevic / trans / en / 030603ME.htm.
12. Tromp, 'The unfinished trial of Slobodan Milošević'.
13. 'Prosecution Response to the 6 May 2003 Submission by Serbia and Montenegro regarding outstanding requests for assistance', 20 May 2003: para. 15: p. 6.
14. Ibid.
15. Tromp, 'The unfinished trial of Slobodan Milošević'.
16. See, for example, exhibit material brought in by General Božidar Delić, ICTY Exh. D300.430 to D300.436.
17. Ibid., T 42100:24-42101:08. See also testimony of Božidar Delić (18 July 2005) T 20408:01-420408:21.
18. Ibid., 11 July 2005, T 42079:0742079:10.
19. Ibid., T 42083:14-42084:19.
20. Tromp, 'The unfinished trial of Slobodan Milošević'.
21. Application of the Convention on the Prevention and Punishment of the Crime of Genocide (*Bosnia and Herzegovina v Serbia and Montenegro*): www.icj-cij.org / docket / index.php?p1=3&p2= 3&code=bhy&case=91&k=f4&p3=0.
22. *Bosnia and Herzegovina v Serbia and Montenegro*, International Court of Justice, Summary of the Judgment of 26 February 2007: www.icj-cij.org / docket / files / 91 / 13687.pdf.
23. A most unusual Specialist Court has since been established by the EU with American support to try these allegations. Indictments and any outcomes are awaited at time of writing.

Chapter 4

1. M. Walzer, *Just and Unjust Wars*, 2nd edn (New York: Basic Books, 1992), pp. 298–99.
2. T. Franck, *State Responsibility in the era of Individual Criminal Culpability* (Austin: University of Texas, 2006) pp. 22–23, p. 26.
3. V. Hüls, *State Responsibility for Crimes under International Law: Filling the Justice Gap in the Congo* (2004), p. 12: http://www.lawanddevelopment.org/docs/justicegapcongo.pdf.
4. C. von Clausewitz, *On War: A Modern Military Classic* (London: N. Trübner, 1873). The best modern edition, ed. & trans. Michael Howard & Peter Paret (Princeton: Princeton UP, 1976), has no index.
5. One of the founders of the International Committee of the Red Cross.
6. J. Willis, *Prologue to Nuremberg: the politics and diplomacy of punishing war criminals of the First World War* (Westport, CT: Greenwood Press, 1982), p. 11.
7. Baron d'Estournelles de Constant de Rebecque, *Le Temps*, 15 May 1915, p. 1; see also Willis, *Prologue to Nuremberg*, p. 14.
8. K. Schlichtmann, 'Japan, Germany and the Idea of The Hague Peace Conferences', *Journal of Peace Research*, Vol. 40, No. 4 (July 2003), pp. 377–94.
9. Its successor, the International Court of Justice (ICJ), deals with some 'criminal' issues, e.g. in state-against-state allegations of breaches of the Genocide Convention.
10. M. Milanović, 'State Responsibility for Genocide', *The European Journal of International Law*, Vol. 17, No. 3 (2006), p. 574: http://ejil.oxfordjournals.org/content/17/3/553.full.pdf.
11. The defence attacked the notion of negative criminality, by which the defendants were to be tried for failing to prevent breaches of law and war crimes by others, as having no basis in international law. The defence also argued, unsuccessfully of course, that Allied powers' violations of international law, including the atomic bombings of Japan, should be examined.
12. See generally B. V. A. Röling and C. F. Rüter, *The Tokyo Judgment: The International Military Tribunal for the Far East (I.M.T.F.E.), 29 April 1946–12 November 1948* (Amsterdam: APA-University Press, 1977).
13. Milanović, 'State Responsibility for Genocide', p. 577.
14. 'The Application of the Convention on the Prevention and Punishment of the Crime of Genocide (*Bosnia and Herzegovina v Serbia and Montenegro*)', Judgment, ICJ General List No. 91, 2007.
15. 'Trial of Pakistani Prisoners of War (*Pakistan v India*)', ICJ Rep. 328 (15 Dec. 1973); 'Bosnian Genocide; Legality of the Use of Force Case (*Yugoslavia v United Kingdom*)', ICJ 124, 132 (2 June 1999); 'Application of the Convention on the Prevention and Punishment of the Crime of Genocide (*Croatia v Yugoslavia*)', ICJ Order 118 (19 Nov. 2002).
16. Scott Shackelford, 'Holding States Accountable for the Ultimate Human Rights Abuse: A Review of the International Court of Justice's Bosnian Genocide Case', pp. 21–22: www.wcl.american.edu/hrbrief/14/3shackelford.pdf.
17. The Kosovo case of Milutinović et al. at the ICTY provides another example of the same difficulty.
18. M. Cherif Bassiouni, *Introduction to International Criminal Law* (Leiden: Brill, 2013, 2nd rev. edn), p. 919.

Chapter 5

1. 'Historically the most lasting impact of "Bloody Sunday" was the effect it had on that generation of young people in Derry, many of whom were on the march that day. As a result, hundreds joined the Provisional IRA, eager to seek revenge for the murders they believed the British Army had committed and the cover-up they were convinced had been perpetrated by Lord Widgery … "Bloody Sunday" had given the Provisional IRA the biggest boost in its history.' Peter Taylor, *Provos: The IRA and Sinn Fein* (London: Bloomsbury, 1998), pp. 126–27.
2. For example, the seven peremptory challenges each defendant had to jurors from the panel meant that in the 1970 'Mangrove 9' trial involving racial allegations against police, 63 challenges were available to ensure the jury ultimately had two black jurors. However, the right to challenge jurors was progressively whittled away and finally abolished altogether. The right to silence when interviewed under caution and in a trial has been reduced to almost nothing, as the prosecution can make adverse comments about those who exercise the right in either setting. The requirements for corroboration in cases involving sex and cases where children were witnesses have been abolished.
3. Desmond Browne, QC, and Tim Dutton, QC, 'Is it only judges that are condemned without the right to be heard?', *The Times*, 28 June 2012.
4. David Barrett and John Bingham, '"Judges lead 'sheltered lives'", warns Britain's most senior female judge', *The Telegraph*, 6 April 2013.
5. This history is dealt with in more detail in Appendix 2 with a review of the correspondence.
6. Expressed another way, the trouble with the modern family of international courts is that there is no supreme / constitutional court to synthesise or correct divergent decisions of the top appellate levels of the various independent courts.
7. During the expenses scandal in 2009 that brought Parliament into disrepute, one MP, Douglas Hogg, was found to have claimed the cleaning of the moat round his country house as a legitimate expense, to the disgust of the public. He was subsequently made a life peer.

Chapter 6

1. 'The term chemical weapon is applied to any toxic chemical or its precursor that can cause death, injury, temporary incapacitation or sensory irritation through its chemical action. Munitions or other delivery devices designed to deliver chemical weapons, whether filled or unfilled, are also considered weapons themselves': www.opcw.org / about-chemical-weapons / what-is-a-chemical-weapon.
2. United Nations General Assembly Resolution 1514 of 14 December 1960, 'Declaration on the Granting of Independence to Colonial Countries and Peoples'.
3. Dwight D. Eisenhower, 'The President's News Conference, 7 April 1954', The American Presidency Project: www.presidency.ucsb.edu / ws / ?pid=10202.
4. See also *Sundus Saleh v George Bush et al*. Dave Eggers, '"These are dangerous times": The man who sued George W. Bush and the Iraq War', *The Guardian*, 11 March 2017.
5. Rodric B. Schoen, 'A Strange Silence: Vietnam and the Supreme Court', *Washburn Law Journal*, Vol. 33, 1993–94, pp. 278–79.

6. Treaty of London of 8 August 1945, Article 6(a) declares that 'waging of a war of aggression' is a 'crime against peace'; individual criminal responsibility followed, with Article 8 only allowing acting pursuant to order of government to be a matter of mitigation.
7. Schoen, 'A Strange Silence', p. 281.
8. A Vietnam War Timeline: www.english.illinois.edu/maps/vietnam/timeline.htm.
9. Alfonso Narvaez, 'Gen. Curtis LeMay, an architect of strategic air power, dies at 83', *New York Times*, 2 October 1990.
10. R. W. Apple, Jr, 'McNamara recalls, and regrets, Vietnam', *New York Times*, 9 April 1995.
11. 'On Civil Disobedience' (pamphlet; London: National Campaign for Youth Disarmament, 1961).
12. Bertrand Russell, *The Autobiography of Bertrand Russell* (Abingdon: Routledge, 2000), pp. 719–20.
13. In its 1993 statute, after these events, the ICTY identified existing law that was also in place at the time of the Vietnam War.
14. *Prevent the Crime of Silence: Reports from the sessions of the International War Crimes Tribunal founded by Bertrand Russell, London, Stockholm, Roskilde* (London: Allen Lane, 1971).
15. See further www.tuantran.org/russelltribunal/#a3.
16. Staughton Lynd, 'The War Crimes Tribunal: A Dissent', *Libération*, Vol. 12, December 1967–January 1968.
17. Something that can be sensed in commentators on the Gaza–Israel conflict, who may be tempted to see the Gazan David as incapable of committing war crimes against the Israeli Goliath – when of course the Gazans (Hamas or not) could be guilty, and should be considered for investigation when appropriate, just as any other party to an armed conflict.

Chapter 7

1. An Iranian detainee and survivor, Shokoufeh Sakhi, participated in this lecture and answered questions put to her by Geoffrey and the audience.
2. Hiroko Tabuchi, 'Japan's Abe: No Proof of WWII Sex Slaves', Associated Press, 1 March 2007.
3. 'The Women's International War Crimes Tribunal for the Trial of Japan's Military Sexual Slavery, Judgment on the Common Indictment and the Application for Restitution and Reparation', Part I, 'Introduction and Background of the Proceedings', 4 December 2001, paragraph 8: http://www.iccwomen.org/wigjdraft1/Archives/oldWCGJ/tokyo.
4. Ibid., Part VIII, 'Conclusion', paras 1093–94.
5. Iran Tribunal (www.irantribunal.com), Judgment, *Prosecutor v Islamic Republic of Iran*, 5 January 2013, para. 93.
6. Ibid., para. 52.
7. Ibid., para. 56.
8. Shokoufeh's testimony was all too clear:

   Q. Each inmate had a space of 80 or 85 cm by two metres to occupy.

   A. Yes.

Q. Next door to each other, were you prevented from oral communication by the person in, if we can call it the first cell, having to sit at the front of the cell facing the wall.

A. Yes.

Q. And the people next door sitting at the back of the two-metre coffin in order that they could not speak.

A. Yes.

Q. How many hours a day did you have to sit facing the wall?

A. Fourteen / fifteen hours.

Q. Were you able to see anything?

A. No, we were blindfolded 24 hours all the time when we were there.

Q. When you went to the lavatory, were you able to take your blindfold off?

A. Only after we went inside, we could take it off, get the job done, and then before stepping out we had to be blindfolded again and cuffed.

Q. As well as blindfolds, was there the use of cotton wool between the blindfolds and the eyes?

A. Yes, sometimes two layers, three layers of blindfold have some cotton balls stuffed there so you cannot see anything.

Q. You have dealt with day time, where the system made it impossible for you to speak to one another.

A. Yes.

Q. At night time how was that achieved?

A. On that occasion I could have contact with the person on the other side ...

Q. My mistake. I will start the question again. At night time in order to avoid you speaking to the person next door, did you sleep head to toe?

A. Head to toe, yes.

Q. Before we move on, you can help us I think now with the business of Morse code.

A. Yes.

Q. Was Morse code used by the women in the prison on a pretty general basis?

A. I can say among the resistant prisoners, yes.

Q. Did you learn Morse code in the time that you were in these coffins or cells?

A. Yes, I did.

Q. Did you learn it at night time?

A. Yes, I did.

Q. When you were head to toe?

A. Yes.

Q. Can you explain as shortly as you can how it was that you were able to learn Morse code?

A. I managed during the day to pass a short note to the person sitting besides me underneath this wood that I need to learn Morse code.

Q. I think that you kept a tiny bit of lead somewhere in your clothing.

A. Just in the hem of my clothes. I found a piece of paper and I went to the bathroom and I mentioned Morse code and I passed it in a moment to her. When we were lying down head to toe she would write the letter on the blanket, because we had the blanket over us, so from under the boards she would write a letter ... the first letter, for example, A, on my toe with her finger and then having a piece of string between us, one in my hand and one in her hand, she would pull one-one, and that would be A. Then the next one B and I would follow the trace of her finger on my toe and then one-one-two and that was B. That is how I learned.

Q. It was possible physically to get a finger underneath the board that lay between you?

A. For the first few months and then the warden found out and they actually fixed that problem with the boarding and they made it impossible after that.

Q. And you had a piece of thread or string, which enabled you to count out the dots and the dashes or whatever it is for Morse codes?

A. Exactly.

Q. You having learned Morse code in that way, was it shared with other prisoners in different methods?

A. Yes.

Q. As well as being able to communicate by thread in this particular example, was it ever possible to tap on walls?

A. Yes.

Q. When prisoners were separated from buildings one to another, but they could see each other or see something of each other in the windows, was it possible to achieve Morse code communication?

A. Yes.

Q. How was that done?

A. Playing with shade and covering the window and just moving objects in front of the window.

Chapter 8

1. The subject of this chapter was the result of a request from a member of my lecture audience that I deal with issues raised by Professor Bogdanor in his Gresham College law lectures: 'The Human Rights Act: Cornerstone of a New Constitution' (25 January 2005), 'The Judges and the Constitution' (30 May 2006), and 'Judges or Legislators: Who should rule?' (16 March 2009).
2. David Dixon, 'Entry to the solicitor's profession 1980–2011' (May 2012): www.lawsociety.org.uk.
3. www.barstandardsboard.org.uk/media-centre/research-and-statistics/statistics/practising-barrister-statistics.
4. 'Every person who has mastered a profession is a sceptic concerning it.' G.B. Shaw, *Mrs Warren's Profession.*
5. Colm O'Cinneide, 'The Human Rights Act and the Slow Transformation of the UK's "Political Constitution"': www.ucl.ac.uk/human-rights/research/working-papers/docs/colm-o_cinneide.
6. Residual powers of the monarch, mostly exercised directly by the government without parliamentary involvement.
7. 'Judges or Legislators: Who should rule?', 16 March 2009.

8. Lord Sumption, 'The Limits of Law', 27th Sultan Azlan Shah Lecture, Kuala Lumpur, 20 November 2013: www.supremecourt.uk/docs/speech-131120.pdf.
9. Compare Lord Justice Leveson's policy recommendations on the press (2012) with Lord Denning's more limited process recommendations in his report on Profumo (1963).
10. www.supremecourt.uk/decided-cases/docs/UKSC_2012_0151_Judgment.pdf.
11. The heading for this section will remind some readers of how, when the *Daily Mail* did not like a judgment delivered over Brexit by three very senior judges, it described them as 'enemies of the people'. Laws and Sumption may reveal differences of view about the UK and Europe, but their lectures show them to be putting their immense knowledge and wisdom to work by the application of reason in the interests of the people.
12. Lord Justice Laws, 'The Common Law and Europe', Hamlyn lectures, 27 November 2013: www.judiciary.gov.uk/wp-content/uploads/JCO/Documents/Speeches/laws-lj-speech-hamlyn-lecture-2013.pdf; Lord Sumption, 'The Limits of Law'.
13. In an earlier lecture in the series Lord Justice Laws had quoted Sir Gerard Brennan, Chief Justice of Australia 1995–98, who said in a lecture at University College Dublin in 1997 that the common law courts have 'no power but the power of judgment, [and] no power base but public confidence'.
14. In his lecture Lord Justice Laws quotes Lord Denning describing the encroachment of law as an incoming tide which it is feared cannot be held back.
15. Lord Sumption, 'The Limits of Law'.
16. '… some degree of judicial lawmaking is unavoidable, especially in an un-codified common law system … Even in a case where the limits have been exceeded, I am not going to suggest that the fabric of society will break down because judges, whether sitting in London, Washington or anywhere else, make law for which there is no democratic mandate. The process by which democracies decline is more subtle than that.'
17. The EU Charter – barely dealt with in my original lecture – has not to date been the anti-UK force those seeking Brexit threatened; few decisions of this court, that reinforces and even enlarges ECHR rights, have imposed changes on UK law. Worldwide changes in the approach to politics happening since these lectures were given may be a further impetus for citizens – even peaceful home-loving types – to turn wherever they can for the assistance of good law if they find themselves living under worryingly authoritarian regimes. And in a disturbing way it can be law more than lawyers that are the last defence. Two-thirds of those sitting round the table at the Wannsee Conference in 1942 that confirmed Nazi plans for the Holocaust were lawyers. They offered no resistance to what German law by then allowed. Once protection of the law itself is gone, lawyers may become far too compliant to save the citizen from harm.

Chapter 9

1. J. E. Singleton, KC, *Conduct at The Bar* (Eastern Press, 1933).
2. W. W. Boulton, *Conduct and Etiquette at the Bar* (Butterworths, 1970).
3. The late Michael Lewis, QC.

4. Hammurabi reigned c. 1792–1750 BCE.
5. Alcibiades in Plato's *Symposium*, translated by Tom Griffith (Marlborough: Libanus Press, 1986).
6. Cicero, *In Verrem* ('Against Verres') I.1.10. English translation from Michael Grant, *Cicero: Selected Works* (London: Penguin Books, 1960).
7. Cicero, *Pro Quinctio* ('For Publius Quinctius') 5. English translation from *The Orations of Marcus Tullius Cicero, literally translated by C. D. Yonge* (London, George Bell & Sons, 1903).
8. See generally Anton-Hermann Chroust, *Legal Profession in Ancient Imperial Rome*, available at: http://scholarship.law.nd.edu/ndlr/vol30/iss4/2.
9. John H. Langbein, *Origins of the Adversarial Trial* (Oxford: OUP, 2003).
10. This followed Viking practices and the Grand Jury procedure established by Henry II.
11. www.bl.uk/magna-carta/articles/magna-carta-english-translation.
12. The same Penn who founded Pennsylvania.
13. Sir John Vaughan, Chief Justice of the Court of Common Pleas, initially held that the writ should not be granted, saying that it was King's Bench that should issue writs of *habeas corpus* in ordinary criminal cases; the other justices, however, issued the writ and Vaughan then ruled that a jury could not be punished simply on account of the verdict it returned.
14. See Graham Turnbull, QC, www.criminalcle.net.au/attachments/closing_address_paper.pdf.
15. During this period, Amnesty International adopted him as a 'Prisoner of Conscience', and, in 1977, he was expelled from the country and moved to the US.
16. Clive Emsley, Tim Hitchcock and Robert Shoemaker, 'Crime and Justice – Trial Procedures', *Old Bailey Proceedings Online*, www.oldbaileyonline.org, 28 February 2017.
17. 'The growing use of lawyers during the 18th century appears to have in part resulted from the growth of commerce. It was merchants and shopkeepers who hired prosecuting counsel in significant numbers.' Emsley, Hitchcock and Shoemaker, 'Crime and Justice – Trial Procedures'.
18. 'Lawyers who appeared at the Old Bailey in the 18th century hardly ever made it to the very top of the legal profession. They were often accused of being ignorant of the law and of a general incivility, something that was also said to characterise their bullying of witnesses. Such accusations were not always unfounded.' Emsley, Hitchcock and Shoemaker, 'Crime and Justice – Trial Procedures'.
19. Section 1, Criminal Evidence Act 1898.
20. In the UK as criminal trials have been seen as more reliable and 'fairer' than formerly, the defendant's right to silence in police station or in court has been very substantially eroded. Other adversarial jurisdictions – the US in particular – have yet to follow this lead.
21. See www.theguardian.com/commentisfree/libertycentral/2009/jul/13/oratory-court-barristers-marcel-berlins.
22. It could be said, now that the Brexit result is with us, that both sides revealed how some of the crudest tricks of advocacy – extravagance of language, deception,

overstatement, etc. – remain alive in political discourse when audiences are emotionally predisposed to conclusions on one side or the other.

23. See cases from the 1990s listed in http://netk.net.au/IRAbombingsHome.asp, e.g. *R. v Judith Ward* (The M62 Bombings), or *Richardson, Conlon, Armstrong and Hill* (The Guildford Four) and issues raised in the '7/11' case, at, e.g. www.dailymail.co.uk/news/article-4282208/The-cover-explode-UK-s-biggest-bomb-trial.html.
24. See 'ground-breaking' judgment of Court of Appeal in *R. v Lubemba, R. v J.P.* [2014] EWCA Crim 2064, presided over by Lady Justice Hallett. Heather Hallett, as she then was, and I were often against each other in the 1970s and 1980s in Kent fighting conventional criminal cases according to the standard rules of procedure and practice. How surprised we might both have been then to understand how the passage of time and accumulation of experience might change our views of fairness of legal process quite as substantially, as I expect, has happened for both of us.
25. In the original lecture, I demonstrated by unrehearsed interrogation of a member of the Gresham staff quite how unfair the adversarial form of questioning can be – seen at minute 33 on www.youtube.com/watch?v=suD8x-gWbeg.
26. Episodes of *Rumpole of the Bailey* are readily available online. In the first – effectively pilot – episode, 'Rumpole and the Confession of Guilt', Rumpole defends a man who has confessed to a killing, but the police have 'over-egged' the 'verbal' confession. Rumpole says pretty well all that needs to be said about the type of courage required at the Bar, the role of instinct and why the virtues of the adversarial system should at least be doubted.
27. I often enough try to shock junior barristers who show some sense of self-importance – but also money-bragging judges – with the proposition: 'You only became a lawyer fiddling around in the affairs of others because you couldn't do a proper job like farming or making a motor car or teaching.' Tongue in cheek? Of course. Grain of truth? Well, they never fight back.

Chapter 10

1. 'Crimes in Burma', a report by the International Human Rights Clinic at Harvard Law School, May 2009: http://hls.harvard.edu/dept/clinical/clinics/international-human-rights-clinic. I was one of the commissioners who endorsed the report.
2. http://burmacampaign.org.uk/belgium-supports-the-establishment-of-a-u-n-commission-of-inquiry-in-burma.
3. In the 2011 case of Ko Mya Aye, brought by London barrister Sappho Dias and others, the United Nations Working Group on Arbitrary Detention reminded Burma of its obligations under international law and highlighted the fact that in 12 previous judgments, the court had pointed out Burma's illegal conduct towards its citizens.
4. See Section III, 'Historical and political context of human rights violations in the Democratic People's Republic of Korea', in the 'Report of the detailed findings of the commission of inquiry on human rights in the Democratic People's Republic of Korea', Human Rights Council, 7 February 2014, © United Nations, for an excellent overview of the relevant history, said by Justice Kirby to have been written by a member of the Commissioners' Secretariat, Christine Chung: www.ohchr.org/EN/HRBodies/HRC/CoIDPRK/Pages/CommissionInquiryonHRinDPRK.aspx.

5. Ibid.
6. Ibid., paras 259–61.
7. Ibid., paras 687–90.
8. Ibid., paras 838–42. Reprinted with the permission of the United Nations.
9. These would now be supplemented by the 2017 assassination in Kuala Lumpur airport of Kim Jong-nam, half-brother of Supreme Leader Kim Jong-un.

Chapter 11

1. Later Judge Seys Llewellyn, QC, senior civil judge of Wales.
2. Later Lord Justice Leveson, of the report into the press.
3. *Barrett v MoD*, 21 December 1994: www.bailii.org/ew/cases/EWCA/Civ/1994/7.html.
4. N. A. M. Rodger, *The Wooden World: An Anatomy of the Georgian Navy* (London: Collins, 1986), pp. 73–74.
5. See Appendix 1 for details of some of these problems.
6. ICTY trial transcript, 27 May 2005: www.icty.org/x/cases/slobodan_milosevic/trans/en/050527ED.htm.
7. ICTY trial transcript, 1 June 2005: www.icty.org/x/cases/slobodan_milosevic/trans/en/050601IT.htm.

Chapter 12

1. Raphael Lemkin, *Axis Rule in Occupied Europe: Laws of Occupation – Analysis of Government – Proposals for Redress* (Washington, DC: Carnegie Endowment for International Peace, 1944), pp. 79–95.
2. Ibid.
3. It is said Lemkin was stimulated to name the unnamed crime in part by a radio broadcast by Winston Churchill in August 1941, following receipt of information about Nazi massacres in Ukraine and Russia, details of which Churchill now knew but could not spell out without compromising his intelligence source: 'Since the Mongol invasions of Europe in the 16th century, there has never been methodical, merciless butchery on such a scale, or approaching such a scale … We are in the presence of a crime without a name.'
4. Benjamin Ferencz, 'Illegal Armed Force as a Crime Against Humanity', June 2015: www.benferencz.org/2010-2015.html.
5. Ibid.
6. Christian Wenaweser and Donald M. Ferencz, *Handbook: Ratification and Implementation of the Kampala Amendments to the Rome Statute of the ICC – Crime of Aggression, War Crimes* (Princeton: Liechtenstein Institute on Self-Determination, n.d.): http://crimeofaggression.info/documents/1/handbook.pdf. 'The crime of aggression is the supreme violation of the *jus ad bellum*, which relates to the legitimacy of using force in the first place. Activating the Court's jurisdiction over this crime will help deter illegal uses of force … Ratifying States will … help fulfil the promise of Nuremberg that never again would those who dare to commit the crime of aggression do so with impunity.'

7. Some would argue this could reflect what happened with Srebrenica when the international community allowed or encouraged Milošević to instruct Mladić to take Srebrenica in order to sort out an insoluble problem.
8. Stephen Engelberg and Tim Weiner, with Raymond Bonner and Jane Perlez, 'Massacre in Bosnia; Srebrenica: The days of slaughter', *New York Times*, 29 October 1995.
9. Dr Nevenka Tromp shared this and the other Srebrenica lecture (and the Gaza lecture) with me, drawing on her learning as an academic political scientist and her unparalleled familiarity with the evidence in the Milošević trial, acquired through her role as principal researcher (Leadership Research Team) for the trial.
10. See www.genocidewatch.org/aboutgenocide/8stagesofgenocide.html.
11. Not itemised here, but discussed in detail in the lecture itself. See www.gresham.ac.uk/lectures-and-events/srebrenica-genocide-and-trials.
12. Anyone interested should go to the ICTY website and look at the interactive map where much detail can be found: www.icty.org/en/cases/interactive-map.
13. The ICJ found, among other things, that Serbia had violated its obligation to comply with the provisional measures ordered by the court as long ago as 1993 by failing to take all measures to prevent genocide in Srebrenica in July 1995, and was in breach of the Convention on the Prevention and Punishment of the Crime of Genocide by having failed to transfer Ratko Mladić to the ICTY.
14. www.icj-cij.org/docket/files/91/13689.pdf.
15. Marlise Simons, 'Serbia's darkest pages hidden from genocide court', *International Herald Tribune*, 8 April 2007.
16. It is worth noting that Hashim Thaçi of Kosovo has recently said that Kosovo is considering bringing a genocide allegation at the ICJ against Serbia. This, too, might be a very strong case that it has not yet been possible fully to articulate for reasons arising from the practical realities of Kosovo establishing its full independence in recent years.
17. See www.icj-cij.org/presscom/files/6/19376.pdf.

Chapter 13

1. UN OCHA June 2015 Report: http://gaza.ochaopt.org/2015/06/key-figures-on-the-2014-hostilities.
2. Avi Shlaim, Iraqi-born British/Israeli historian, Emeritus Professor of International Relations at the University of Oxford and a Fellow of the British Academy; General Sir Nick Parker, KCB, CBE, Commander-in-Chief Land Forces for the British Army from 2010 until 2013; Dr Nevenka Tromp, a political scientist who worked for 12 years at the prosecutor's office of the ICTY and was senior researcher for the Milošević trial; Rodney Dixon, QC, lawyer specialising in international war crimes.
3. See Theodor Herzl, *Complete Diaries*, ed. Raphael Patai, trans. Harry John (New York: Herzl Press and Thomas Yoseloff, 1960), Vol. II, p. 711.
4. Yoram Meital, *Peace in Tatters: Israel, Palestine, and the Middle East* (Boulder, CO: Lynne Rienner, 2006), pp. 43–46; Avi Shlaim, 'The Rise and Fall of the Oslo Peace Process', in Louise Fawcett (ed.), *International Relations of the Middle East* (Oxford: OUP, 2005), pp. 241–61.
5. Benjamin Netanyahu, *A Place among the Nations: Israel and the World* (London: Bantam Press, 1993).

6. *Likud Party Charter*, 1999: 'The Jewish communities in Judea, Samaria and Gaza are the realization of Zionist values. Settlement of the land is a clear expression of the unassailable right of the Jewish people to the Land of Israel and constitutes an important asset in the defense of the vital interests of the State of Israel. The Likud will continue to strengthen and develop these communities and will prevent their uprooting.' See http://mondoweiss.net/2011/11/netanyahu%E2%80%99s-party-platform-flatly-rejects-establishment-of-palestinian-state#sthash.lUWvvMLM.dpuf.
7. Avi Shlaim, 'Prelude to the Accord: Likud, Labour and the Palestinians', *Journal of Palestine Studies*, Vol. 23, No. 2, Winter 1994, pp. 5–19.
8. 'Palestinian Elections: Trip Report by Former U.S. President Jimmy Carter', 30 January 2006: www.cartercenter.org/news/documents/doc2287.html.
9. Palestine Papers obtained by Al Jazeera and released 23–26 January 2011: www.aljazeera.com/palestinepapers/2011/01/201112214310263628.html.
10. Nathan Thrall, 'Hamas's Chances', *London Review of Books*, 21 August 2014.
11. Robert Tait, 'Hamas kidnapping: Islamist group to blame for youths' "kidnapping", Benjamin Netanyahu says', *The Telegraph*, 15 June 2014.
12. Editorial: 'Gaza: A war that should never have been fought', *The Guardian*, 25 September 2014.
13. David Shulman, 'Gaza: The Murderous Melodrama', *New York Review of Books*, 20 November 2014.
14. See also 'Operation Projective Edge by the Numbers': www.idfblog.com/blog/2014/08/05/operation-protective-edge-numbers.
15. Leading expert in the area and co-editor of *Archbold International Criminal Courts*, the authoritative textbook on that subject.
16. From a paper prepared by Rodney Dixon for me, his contribution to the work of the multi-disciplinary team.
17. See www.middleeasteye.net/news/israel-concludes-deadly-gaza-beach-bombing-was-legal-894438693.
18. http://gisha.org/press/2447.
19. Some 1.86 million in 2014.
20. The largest numbers of Palestinian refugees originate from areas inside the state of Israel and were displaced during the 1948 Israeli–Arab War: www.forcedmigration.org/research-resources/expert-guides/palestinian-refugees-in-the-west-bank-and-the-gaza/alldocuments.
21. www.jewishvirtuallibrary.org/jsource/brief/IDF.html.
22. www.idfblog.com/about-the-idf/idf-code-of-ethics.
23. Giora Eiland, 'In Gaza, there is no such a thing as "innocent civilians"', *Ynet News*, 8 May 2014: www.ynetnews.com/articles/0,7340,L-4554583,00.html; 'Israeli general: No civilians in Gaza', *The Daily Beast*, 4 August 2014: www.thedailybeast.com/cheats/2014/08/04/israeli-general-no-civilians-in-gaza.html.
24. http://news.bbc.co.uk/2/hi/middle_east/1270038.stm.
25. http://jewishweek.timesofisrael.com/war-of-the-words.
26. www.haaretz.co.il/misc/article-print-page/1.2228666, 28 January 2014.
27. www.timesofisrael.com/idf-commander-calls-on-troops-to-fight-blasphemous-gazans.

28. http:// mondoweiss.net / 2015 / 05 / netanyahu-palestinians-government.
29. Source: www.youtube.com / watch?v=OMG7Fze6sgQ; viewed on 16 July 2014.
30. And although a far, far remove from events in the Middle East, the killing of MP Jo Cox by a pro-Brexit criminal in 2016, *arguably* responsive in part to the excessive language used in the Brexit 'debate', is an indication of quite how dangerous freedom of speech can be when abused.
31. For long enough the Palestinian Authority, under Mahmoud Abbas, failed to take steps to refer the conflict to the International Criminal Court with both sides of the conflict being investigated. His approach may have reflected threats by the US and Europe to penalise Gaza and the West Bank should there be a referral to the court by the PA. The PA has now effectively referred the matter to the court. The November 2016 Annual Report of the ICC Prosecutor indicates investigations continuing with no date forecast for any decisions: www.icc-cpi.int / iccdocs / otp / 161114-otp-rep-PE_ENG.pdf.
32. http:// avalon.law.yale.edu / 20th_century / hamas.asp; 'softened' by the revised charter – see http:// mondoweiss.net / 2017 / 04 / translated-leaked-charter.
33. See, for example, www.theguardian.com / commentisfree / 2014 / nov / 20 / hamas-charter-israeli-civilians-dying-ahmed-yousef.
34. How this works is made clearer in the full text of General Parker's contribution to the original lecture, available to view on the Gresham College website, with accompanying PowerPoint presentation.

Chapter 14

1. 'The Mission expresses its profound regret that, notwithstanding a most cordial meeting on 18 August 2010, the Permanent Representative of Israel advised in writing at the end of the meeting that the position of his Government was one of non-recognition of, and non-cooperation with, the Mission.'
2. UN General Assembly, Human Rights Council, 'Report of the international fact-finding mission to investigate violations of international law, including international humanitarian and human rights law, resulting from the Israeli attacks on the flotilla of ships carrying humanitarian assistance', 27 September 2010, www2.ohchr.org / english / bodies / hrcouncil / docs / 15session / A.HRC.15.21_en.pdf.
3. 'The Gaza Cheat Sheet – Real data on the Gaza Closure': www.gisha.org / userfiles / File / publications / Info_Gaza_Eng.pdf.
4. 'The Public Commission to Examine the Maritime Incident of 31 May 2010', Turkel Commission: http:// turkel-committee.gov.il / files / wordocs / 8808report-eng.pdf.
5. International Committee of the Red Cross, 'Gaza Closure: Not Another Year!' 14 July 2010: www.icrc.org / eng / resources / documents / update / palestine-update-140610.htm.
6. 'Gaza: Humanitarian Implosion', 1 March 2008: https: // unispal.un.org / DPA / DPR / unispal.sf / 0 / 321236597C8E413785257404005247DB.
7. Founded in 2006 and with a stated purpose on its website (www.freegaza.org) to 'break Israel's illegal siege on Gaza's 1.8 million civilians, since it inflicts collective punishment on the Palestinians who live there and has destroyed its economy'.

8. Details of each of its voyages are available on the Free Gaza Movement's website: www.freegaza.org/trips.html.
9. The precise number of passengers is unclear; the UN Human Rights Commission reports 748, whereas other sources have indicated more than this number.
10. 'Summary of equipment and aid aboard the Gaza flotilla', Israeli Ministry of Foreign Affairs, 7 June 2010: www.mfa.gov.il/MFA/Government/Communiques/2010/Equipment_aid_Gaza_flotilla_7-Jun-2010.htm.
11. Two of the vessels to set sail, the *Challenger II* and *Rachel Corrie*, were not present due to engine failure and late departure respectively.
12. 'Report of the international fact-finding mission to investigate violations of international law, including international humanitarian and human rights law, resulting from the Israeli attacks on the flotilla of ships carrying humanitarian Assistance', UN Human Rights Council (hereafter 'UNHRC Report'), A/HRC/15/21, 27 September 2010, para. 128, p. 26.
13. James Kirkup, 'David Cameron makes historic visit to Amritsar – but stops short of making apology', *The Telegraph*, 20 February 2013.
14. International Covenant on Civil and Political Rights, adopted and opened for signature, ratification and accession by General Assembly Resolution 2200A (XXI) of 16 December 1966, entry into force 23 March 1976, in accordance with Article 49: www.ohchr.org/EN/ProfessionalInterest/Pages/CCPR.aspx.
15. 'Legal Consequences of the Construction of a Wall in the Occupied Palestinian Territory', International Court of Justice, Advisory Opinion of 9 July 2004: www.icj-cij.org/docket/files/131/1671.pdf.
16. UNHRC Report, p. 28.
17. 'Situation on the Registered Vessels of the Union of the Comoros, the Hellenic Republic and the Kingdom of Cambodia: Decision on the request of the Union of the Comoros to review the Prosecutor's decision not to initiate an investigation', Pre-Trial Chamber I (the 'PTC Decision'), 16 July 2015, p. 14.
18. UNHRC Report, pp. 41–42.
19. Jonathan Ferziger, 'Israeli army inquiry says mistakes made in Gaza raid', 12 July 2010: www.bloomberg.com/news/articles/2010-07-12/israeli-inquiry-says-intelligence-other-mistakes-made-in-raid-on-flotilla.
20. Turkel Report, p. 279.
21. UNHRC Report, p. 53.
22. 'Report of the Secretary-General's Panel of Inquiry on the 31 May 2010 Flotilla Incident', September 2011, p. 117.
23. Flag state of the *Eleftheri* was Greece and of *Rachel Corrie* was Kingdom of Cambodia, both signatory states to the Rome Statute.
24. Office of the Prosecutor, International Criminal Court, 'Situation on Registered Vessels of Comoros, Greece and Cambodia Article 53(1) Report', 6 November 2014, pp. 56–60: www.icc-cpi.int/iccdocs/otp/OTP-COM-Article_53(1)-Report-06Nov2014Eng.pdf.
25. In the presence of an unlawful blockade, there was reasonable basis to believe that the war crime of intentionally directing an attack against civilian objects pursuant to Article 8(2)(b)(ii) of the Rome Statute was committed by IDF soldiers in relation

to the non-consensual boarding and takeover of the *Mavi Marmara* and the *Eleftheri Mesogios*.

26. 'Application for Review pursuant to Article 53(3)(a) of the Prosecutor's Decision of 6 November 2014 not to initiate an investigation in the Situation' (the 'Review Application'), 29 January 2015, pp. 23–26.

27. Ibid., pp. 33–59.

28. PTC Decision, pp. 8, 9, and 22.

Chapter 15

1. Mary Whitehouse, a conservative Christian schoolteacher, became an activist from about 1963 against the developing liberalism she saw in her country, especially on its television. She campaigned against many changes, mostly concerning sex but also about bad language and violence. She was regarded by many as a joke, a figure of fun, out of date. She had supporters throughout, however, and more recently may be seen as a brake on changes that were going too far.
2. *Round the Horne*, a 1960s BBC radio comedy series full of sexual *double entendres* delivered especially by gay Kenneth Williams, whose lines would have teenagers imagining their parents did not understand the filthy things being said and parents pretending they didn't.
3. In 'Sexual fantasizing in males and females', *Journal of Research in Personality*, Vol. 18, No. 4, pp. 451–62, Danielle Knafo and Yoram Jaffe found that university males were more likely to endorse the fantasy 'I imagine that I rape or humiliate a woman or women,' for example, whereas women more frequently reported the fantasy 'I imagine that I am being overpowered or forced to surrender.' Interestingly, Kanin's study of women's 'rape fantasies' suggests that, in many cases, these fantasies were 'something quite different from rape … they appeared to be reporting erotic fantasies about being aggressively approached and sexually engaged, but in situations where they offer only token verbal resistance, if any, to a highly desired encounter' (E.J. Kanin, 'Rape as a function of relative sexual frustration', *Psychology Reports*, Vol. 52, pp. 133–34).
4. After this lecture was delivered, Donald Trump's boasting of groping women sexually showed how, as a minimum, his imagination crossed the line, how his actions may have crossed the line and suggested that, from his boast, he knowingly and criminally disregarded the law.
5. C. Hoyano and C. Keenan, *Child Abuse: Law and Policy across Boundaries* (Oxford: OUP, 2007), p. 7.
6. The Dame Janet Smith Review, Chapter 3, 'Changing attitudes and sexual mores', Volume 2, The Jimmy Savile investigation report, The BBC Trust, 25 February 2016: http://downloads.bbci.co.uk/bbctrust/assets/files/pdf/our_work/dame_janet_smith_review/savile/chapter_3.pdf.
7. The Dame Janet Smith Review, 'Opening Statement': www.damejanetsmithreview.com/wp-content/uploads/2016/02/Opening-Statement-of-Dame-Janet-Smith-25.02.16.pdf.
8. Charles Moore, 'Sixties liberalism swept away our shared sense of decency', *The Telegraph*, 6 June 2015.

Chapter 16

1. In Switzerland the complex process of *Vernehmlassungsverfahren* (procedure to hear opinions) is said to be responsive to the reality that even the most sophisticated system of proportional voting cannot guarantee that the opinions of the members of parliament are a true representation of people's opinions in any possible political question: http://direct-democracy.geschichte-schweiz.ch/switzerlands-system-referendums.html.
2. Denis MacShane, 'Why UK's EU referendum will be nothing like the last', *Politico*, 14 January 2016.
3. Which is why Swiss Direct Democracy moves by stages to avoid confrontation in referendums.
4. Sir Nicolas Bratza, 'European judge slams UK "xenophobia"', *The Guardian*, 23 November 2011.
5. Steven Greer, 'The margin of appreciation: interpretation and discretion under the European Convention on Human Rights', Council of Europe Publishing, 2000.
6. For the House of Lords judgment see: http://swarb.co.uk/a-v-secretary-of-state-for-the-home-department-and-x-v-secretary-of-state-for-the-home-department-HL-16-Dec-2004.
7. *Vinter and Others v the United Kingdom*, judgment (Grand Chamber) of 9 July 2013, Sections 119–122.
8. Damian Chalmers et al., *European Union Law: Text and Materials* (Cambridge: CUP, 2nd edn, 2010) pp. 257–58; Paul Craig and Gráinne de Búrca, *EU Law: Text, Cases, and Materials* (Oxford: OUP, 5th edn, 2011), p. 359.
9. See also 'Opinion of Advocate General Trstenjak', delivered on 22 September 2011: http://eur-lex.europa.eu/legal-content/EN/TXT/?uri=CELEX%3A62010CC0411.
10. Rights Info: Human Rights News, Views & Info, https://rightsinfo.org.
11. www.bailii.org/uk/cases/UKHL/2004/56.html.
12. In the case of *Goodwin v the United Kingdom*: www.bailii.org/eu/cases/ECHR/1996/16.html.
13. Case of *Pretty v The United Kingdom* (Application no. 2346/02) Judgment 29 April 2002: www.bailii.org/eu/cases/ECHR/2002/427.html.
14. Sir Nicolas Bratza – 'The relationship between UK courts and Strasbourg', *European Human Rights Law Review* (2011) No. 5, pp. 505–12.
15. www.theguardian.com/law/2014/dec/17/britain-withdraw-human-rights-convention.
16. And UK newspapers describing UK Court of Appeal judges as 'Enemies of the People' over their Brexit decision shows how far those seeking political change by means fair or foul will go to manipulate the public.

Chapter 17

1. www.supremecourt.uk/docs/speech-160303.pdf.
2. Ibid.
3. Francis FitzGibbon, 'Joint Enterprise', *London Review of Books*, Vol. 38, No. 5, 3 March 2016.

4. Richard J. Evans, *The Third Reich in Power, 1933–1939* (London: Allen Lane, 2005).
5. Lord Neuberger, 'Keynote closing address to the International Council of Advocates and Barristers', World Bar Conference 2016, para. 14.
6. Lord Neuberger, 'Technology and the Law. Closing Keynote Address', British Irish Commercial Bar Association Law Forum, 21 April 2016, para. 15.
7. Curiously, lawyers working in Scotland's separate legal system probably earn significantly less than London and other English lawyers, something never really explained.
8. Pro bono work by lawyers and other professionals of 'developed' countries is a pattern of behaviour not entirely easy to explain; but it is a reality. Excluding altruism as the driver, it may be that having some professional skill – say, of ophthalmic surgery, or of water engineering in desert lands – demands of the professional that her/his skill is turned to use? It is almost as if the professional skill itself *requires* to be used rather than that the professional wishes to do good. It is sometimes an imperative that cannot quite be resisted.
9. www.icty.org/en/press/trial-judgement-in-the-case-of-vojislav-seselj-delivered.
10. 'Information on the Partially Dissenting Opinion of Judge Lattanzi in Judgment in the case of Vojislav Šešelj', 31 March 2016: www.icty.org/en/press/information-on-the-partially-dissenting-opinion-of-judge-lattanzi-in-judgement-in-the-case-of.
11. Charles Darwin, *The Descent of Man* (London: John Murray, 1871).
12. Nigel Farage, 'Fruitcakes can be good for you', *The Guardian*, 13 April 2009.
13. His only son predeceased him; he provided for his widow and left a very large amount of money and continuing income for the creation of Gresham College where eight professors would give lectures, free of charge, in their eight different subjects, one of which was – and is to this day – law.

Postscript

1. From 'Death's Duel', the last sermon of poet John Donne, Dean of St Paul's, given at Whitehall in Lent, 1630: 'But then this *exitus à morte* is but *introitus in mortem*; this issue, this deliverance, from that death, the death of the womb, is an entrance, a delivering over to another death, the manifold deaths of this world; we have a winding-sheet in our mother's womb which grows with us from our conception, and we come into the world wound up in that winding-sheet, for we come to seek a grave.'
2. And by an armchair occupant who was privileged from birth, not by inherited wealth or rank but in all other ways, who usually was able to add good luck to privilege even when things might have gone wrong and who could lead a comfortable 'thin' life, never going to a rock concert or learning the rules of football, feeling (following Dr Johnson) 'meanly of himself' for never being in the armed forces and, in truth, never having to do anything too dangerous or brave.
3. Would *you* torture someone you believed to know the whereabouts of an atomic device, due to go off in a major city in 30 minutes' time, if the torture *might* 'work'?
4. Former Conservative Attorney General, sacked by Prime Minster David Cameron for being a supporter of the ECHR.
5. Afterwards the language used in the public debate was discussed in the media, often dismissing its connection to the killing.

6. 'I disapprove of what you say, but I will defend to the death your right to say it.' Not Voltaire's precise words, but a summary by Evelyn Hall of Voltaire's meaning in his *Essay on Tolerance*: 'Think for yourselves and let others enjoy the privilege to do so too.' See Halls's explanation in *Saturday Review* (11 May 1935), p. 13.
7. Patrick Leigh Fermor, *A Time of Gifts* (London: John Murray, 1977). 'I was at the age when one's memory for poetry or for languages – indeed for anything – takes impressions like wax and, up to a point, lasts like marble.'
8. Stanza XXVII, *The Rubáiyát of Omar Khayyám*, translated by Edward FitzGerald. First taught me by my father, blue-collar reader of some poetry and actually, so I learnt, something of an orator in the workplace.
9. Tom had a beautiful Welsh voice, lived in Bloomsbury and 'anti-commuted' to my school in suburban Catford. It was he who ensured my spoken voice was not wasted: he trained me to speak better. And by spending time with his family I enjoyed blue-collar free-thought complementing intellectual free-thought at opposite ends of the 'Catford Loop Line' train.
10. Campaign for Nuclear Disarmament: CNDUK.org.
11. L. F. Morris, *A History of St Dunstan's College* (London: Adams Bros. and Shardlow Ltd, 1970), pp. 199–200.
12. Of course, many educated at such a school will have laughed at completely inappropriate anti-diversity jokes over time; I know I have. But in essence the way I was educated means that I have no hostility to diversity of race, religion or whatever. And any instinctive or instilled hostility I *do* sense in myself from time to time has, I know, to be countered, and I may be reasonably effective at achieving that.
13. Tom Earley, *Welshman in Bloomsbury* (London: Outposts Publications, 1966), p. 10.

Introduction to Appendices

1. Maybe it is this that has many people resisting, *in advance*, claims they fear may be made on their behalf after death that they had 'a long fight' with some disease. *They* did not. Their *bodies* – helped sometimes by doctors – did the fighting. The individual who survives serious illness knows this by looking back on what they did during the worst of it that was completely beyond what could ever have seemed possible before or after ill health struck.
2. I have been given generous credit in public, and whenever we meet privately, by my opponent in a child sex case I prosecuted to conviction just before I took silk. I became aware after the trial of how both counsel and the judge had missed something that would lead to an acquittal on appeal but that might well not be exposed by the appeal actually being launched. It took me some time to do what I knew I had to do and write to my opponent explaining the error (for which the judge and I were most to blame), the action for which I have since been given such credit by my opponent. In truth the temptation to let it go and avoid personal embarrassment had been very strong.

Appendix 1

1. From 1999–2004 Justice of the Supreme Court of Canada; from 2004–2008 United Nations High Commissioner for Human Rights; from 2009–2014 President and CEO of the International Crisis Group; from 2017 UN Special Representative for International Migration.
2. We did meet occasionally at embassy receptions after this was all over. Judge Jorda was always courteous and charming, once even offering to explain why they acquitted of genocide. I genuinely did not want to hear and politely declined the offer – and in any case, one of Jorda's fellow judges had already given the game away to a colleague of mine the day after the acquittal, saying they 'wanted to keep the ICTY's first genocide trial verdict for a bigger fish'.
3. In the last couple of decades substantially increased rights of audience for solicitors in UK law firms have changed this particular characteristic of the legal culture with which I was familiar.
4. The UK's Crown Prosecution Service (CPS) is a very large law office, sometimes using independent counsel, sometimes using its own lawyers to prosecute cases. It is likely to be subject to *some* of the same tensions although protected from them, to an extent, by the culture of independence of UK lawyers and by media that would be unforgiving of political interference in prosecutorial decisions.
5. Del Ponte seemed to have no interest in the people of the region and could not understand how Nena Tromp and I would want to learn what we could of Serb culture or to make friendly contacts with Serbs in Belgrade and elsewhere. She 'gated' me from going to operas or art exhibitions if I had any free time on weekend fact-finding missions to Belgrade, nominally on grounds of risk. I was told the proper course was to stay in a hotel or the ICTY office and to go nowhere else. I did not visit Belgrade again until after Milošević had died, when, free of the 'close protection' imposed on me as an employee, I found the Serbs in the street entirely open and friendly.
6. Louise Arbour, of course, had the same powers available to her when she made difficult decisions but normally achieved a willing, office-wide consensus.
7. Apart form other sources, US Vice President Al Gore is recorded reading them out to colleagues in part of the authoritative Dutch (NIOD) report into Srebrenica. See Dr Cees Wiebes, 'Srebrenica: a "safe" area. Appendix II – Intelligence and the war in Bosnia 1992–1995: The role of the intelligence and security services', Nederlands Instituut voor Oorlogsdocumentatie (NIOD), p. 221. http://www.niod.knaw.nl.
8. See also the writings of Andreas Zumach, journalist. Andreas Zumach, 'US Intelligence knew Serbs were planning an assault on Srebrenica', *Basic Reports*, No. 47, 16/10/95. And: 'VS wisten van komende val Srebrenica' (US knew of impending fall of Srebrenica), *Nederlands Dagblad*, 13/10/95 and 'VS wisten al weken tevoren van val Srebrenica' (US knew about fall of Srebrenica weeks in advance), *De Gelderlander*, 13/10/95. Source: 'Srebrenica: a 'safe' area. Appendix II – Intelligence and the war in Bosnia 1992–1995: The role of the intelligence and security services', Nederlands Instituut voor Oorlogsdocumentatie (NIOD), p. 193, footnote 1026.
9. In May 2008 Delić stood for election on behalf of the party of far-right ICTY indictee Vojislav Šešelj and was named as a potential Minister of Defence. The Serbian daily newspaper *Blic* published an account of his dealings with the ICTY Prosecutor and Delić's political career ended.

10. Dr Nevenka (Nena) Tromp, senior researcher throughout the Milošević trial and co-founder of the Geoffrey Nice Foundation.
11. In fact it would always be hard to find such high-quality lawyers to serve as prosecutors, as these foreign courts are often regarded as second-rate and intellectually unappealing for the most cerebral of lawyers. Similar difficulties were once encountered by the international judiciary, although the UK's appointments of the famously fair Lord Iain Bonomy to the ICTY in succession to the truly excellent late Sir Richard May, and radical Sir Adrian Fulford to the International Criminal Court (ICC), were important exceptions.

Appendix 2

1. I operated a similar process of written notes of argument for the sentencing determination by the 'Superior Number' – the two trial Jurats, plus three others – to avoid my having any influence on sentencing beyond advising of the law and any sentencing guidelines. And again it worked. I felt that these systems could readily have been adopted in Jersey. None of those in authority showed any interest. I can only hope 'nudging' of Jurats is a thing of the past.
2. Interestingly, in his 2017 announcement of vacancies for his and other seats on the Supreme Court, Lord Neuberger radically enlarged the categories of people who could apply; not quite to include non-lawyers, but I do wonder whether his experience in the Jersey case and my suggestion to him that a reasonably intelligent person would not have missed the points the Privy Council overlooked may have helped him take the approach he did.
3. As in the 1984 film *Another Country* but also described to me directly by public schoolboys abused at schools as recently as the 1960s or 1970s in similar ways.
4. Jersey has been the subject of regular revelations since the trial about its compliant financial culture, coming to something of a head in 2016 at the time of the 'Panama Papers' disclosures about the Panamanian law firm Mossak Fonseca. https://panamapapers.icij.org.
5. To revert to boys' club culture, on one occasion, as I 'downed' a very large analgesic Scotch at the hotel after court, I was met by another of Jersey's Commissioners whom I had not met before. Within 20 minutes he showed me pictures of his younger wife in underwear, assuming I would feel a club-like affiliation with him, rather than revulsion. How could it be that the Island employed this kind of 'rumbustious' judge, with whom, I discovered, the women greffiers – court clerks – objected to working? Into what out-of-date culture had I been drawn? I finished my drink, made an excuse and left.
6. The only event that could have revealed I was in pain – immense pain as it happened – was when I read a prepared judgment on an interlocutory issue. The pain was rising to the point where it was becoming unbearable so I accelerated delivery to a very, very fast speed and rose immediately to do whatever I could to kill the pain in privacy. There was nothing else unusual in my public performance at any point of the trial. Counsel who seem to have taken liberties with the transcript had no idea. Nor, indeed, did Caitriona Fogarty, until long after she had written the critical letter to the Privy Council that finally drove them to a limited recognition of reality.
7. Brown in his judgment just acknowledges this as a difficulty for the court by saying that the Jurats showed by their conviction on this count that they were

D

E

V

W

XYZ